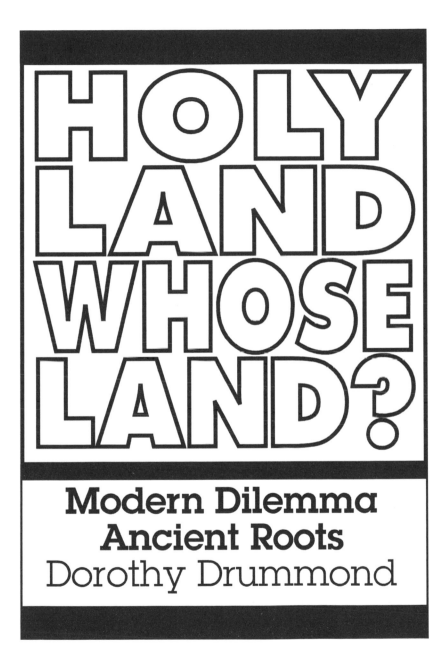

HOLY LAND WHOSE LAND?

Modern Dilemma
Ancient Roots

Dorothy Drummond

Published by:
Educare Press
2208 NW Market Street, Suite 308
Seattle, WA 98107

Printed and bound in Canada.
10 9 8 7 6 5 4 3

First Edition
Library of Congress Control Number: 2002100803

ISBN:O-944638-30-9

Holy Land, Whose Land?

Modern Dilemma, Ancient Roots

CONTENTS

MAPS

PHOTOGRAPHS

ACKNOWLEDGEMENTS

No work begins in a vacuum. It is the outgrowth of ideas accumulated, often subliminally, over a lifetime. Nevertheless, I want to acknowledge especially those persons who have been influential in the making of *Holy Land, Whose Land?* My interest in the Holy Land started when I was on a Fulbright fellowship in Burma, more than forty years ago. At that time, I met Dr. Daniel Hillel, an Israeli agronomist temporarily detailed on an advisory mission. He had grown up in Israel before World War II and many of his friends were Arabs. I never forgot our long conversations, nor my subsequent experiences as a guest in his young country the year that Israel celebrated its tenth anniversary. He went on to become a world-renowned soil scientist, something I could have predicted from his brilliance, his energy, and intensity, even then. I am grateful to my friend Jane Hazledine, who headed me in the direction of the Hashemite Kingdom of Jordan nearly a decade ago. That experience initiated my research on the Decapolis, and led me to want to return to Jordan, and to Israel as well, at an early opportunity.

My interest in Middle East history is long-standing, but for a focus on the history of the Holy Land, and of the Biblical accounts that are critical to its understanding, I credit author Thomas Cahill, whose two books, the *Gift of the Jews* and *Desire of the Everlasting Hills,* gave me a new way of seeing. Also immensely helpful was Karen Armstrong's *A History of God.* I think, however, that my intense interest in the Biblical accounts, and their relationship to the Holy Land today, began with weekly discussions on the Book of Genesis led by Dr. Wm. Dando, who saw all the comings and goings of the Patriarchs through his geographer's eye.

Through the years, I have been blessed with friends who on a personal level have given me insights into the Israeli/Palestinian dilemma. Friends in my town travel often to Israel to visit their families, and I have come to know the grief and anxiety and outrage that they feel. A Holocaust Museum is in my town, the personal creation of a remarkable woman, Eva Kor, who as a young twin survived the vicious Auschwitz experiments of Dr. Josef Mengele. She has traveled widely to bring her message that one can live to overcome bitterness. Years ago, I shared discussions with Elsie Mayyasi, whose Palestinian husband was working in my town as a chemist. Through Elsie and her husband, I began to sense what it meant to be uprooted and stateless. But it was Irmgard Fuchs who first introduced me to the horror of forced displacement. She wore a concentration camp tattoo on her forearm. In the 1980s, a Palestinian geographer colleague in Iowa spoke and wrote about the Palestinian tragedy at every opportunity, but at that time few were listening, and he died before the full impact of what he was saying revealed itself. Another colleague, Dr. Akhtar Siddiqi, sharpened my awareness of Arab contributions to scholarship through his publications on Muslim geographers of the Middle Ages. Dr. Siddiqi was loyal to his Muslim roots, but alas he too died before I could have the talks with him that would have helped me in writing this book.

Two authors who most helped me to understand the volatility of today's Holy Land wrote more than a decade ago, but their accounts seem fresh today: Thomas Friedman, *From Beirut to Jerusalem,* and David K Shipler, *Arab and Jew: Wounded Spirits in a Promised Land.*

Bernard Lewis has published extensively on the Middle East and on Islam, and his clarity and insights were of immense value to me.

I cannot possibly do justice to the magnificent effort put forth by a thoroughly knowledgeable and sensitive Israeli guide named Yossie Weiss, as well as by John Reitan, whose itinerary maximized coverage in a limited time frame. I appreciate the willingness of my sister, Arlene Weitz VanderKlomp, and our mutual friend, Karen McCullough, to harbor me as a triple in a succession of rooms meant for two, and I treasure the conversations we had that ultimately triggered this account. I owe a debt to my three daughters, Kathleen, Gael, and Martha. It was so they and their husbands could share my Holy Land experiences that I set out originally to write a modest journal, and it was they who first urged me to expand it.

I am especially grateful to my friend the Rev. Arthur Simon, founder of Bread for the World, and to my publisher/friend Geographer Kieran O'Mahony of Educare Press, both of whom early had faith and gave encouragement at every step. My editor, Ms. Marianne Van de Vrede, helped give form to substance but tried valiantly not to impose her sense of style on mine. The creative stamp of artist-mapmaker-designer Jeff Reynolds is on every page. In addition I am indebted to the Rev. Joseph H. Chillington, Dr. Christine Drake, the Rev. Dr. Mark Kane, Ms. Kathleen Lindstaedt, the Rev. Barbara Nolin, Ms. Carol Rueckert, and Ms. Jonnee Weston, all of whom have given valuable critique. Errors of commission are mine. This account is also flawed by omission, and no one knows this better than I. But I know, too, that in writing it I have gained a world of understanding. It would please me to know that the reader may feel likewise enriched.

FOREWORD

The idea that grew into this book seemed simple enough on first resolve. It was late March of the millennial year. I was sitting on Suleiman's Wall, overlooking the Old City of Jerusalem, on the last day of my most recent visit to the Holy Land. As I was churning over in my mind how to condense my experience so that I could both retain it and share it, I realized that this was not going to be an easy task. I would first have to dig into the past to make sense of the Holy Land as it is today. I resolved to do so. Soon after, the urgency of the Intifadeh and the collapse of the peace process placed an added layer on my resolve.

On the Wall I was idly musing, "How did it happen that the land holy to three faiths can be kept secure only at gunpoint?" Today this question is irrelevant, for soldiers and firepower no longer guarantee peace. They only serve, as guns always do, to inflame. Why is the Holy Land—today again, as so often in the past—a cauldron of conflict? Seeking answers, I have had to delve deeply. What started as a simple account of my travels has become far longer and more complicated than I had originally intended.

The Holy Land has a complex story, played out in a varied landscape, where the past is continually intruding into the present. Piecing it together has taken me more time than I had anticipated. Many lights have gone on in the process, leading my research continually in new directions. But the story of the Holy Land has not yielded easily to generalization.

This account is no longer centered on my travels. It is the story of the Holy Land, with my own experiences interspersed in italic. I offer it now to anyone who may be contemplating a journey to the Holy Land or who may simply want to understand the complicated story—both sacred and profane—of this unique, beautiful, and tortured land.

Dorothy Weitz Drummond
Terre Haute, Indiana
January 22, 2002

PROLOGUE:
FROM SULEIMAN'S WALL

On a warm spring day at the start of the third millennium, I am leaning against a shaded niche on the parapet of the Wall that Suleiman the Magnificent built five centuries previously to enclose the Holy City. My most recent travels in Israel and Jordan, the land where Abraham, Jesus, and probably Mohammed walked, are nearly at an end. I am thinking of the millions who have come before me, pilgrims of three faiths and of no faith at all, drawn like iron to the magnet of Jerusalem, this ancient city at the crossroads of civilizations.

I try to recall bits and pieces of the long history of empires and armies that in the past four thousand years have struggled for control of the Fertile Crescent passageway at the eastern end of the Mediterranean Sea: the Egyptians, the Hittites, the Philistines, the Hebrews, the Assyrians, the Babylonians, the Persians, the Phoenicians, Alexander the Great, the Romans, the Byzantines, the Arabs, the Crusaders, the Seljuk Turks, the Ottoman Turks, and the British.

Below me, interspersed among the crowd thronging continually wary power—the modern state of Israel—committed to guarding and protecting all pilgrims who come to its land, of whatever faith.

I am thinking, too, of the peoples of the past who were caught in the continual upheavals as superior forces invaded their territories: the Canaanites and Hebrews in the central highlands, the Philistines and the Phoenicians on the coast, and the peoples of Moab and Edom on the plateau rising starkly east of the Jordan River. Currently, the most tragic are the stateless Palestinian Arabs who lost their homes as Jewish refugees from the Holocaust flooded into the Palestine Mandate after World War II and into the new state of Israel after 1948. One human tragedy begets another. How to address the grievances of the displaced Palestinians is no closer to a solution today than it was in 1948. As the Jews keep the memory of the Holocaust alive, so the Palestinians cry out that they too are the victims of injustice. The Palestinian issue has pitted Israel against the Arab nations. It has involved the United States time and again as broker in the peace process. And, as I write, it is still confounding the efforts of good people on all sides to bring about peace. Only now, the urgency is all the greater, for nuclear weapons are positioned in the region.

On this day, however, there is peace in Jerusalem. Pope John Paul II worshipped the day before at the Church of the Holy Sepulchre, and he is shortly to conclude his own intense and difficult pilgrimage to Holy Land sites. Israelis, Palestinians, Jordanians, and Egyptians have spared no security efforts, and the visit has been without incident.

Armed Israeli soldiers stand guard to protect the thousands of pilgrims who have come for the millennial year. They protect Pope John Paul II as he prays at the places holy to his faith, and they protect the pilgrims loyal to other Christian traditions. They protect the Jews who come to the Western Wall to bewail the fate of their twice-destroyed Temple; they protect Muslim pilgrims who come to the Haram al-Sharif to pray at the Al-Aqsa Mosque, where the outer courtyard of the Temple once stood; and they protect visitors like me. I doubt that I need protection, for the tightly packed crowds here today are peaceful. But the city is volatile, no less today than in the past, and the Israelis are determined that the shrines of this Holy City shall be kept open to all who wish to visit.

The story of the Holy Land that follows is not intended to answer the question posed in the title of this book. Rather, by shedding light in dark corners, it attempts to bring understanding. The story is in three parts: The first details the present Israeli/Palestinian conflict and puts it into modern context. The second surveys the roots of conflict in the Holy Land, traveling four thousand years into the past to unravel the tangled web of religion, conquest, and politics that has made the land unique and its future consequential far beyond its borders. The third takes a broader worldview, examining how and why the conflict has been co-opted, and why there is no alternative to negotiation. In all three parts, I use the present tense to give an immediacy to all that has happened, for in truth, the past is always present in the Holy Land.

Part I
The Present:
Turmoil in
the Holy Land

The Holy Land, holy to the world's three monotheistic faiths—Judaism, Christianity, and Islam—must be defined geographically. Broadly speaking, it encompasses most of the territory where events chronicled in the Hebrew Scriptures (foundational to the faith of Jews, Christians, and Muslims alike) and the first five books of the New Testament took place.

The heartland of the Holy Land is the region commonly known as *Palestine*, a name given to it by the Romans in the second century. West to east, Palestine extends from the Mediterranean Sea coastlands through hill country rising to 3,000 feet, then plunges to the geological trench occupied by the Sea of Galilee (Lake Kinneret), the Jordan River, and the Dead Sea. North to south, it extends from the source of the Jordan in Mount Hermon to the Dead Sea and the northern part of the Negev Desert. In the time of Jesus and before, there was no such named region. Instead, there was Galilee in the north, Samaria in the center, and Judea in the south, all governed by Rome. Because Biblical narratives took place not only in Palestine but also on the plateau east of the Jordan River, southward within

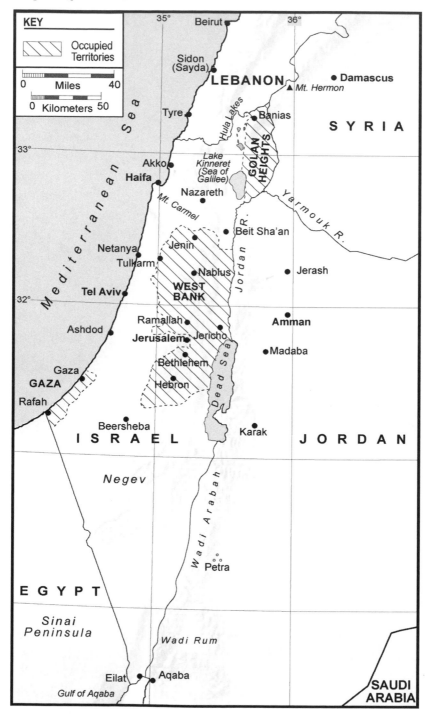

Map 1. The Holy Land today.

the Negev and Arabian Deserts, and west of the Negev Desert into the Sinai Peninsula, the Holy Land traveler must be prepared to traverse these lands as well.

Defined in this broader sense, the Holy Land today is under the political jurisdiction of six entities. It includes all of Israel and that part of the Occupied Territories governed by Israel, all of the fragmented territory governed by the Palestinian Authority, the coast of southern Lebanon, southwestern Syria, western Jordan, and Egypt's Sinai Peninsula. The threads of religious heritage could well weave this region into one, but the Holy Land has never been more fractured politically.

Today, one cannot travel between Israel and Lebanon or between Israel and Syria. At this writing, however, one *can* travel between Israel and Egypt and between Israel and Jordan, but only by using selected border crossings. Even travel within Israel and the territories that Israel occupies is restricted. For the most part, visitors are still free to travel everywhere. Technically, Israelis are also, but they are not welcome in the cities governed by the Palestinian Authority. Palestinians in the West Bank and Gaza essentially cannot travel. For the many months of the present Intifadeh, Israel has forbidden Palestinians to cross the figurative "Green Line" that separates Israel proper from the territories it has occupied since 1967. And only with greatest difficulty can Palestinians move through Israeli barriers from one part of their fragmented Authority to another.

The first time I was in Israel I looked over a wall into the Old City of Jerusalem and stared into the muzzle of a Jordanian gun. That was in 1958, the year Israel celebrated its tenth anniversary. The most fervent wish of Israelis in that anniversary year was for all of Jerusalem to be part of Israel. In another nine years, this wish would be fulfilled. More than forty years later, I wonder again about the future of the Holy City.

1

BIRTH OF A
JEWISH STATE

*Had the Arabs accepted partition, Israel would have
ended up with considerably less territory than it gained
through their rejection. [The Arab armies] provided the
Jews with the most severe motive in battle: survival.*
David K. Shipler,
Arab and Jew

*Although its roots are deep and immemorial, the young
State is foredoomed to many grave trials.*
David Ben-Gurion,
The Call of the Spirit in Israel

Desperate for a place to settle at the end of World War II, 1945-
Holocaust survivors are languishing dazed and weak in 1946
makeshift refugee camps in Europe. Young Jews from the
British Mandate of Palestine, healthy and bright-eyed, visit the
refugees. "Come to the Promised Land, Eretz Israel," they say. "We
will help you get there, and you can help us build a new Israel." The
young Jews are operating illegally. They represent the underground
organization known as *Haganah*, dedicated to bringing Holocaust
survivors to Palestine. The British do not want any more Jews in
their Mandate. Over the preceding sixty years, Arab Palestinians have

7

seen more and more of their farmland purchased by Israeli settlers. Since the Nazis came into power, Jewish immigration into the Mandate has swollen. The Arab Palestinians are feeling threatened. For the past twenty years, intermittently, a Palestinian underground has been harassing Jewish settlers, and the Jewish underground has been retaliating. The settlers keep arms close at hand. The situation is volatile. The British conclude that Jewish immigration must be restricted.

The British Dilemma

Britain is in a quandary. It is tied by its Mandate to protect the rights of Arab Palestinians and to maintain order. At the same time, when the Mandate is established after World War I, one of its goals is to further Jewish settlement, in accordance with a British government policy (the Balfour Declaration) that dates from 1917. It is clear that if masses of Holocaust survivors settle in Palestine, Arabs will be displaced. Already a trickle of Arabs is beginning to flee. As the first wave of refugees reach Palestine, militant Jewish settlement groups intimidate and harass Arab property owners. The militants want the Arabs out of the Promised Land, and they make no secret of this. Not all Jewish settlers share this view, however. Most hope for a Palestine in which Arabs and Jews can live peacefully, side by side.

Jewish settlers have been coming to Palestine since the Zionist movement of the 1890s. Zionism wants a national homeland for Jews in the land that gave birth to Judaism, the Promised Land, Eretz Israel. With early financing from Zionists in England (soon also from the United States and other Western countries), more and more Jewish pioneers come to Palestine. They buy land from the Arabs and begin to farm. They set up shops in the cities. Slowly they prosper. The Jews are Europeans; the Palestinians are Arabs. Their ways are different. By the end of World War II, 300,000 Jews are living in Palestine. Although Arabs still constitute the majority of residents in the British Palestine Mandate, they fear that the onslaught of Jewish refugees will change Palestine forever, and Arab Palestinians will be a minority in their own land. The Arabs look to the British for support. The British try to hold back the tide, preventing boatloads

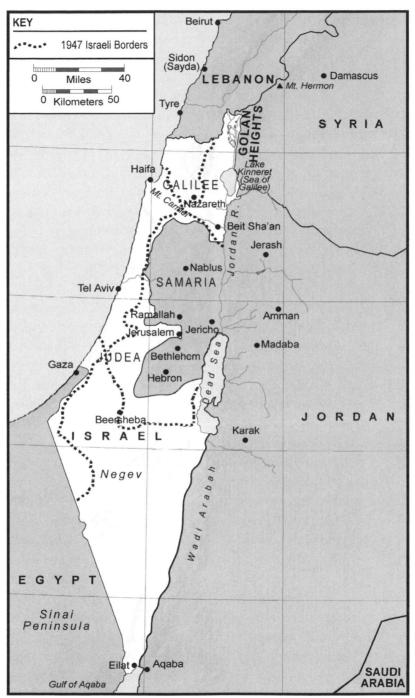

KEY

┅┅┅ 1947 Israeli Borders

0 ___ Miles ___ 40

0 ___ Kilometers ___ 50

Beirut

Sidon
(Sayda)

● Damascus

LEBANON ▲ Mt. Hermon

S Y R I A

Tyre

GOLAN HEIGHTS

Haifa

GALILEE

Lake
Kinneret
(Sea of
Galilee)

Mt. Carmel

Nazareth

Beit Sha'an

Jordan R.

Jerash

● Nablus

SAMARIA

Tel Aviv

Ramallah

Amman

Jerusalem   Jericho

● Madaba

JUDEA   Bethlehem

Dead Sea

Gaza

Hebron

Beersheba

I S R A E L

Karak

J O R D A N

Negev

Wadi Arabah

E G Y P T

*Sinai
Peninsula*

Eilat   Aqaba

**SAUDI
ARABIA**

Gulf of Aqaba

**Map 2. Borders of Israel, 1947 (U.N. proposed) and 1949
(following armistice).**

of refugees from landing, for the landings are indeed illegal. But the landings continue. The Haganah has learned to work around the British.

Meanwhile, within Palestine, a radical Jewish underground organization called *Irgun*, formed originally to protect settlers from Arab militants—and to make life so uncomfortable for Arabs that they will leave Palestine—now realizes that for the time being their enemy must be the British. They do all they can to disrupt the British, going as far as blowing up the King David Hotel in Jerusalem. The flood of refugees continues, Arab indignation rises, the Irgun destroys British headquarters, and the British in the end can do little to stop the violence. They seek help from the United Nations.

Independence and the First Arab/Israeli War: 1948

1947

In November of 1947, the United Nations (UN) passes a resolution partitioning Palestine into a Jewish state and an Arab state. Jerusalem is to be a UN protectorate. All Arab countries oppose this resolution, but a majority of other countries support it. Official partition is to take place in September of 1948. But the Jewish settlers in Palestine—whose very presence is by this time vehemently opposed by the surrounding Arab states—act unilaterally. On May 14, 1948, they proclaim Israel as an independent country. At the same time,

1948

the British give up their troubled Mandate over Palestine.

A day after Israel proclaims its independence, its Arab neighbors declare war. The Israelis anticipate this action. The territory they were to receive under the UN partition includes only a portion of "Eretz Israel," the land of the Zionists' dreams. It is not even enough, Israelis say, to serve as the basis for a viable state. If they are to gain more territory, indeed if they are only to keep what has been granted them in the partition, they must fight. Units of the Haganah and Irgun form the core of a hastily mobilized Israeli army. As Arab forces enter the territory of the former British Mandate, they are determined to push the Israelis into the sea. The Jordanians, with their crack British-trained Arab Legion, fight well, advancing across the Jordan River to take the land known today as the West Bank. Israeli troops, harassed from all directions, are held to the borders shown in the map on page twenty-nine.

Egypt takes the Gaza Strip, and Syria retains the Golan Heights, overlooking Lake Kinneret (the Sea of Galilee). The Israelis make their strongest stand in Jerusalem; there the Jordanians are able to take only the eastern half of the city. But this half includes the Old City and, above all, the Temple Mount, where Solomon's Temple once stood. The Temple Mount has not been a site of Jewish worship since the Roman destruction of the rebuilt Temple in 70 CE (Common Era). Now called the Haram al-Sharif by Muslims, the former Temple Mount contains the Dome of the Rock, the third of the three most holy sites of Islam (after Mecca and Medina in Saudi Arabia). Nearby is the Western Wall, the only portion of the Temple complex that escaped Roman destruction. Now the Jews of Israel will no longer have access to this sacred site.

UN-Brokered Territorial Settlement: 1949

The UN brokers a peace settlement in 1949. Under this settlement, Israel begins its life with fifty percent more territory than it would have had under the UN partition plan. It has control of the entire eastern Mediterranean coast south of Lebanon (except for the Gaza Strip), the northern (Galilean) and southern (Judean) portions of the bordering hill country, and the western portion of Jerusalem. Samaria (subsequently called the West Bank) is in Jordanian hands, as is almost the entire Jordan Valley. Egypt controls the Gaza Strip, and Syria the Golan Heights. Southward, Israel controls the Negev Desert, from the Dead Sea westward to the Sinai Peninsula. But its spiritual heart, the Old City of Jerusalem, remains in Arab hands.

1949

War and Israeli Territorial Gains: 1956 and 1967

In 1956, Egypt blockades the Straits of Tiran, Israel's only outlet to the Red Sea, cutting off its access to petroleum. Israel invades Egypt and takes over the Sinai Peninsula and the Gaza Strip. Subsequently, it agrees to hand back these territories to a UN Peacekeeping Force. But in succeeding years, the Egyptians refuse

1956-
1949

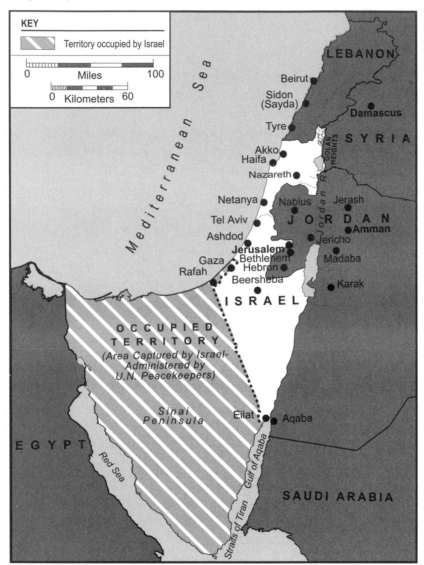

KEY

Territory occupied by Israel

0   Miles   100

0   Kilometers   60

Mediterranean Sea

LEBANON

Beirut

Sidon
(Sayda)

Damascus

Tyre

S Y R I A

Akko
Haifa

GOLAN HEIGHTS

Nazareth

Netanya   Nablus   Jerash

Jordan R.

Tel Aviv   J O R D A N

Ashdod   Amman

Jericho

Jerusalem

Gaza   Bethlehem   Madaba
Rafah   Hebron

Beersheba   Karak

I S R A E L

O C C U P I E D
T E R R I T O R Y
*(Area Captured by Israel-
Administered by
U.N. Peacekeepers)*

*Sinai
Peninsula*   Eilat   Aqaba

E G Y P T

Red Sea

Straits of Tiran   *Gulf of Aqaba*

SAUDI ARABIA

Map 3. Israel following 1956 war.

Israel the use of the Suez Canal, move troops into the Sinai, and
demand the withdrawal of the UN Peacekeeping Force. Meanwhile,
the Syrians are shelling Israel from the Golan Heights. Thus provoked,
on June 5, 1967, Israel strikes targets in Egypt, Jordan, and Syria.
1967 The war lasts just six days before all parties accept a UN Security
Council ceasefire. From this action, Israel gains control of the Sinai

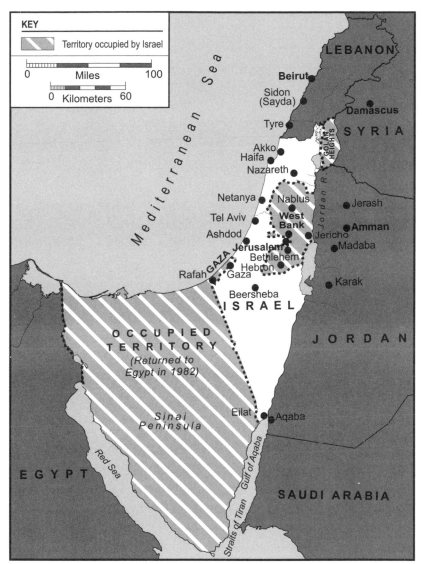

KEY

Territory occupied by Israel

0   Miles   100

0   Kilometers   60

Map 4. Israel following the Six-Day War, 1967.

Peninsula, the Gaza Strip, the Golan Heights, and all land west of
the Jordan River (the West Bank), including all of Jerusalem. In 1979,   1979
urged on by the carrot of U.S. aid, Egypt makes peace with Israel,
and in 1982, Israel hands back the Sinai Peninsula. But the rest of the   1982
gains of the Six-Day War remain under total or partial Israeli control
to this day.

2

OCCUPIED TERRITORIES

*Only through the [1988] intifadeh did the West Bankers
and the Gazans really emerge as a nation in the fullest
sense. The intifadeh transformed [them] from Jordanized
and Egyptianized Palestinians into Palestinians–period.*

**Thomas L. Friedman,
From Beirut to Jerusalem**

On most maps created outside Israel, including United
Nations maps, the West Bank and Gaza are separately
designated as areas of disputed ownership, or *Occupied
Territories*. Their status, the status of the Golan Heights, and the
status of Jerusalem are thorny issues that no peace initiative has been
able to resolve.

The West Bank

1967

At first, after Israel wins the Occupied Territories in 1967, a
liberal Israeli government leaves the West Bank more-or-less alone,
with the exception of a military presence. Ruled by Jordan since 1948,
the West Bank is economically underdeveloped, for the young country
of Jordan is overwhelmed by the influx of Palestinian refugees on its

Photo 1. Irrigated farmland in Israel, along the Jordan River.

soil. Nevertheless, the West Bank has a relatively efficient administrative infrastructure. Its people are Jordanian citizens, free to work in Jordan and continue their links with Jordan, even using Jordanian currency. A few Israeli kibbutz settlements are built in a lightly occupied strip along the west bank of the Jordan River, keeping a relatively low profile.

As I pass northward in the West Bank along the Jordan Valley, I see how Jewish settlers are making the land highly productive by combining technology with hard work. Only later do I realize that the irrigation water they are using, the result of a huge Israeli investment in water development, is often denied to neighboring Arab farmers.

A conservative government follows. Its members consider that the Occupied Territories are part of the Biblical Promised Land and must be absorbed. Israeli settlements soon spread to the Samaritan hill country, and the West Bank is linked economically with Tel Aviv. The conservative government is determined that the West Bank shall be in integral part of the Jewish state.

Jewish Settlements

By 1970, the Israeli government is confiscating land and building homes in the heavily settled areas of the West Bank. Palestinian villages and neighborhoods are being bulldozed to make way for new construction, and olive groves are being uprooted. The settlement program makes it clear that the intention is not only to create new settlements, but also to destroy evidence of previous Palestinian occupancy. Although some Israeli settlers come for ideological reasons, to help give permanence to Israeli occupation, most are attracted by the favorable terms (low taxes, low-interest loans) under which they receive housing and land. Serving a defensive purpose as well as providing housing, most West Bank settlements are sited on hilltops, overlooking Palestinian villages or towns. As the planned settlements grow, they reach outward in the direction of the settlement on the next hill, with the intention that eventually the two will merge.

About 174,000 Jewish settlers now live in the West Bank in 137 separate settlements, ranging in size from two hundred to several thousand. Another 20,000 live in enclaves too small to be called settlements. The rate of Jewish population growth in the West Bank, over eight percent per year, far outpaces Israel's 2.5 percent average rate of growth.

In 2001 the Israeli government agrees to halt the building of new settlements except in the vicinity of Jerusalem. But it has pledged to continue to care for those already in place. The Israelis are building a network of high-speed roads by-passing Palestinian towns to connect the settlements with each other and with Israel proper. Settlers use the by-pass roads to get to their jobs in Israel's cities, but Palestinians are not allowed to travel on these roads. The roads separate Palestinian villages from each other as effectively as the Interstate Highways, cutting through cities in the United States, once tore apart urban neighborhoods.

To build the settlements, the by-pass roads, and the military installations dotting the West Bank, Israelis confiscate land from Palestinian owners. Israeli law requires payment for land confiscated, but Palestinians are generally denied building permits to replace the homes the Israelis destroy. Many villagers have been separated from

1970

2001

17

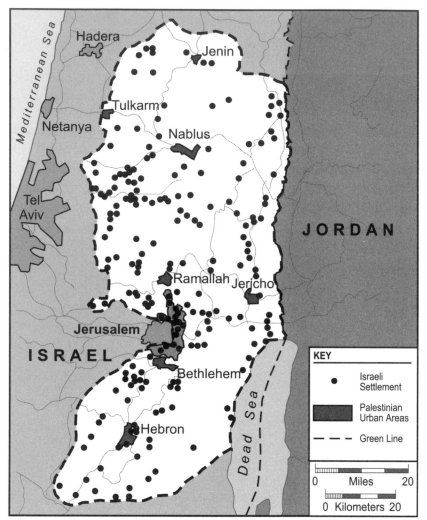

Map 5. Israel settlements in the occupied territories since 1967; The West Bank

their farmland by a by-pass road. If they try to put up a building on their separated plots, so that they can once again farm their land, the building permit is denied. But if the land remains idle for three years, it can be confiscated. Rarely is a building permit issued to a Palestinian; yet if he goes ahead and builds without a permit, and many do, he risks having his structure torn down. In ways such as this, the Israeli settlement program sends a message to West Bank Palestinians: This land is ours, we intend to stay, and you may leave if you wish. In the

West Bank, eight percent of the total West Bank population of nearly 2.3 million is now Jewish. The settlers are among the most militantly anti-Arab of Jewish voters.

The settlements require military protection, an infrastructure of schools and medical care, water and sewer lines, as well as connecting roads. The settlers receive water rights denied to Palestinians. Palestinians are denied access both to the settlements and to the infrastructure that serves them. By contrast with nearby Palestinian villages, the West Bank settlements appear conspicuously affluent. Their occupants are employed and prospering but are unwelcome and unloved except by one another. Their presence is deeply resented by the Palestinians.

To protect the settlements, Israelis have set up roadblocks and check points, which have now been given a measure of permanence, with steel bars and metal grating delimiting the areas where people must queue. Palestinians must endure frequent security checks if they wish to travel between their own communities. Settlers, by contrast, are waved through checkpoints as they travel between settlements or out of the Occupied Territories into Israel proper. The Jewish settlers and the Palestinians have almost no communication. They speak different languages, and their children learn different histories and different religions in separate school systems. Distrust and mistrust prevail.

Jerusalem

Israel does not consider East Jerusalem to be part of the Occupied Territories. In all other areas, except for Jerusalem, the Occupied Territories represent the land won by Israel in the Six-Day war of 1967. But the Green Line does not run through Jerusalem. Instead, it runs east of the city. Shortly after the 1967 armistice the entire city is placed under Israeli civil administration (in contrast with the West Bank and Gaza, which are under military administration). In 1980 the Knesset, Israel's parliament, explicitly annexes East Jerusalem, despite a host of UN resolutions censuring Israel for doing so. Israeli policy toward Jerusalem is two-fold: 1) to guarantee the security of all religious structures and those who worship there; and 2) to increase the percentage of the population in East Jerusalem that is Jewish in order to validate Israel's claim to the entire city. On both policies Israel is succeeding. As far as worshippers are concerned, of any faith, Jerusalem is an open city (although for security reasons no Muslim under the age of 45 is allowed access to the Al-Aqsa Mosque). But as far as the Palestinian population is concerned, life in Jerusalem presents a host of difficulties.

Although Palestinians in East Jerusalem represent thirty percent of the city's population, they are allotted only ten percent of the city's municipal services budget. They are crowded into an area where forty percent of the houses are substandard, but they are not allowed building permits to upgrade their housing. They are given identity cards, which can be revoked. On the northern, eastern, and southern outskirts of the city, where municipal boundaries have been expanded, there are now ten major Jewish settlements, housing more than 200,000 settlers. To build these settlements, one-third of the Palestinian-owned land in east Jerusalem has been confiscated. Payment is made for land confiscated, but building permits are not issued to build new dwellings. The ring of settlements effectively separates Palestinian residents of the Old City from Palestinians in the West Bank. In terms of population, Jerusalem—now a city nearing 700,000—is becoming ever more a Jewish city.

What about the future of Jerusalem? Israel's position is that there is no room even for negotiation; the entire city must remain as the capital of Israel. The position of the Palestinian Authority is that Jerusalem should be an Open City, but that administration should be divided between Israel and Palestine, on pre-1967 boundaries; East Jerusalem must be the capital of Palestine. The European Union, and many world statesmen, support the idea of Jerusalem as an international city, as proposed in the 1947 United Nations partition plan—a city that would be administered by a governing body separate from either Israel or Palestine. Meanwhile, for now Israel's control is defacto and absolute.

The Gaza Strip

When the Israelis take over the Gaza Strip from the Egyptians in 1967, it is already one of the world's most crowded areas and is

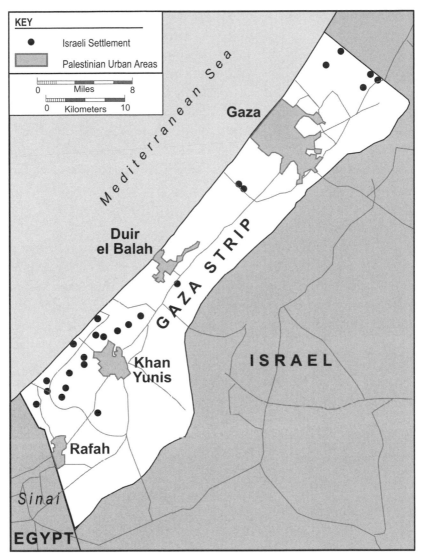

Map 6. Israeli settlements in the occupied territories since 1967; The Gaza Strip.

seething with discontent. The people of Gaza, most of whom lost their homes in Israel, had not been granted Egyptian citizenship, nor had they been allowed to work in Egypt. In effect, the majority were (and still are) wards of the UN, living in crowded refugee camps. From the first, Israel imposes harsh security measures in Gaza to quell unrest. Now, with a population of 1.2 million, three times its 1967 size, the Gaza Strip has a density averaging more than 2,500

1967

21

people per square mile. Eighty-nine percent of the working force is unemployed. Yet, unbelievably, a few Israeli settlers, most of them religious zealots, have been enticed to live there. The majority of Israeli settlements are on the rich agricultural lands of the southern coastal plain, where land was confiscated. The 6900 Jewish settlers form half of one percent of the population, but their landholdings and the security measures needed to protect them include thirty percent of the Gaza Strip. This includes a security zone along the border, in which no building is permitted. There is little reason in Gaza for tempers to cool.

2002

A "Hot Button"

The presence of the settlers in the West Bank, East Jerusalem, and Gaza is one of the "hot buttons" that Palestinians keep pressing, knowing that Israelis themselves are divided on whether the settlers should remain. Sixty percent of all Israelis now feel that settlers and Israeli military personnel should be withdrawn from the Occupied Territories, (but not from East Jerusalem). An increasing number of Israelis feel that a wall should be built to separate the two countries, reminiscent of the wall that divided Jerusalem before 1967. However, the Israeli government is a democracy run by coalition, and the controlling votes in government are those of the religious right. To the extent that the religious right is in control, Israel can be viewed as much a theocracy as a democracy. Its very justification for existence is based on the Hebrew Scriptures. Eretz Israel is the ancient Promised Land, and the Palestinians are the Canaanites who must be expelled. There is little prospect that the government will abandon the settlers.

A "Land-for-Peace" Solution?

United Nations Security Council Resolution 242, adopted on November 22, 1967, presents a "Land-for-Peace" solution that Palestinians say they can support. It calls for the establishment of a just and lasting peace based on Israeli withdrawal from territories occupied in 1967 in return for the end of all states of belligerency, respect for the sovereignty of all states in the area, and the right of all

1967

people to live in peace within secure, recognized boundaries. In effect, the resolution commits Arab countries to the acceptance of Israel as a sovereign state. The dangling carrots of peace and acceptance have led 1970 many Israelis to favor this resolution, with the caveat that Jerusalem is non-negotiable. But they point to Palestinian statements in the printed media and on the Internet that decry the very existence of Israel, and they say the Palestinians are not sincere. Palestinians, on the other hand, point to the Israeli settlements within the Occupied Territories and the commitment of the religious right to the expansion of Eretz Israel as proof that the Israeli government has no intention of leaving, ever. Since September 2000, Palestinians have responded with the pent-up fury of stone-throwing, mortar fire, and suicide bombing that is known as the *Intifadeh* (an Arabic word meaning "shaking off the dust and burden"). The Israelis have answered with force. The death toll mounts on both sides, but it is far heavier among the Palestinians. The first *Intifadeh* lasted from 1988 until 1993. 1988-Now a new wave of violence exists in the Holy Land, far more deadly 1993 than its predecessor. At this writing more than a thousand coffins have been filled, two-thirds of them Palestinian, one-third Israeli. No end to the violence is in sight.

3

ARAFAT'S ISLANDS

To end the occupation and all that has gone with it is a
clear enough imperative. Now let us do it.
Edward Said,
Al-Ahram Weekly, January 11, 2002

Hamas does not recognize the right of Israel to exist. Its
long-term aim is to establish an Islamic state on land
originally mandated as Palestine.
Martin Asser,
BBC News, December 3, 2001

In the recent past, there have been measured steps toward peace.
Today there is a Palestinian Authority with jurisdiction over
fragmented portions of the Occupied Territories that skeptics
call *Arafat's Islands*. The steps that lead to the creation of the Palestinian
Authority begin in 1979 when United States President Jimmy Carter
brokers a peace with Egypt (called the Camp David Accord), followed
by Israel's return of the Sinai in 1982. In 1993, the Oslo Accord
recognizes Israel's right to exist and Palestinian rights to the Occupied
Territories. This landmark Accord is brokered by Norwegian
diplomats in Oslo in 1992 and signed the next year in Washington.
The signers are Israeli Prime Minister Yitzhak Rabin (who later is
assassinated by a crazed right-wing Israeli attempting to undermine

1979

1993

the peace process) and Palestinian leader Yasser Arafat, both of whom are awarded the Nobel Peace Prize the following year. Arafat comes to the negotiating table as head of the Palestinian Liberation Organization (PLO), once a terrorist organization but legitimized after Oslo. He has been the spokesman for all displaced Palestinians, but now he represents specifically those living in the West Bank and Gaza.

1994

1995

The first benefit to Israel is the establishment of diplomatic relations with Jordan in 1994. The Palestinians see no benefit until a year later, a benefit granted by the Israelis only after prodding from U.S. President Bill Clinton and a further Oslo II Accord brokered in Washington. Israel begins withdrawing its military forces from all West Bank cities in 1995. At the same time, a *Palestinian Authority* is created. As the Israelis gradually withdraw from West Bank cities, the Palestinian Authority, headed by Arafat, takes over governance. In addition, the Palestinian Authority begins to govern in some of the rural areas where many Palestinians live, but in these areas Israel retains security responsibility. By Oslo Accord terms, nearly three-fourths of the West Bank remains under total Israeli control.

A Broken Framework

The Oslo Accord provides for other steps as well—negotiations over shared sovereignty of Jerusalem, the status of Palestinian refugees, further territorial withdrawal, security arrangements, and disputed boundaries—but on these issues there has been little progress. A conservative Israeli government in power since 1996 opposes the Oslo Accords in principle and drags its feet on further negotiations. The Palestinians, wary of Israeli objectives and insisting on Jerusalem as their capital, likewise stall. As the Israelis furiously build new settlements in the West Bank, the Palestinians feel betrayed. At the same time, a powerful radical wing within the Palestinian Authority remains opposed to Israel's right to exist. It is this radical wing that sows terror, to which Israelis retaliate, likewise spreading terror.

The 5-year period after Oslo, allotted for the achievement of Palestinian independence, passes by in 1998 without accomplishment. Nevertheless, diplomacy continues, most with no results, but some

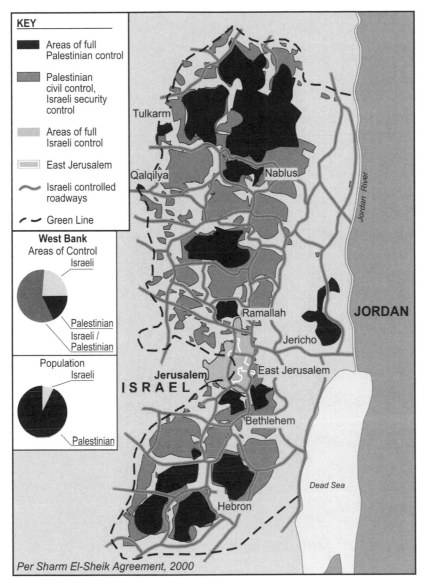

KEY

- ■ Areas of full Palestinian control
- ▨ Palestinian civil control, Israeli security control
- ▨ Areas of full Israeli control
- ▨ East Jerusalem
- ∼ Israeli controlled roadways
- ⌒ Green Line

West Bank
Areas of Control
Israeli
Palestinian
Israeli / Palestinian

Population
Israeli
Palestinian

Tulkarm

Qalqilya

Nablus

Jordan River

Ramallah

Jericho

JORDAN

Jerusalem

East Jerusalem

ISRAEL

Bethlehem

Dead Sea

Hebron

Per Sharm El-Sheik Agreement, 2000

Map 7. West Bank administrative areas, as of March 2000.

with measured success. In 2000 the Sharm el-Sheikh agreement increases the amount of West Bank territory over which the Palestinians have absolute control and reduces Israel's area of control. But today the majority of the Israeli electorate is convinced that Israel's security will be compromised with further concessions. The Palestinian

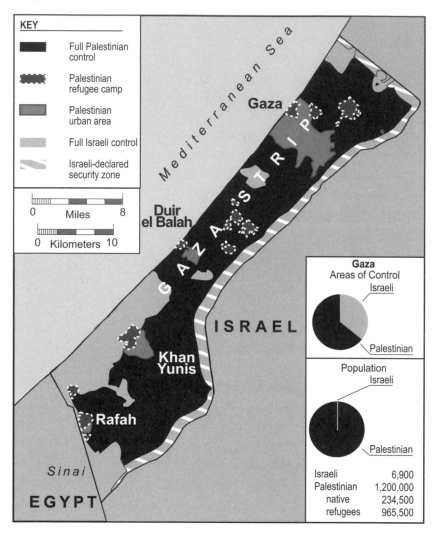

KEY

- ■ Full Palestinian control
- ▓ Palestinian refugee camp
- ▓ Palestinian urban area
- ░ Full Israeli control
- ▨ Israeli-declared security zone

0 Miles 8

0 Kilometers 10

Mediterranean Sea

Gaza

GAZA STRIP

Duir el Balah

GAZA STRIP

ISRAEL

Khan Yunis

Rafah

Sinai

EGYPT

Gaza
Areas of Control

Israeli

Palestinian

Population

Israeli

Palestinian

Israeli	6,900
Palestinian	1,200,000
native	234,500
refugees	965,500

Map 8. Gaza Strip administrative areas, as of March 2000.

Authority's governance of a fragmented portion of the Occupied Territories is the only part of the Oslo Accords that remains.

The Palestinian Authority

In all cities of the Occupied Territories, the Palestinian Authority is sovereign in local matters. It regulates civic affairs, and its police force is in charge of security. These urban sites represent a fragmented and noncontiguous area of about eighteen percent of the Occupied

Territories, creating the almost ungovernable territory termed by some as Arafat's Islands. In another twenty-two percent of the Occupied Territories, mostly towns and villages, the Palestinian Authority is sovereign over civic affairs, but Israel is responsible for security. That leaves seventy-one percent of the Occupied Territories (including East Jerusalem and all of the Jewish settlements) in which Israel is totally sovereign. This, say the Palestinians, is unacceptable. To which the Israelis answer that the security of their settlers and their capital of Jerusalem are at stake. The differences seem unbridgeable.

The cities in the West Bank and Gaza now governed by the Palestinian Authority include places sacred not only to Jews and Christians but also to Muslims, who share ancient traditions with Jews and who consider Jesus Christ as a major prophet: Bethlehem, the birthplace of Jesus; Hebron, where Abraham was buried and where David assumed the kingship; Nablus (ancient Shechem), where Abraham first camped when he reached the Holy Land and where the Israelites later crowned their kings; and Jericho, the first Canaanite stronghold taken by Joshua and his Hebrew soldiers. Other cities within the Palestinian Authority are Gaza, Jenin, Khan Yunis, Rafah, Ramallah, and Tulkarm. At the outskirts of all these cities today, Israelis have erected barricades and have sometimes positioned tanks. Significantly, the Palestinian Authority has no jurisdiction over Jerusalem, the city both Palestinians and Israelis claim as their capital. Hebron, one of the largest cities in the West Bank, is an exception to the Oslo plan. With a small but militant Jewish population, Hebron exists as a divided city. Palestinians have control over eighty-five percent of Hebron, but Israel retains governance of the fifteen percent where 400 extremely conservative Jewish settlers have established their homes.

Terrorist Organizations

With Arafat committed to negotiations with the Israelis, the extremists among the Palestinians (those who feel that the Palestinians will never receive justice so long as Israel exists) now align themselves with either Hamas or the Islamic Jihad. Both have been termed terrorist organizations by Israel and the majority of the non-Arab international community, but to Arabs they are "freedom fighters." Both Hamas and the Islamic Jihad receive support from sympathizers in other Arab countries. The Islamic Jihad is closely related to militant Islamic fundamentalist counterparts in Egypt. Because Hamas is homegrown, and Islamic fundamentalist as well, it has a somewhat more popular following than the Islamic Jihad, whose main base of support is in Gaza. Leaders in both organizations have trained abroad, some under Osama bin Laden in Afghanistan.

It is young Palestinians inspired and directed by Hamas or the Islamic Jihad who blow themselves up in Israel's cities, on buses, in shopping districts, in cafes, or wherever they can most effectively sow terror. The two terrorist organizations want to weaken Israel's resolve to remain in the Middle East, a cancer, as they see it, among Muslim states. They collect donations and disperse a number of needed social services within the Palestinian Authority to stay in line with their commitment to Islam and its mandate to perform acts of charity. In this way, they win favor with Palestinians. They are extremists, religiously fundamental, and politically radical. A growing number of Palestinians share their vision.

Hamas and the Islamic Jihad have power, weapons, and influence over Yasser Arafat, whose prior unyielding credentials (like those of Israel's Prime Minister Ariel Sharon) have brought him to his present position of leadership. (Later in this book Sharon and Arafat are profiled, their backgrounds compared.) Toward Palestinians whom they suspect of collaborating with Israel, Hamas and the Islamic Jihad are brutal. If and when Palestine becomes a sovereign country, they intend to provide its leadership and direction. To this extent, they are also a threat to Arafat and his currently more-moderate Fatah party. Also a threat to Arafat's leadership, however, are leaders of the armed wings within the Palestine Liberation Organization, which he heads. The PLO is formed of two major factions, Fatah and the Popular Front for the Liberation of Palestine. Within Fatah is an armed group known as Tanzim, which embraces terrorism despite Fatah's official commitment to negotiation. The PFLP has never shared Fatah's commitment and over the militant PFLP Arafat has little personal control. Sharon, by default, must negotiate with Arafat, who at least recognizes Israel's right to exist. But with the growing strength of the

Photo 2. Visitors at the Church of the Nativity in Bethlehem.

Palestinian terrorist organizations and Arafat's seeming reluctance or inability to quell terrorist activities, the Israelis are now determined to hold on to their military presence in the Occupied Territories and to exert force as they deem necessary. On both sides, the will to negotiate is weak.

The present Intifadeh begins in September of 2000. Its immediate trigger is the appearance of then Israeli Defense Minister Ariel Sharon on the Haram al-Sharif, which Sharon and all Israelis never cease to call "the Temple Mount." Although technically he has a right to be there, Sharon's presence is inflammatory, as he must know it will be. The first group of boys begins to throw rocks, the first retribution results in a Palestinian death, and the *Al-Aqsa Intifadeh* (named after the mosque on the Haram al-Sharif) is underway. Violence intensifies with each suicide bombing and each further retribution. It continues unabated as I write. Sharon requires seven days without violence as a precondition for further negotiations. But it is in the interest of Hamas and the Islamic Jihad that violence continues. Sharon is well aware that his terms may not be met.

Before the present Al-Aqsa Intifadeh begins, Arafat declares that by September of 2000 Palestinians will proclaim their fragmented territory as an independent country. That does not happen, and the thorny questions of the Jewish settlements, compensation to Palestinians for seized property, resettlement of Palestinians in Israel, and the status of Jerusalem now seem beyond resolution. In Israel, it is the reactionary Jewish religious right who call the shots; in the Palestinian Authority, it is, de facto, the radical Islamic extremists.

Economic Woes

The places governed by the Palestinian Authority today are under-funded, lacking in economic opportunity, and a breeding ground for frustration and recruitment of young men into radical movements.

My experiences in the Palestinian Authority are positive but also indicative of the contrast between Israel and the Authority. The day I visit Bethlehem, in March of 2000, my view is totally blurred by the thousands of tourists who come to the city of Jesus' birth on the day following the Papal visit. But human and automobile movement carries on apace, and the Palestinian Authority in Bethlehem seems to be coping. Not so its Arab citizens however. I talk with a man in suit and tie who convinces me that, despite working two jobs, at the end of the month there is nothing left to pay for much-needed dentistry, to send a cherished three-year-old to nursery school, or to replace a frayed shirt with a new one. "No matter which way I turn, I feel I am in a box," he tells me. Driving through Jericho in early evening, I find the streets poorly paved, the storefronts shabby, and the overhead lights dim to save on electricity.

The Palestinians claim that what they most need is investment in industry. But few investors are willing to commit to Palestine until both peace and the rule of law are certain. Nongovernmental organizations, representing the gamut of religious and political affiliations, give much-needed help. In addition, before the present Intifadeh, there were encouraging examples of Israeli and Palestinian businessmen working together on an individual basis. Although in general the private sector is steering clear of Palestine, there is one notable exception: A luxurious casino is going up in Jericho, privately funded by Palestinian and Israeli investors. There is as yet no other in the Holy Land, and if the Jericho casino attracts hordes of Israeli gamblers, as the Palestinian Authority expects, the taxes, they say, will go into the public coffers.

I do not enter the Gaza Strip, but I have one unforgettable encounter with an Arab woman from Gaza. An attractive young woman, she and her three sickly children are sitting in the lobby of the Jerusalem hotel where I am staying. Through an interpreter, I learn that she is twenty years old, from Gaza, and that her husband has beaten her. Her parents will not shame themselves by letting her come home, so the Israeli police have taken her to the hotel as a safe house for one night while her husband cools off. When she returns, she expects to be beaten again. She has no money, no food, and it is obvious the children are sick. I share what food I have with her, but the feverish children only nibble on it. In the morning, I search for her, to give her some money, but the police have already taken her back. She still haunts me. (At that time, the Israeli and Palestinian police were cooperating, but I doubt if such cooperation is possible now.)

Israeli national statistics do not include the West Bank and Gaza as an integral part of Israel. On the one hand, this is an admission that the areas are separate from Israel proper. But there may be another reason. By all measures, the Occupied Territories rank among the world's poor nations. Their birth rates and death rates are high, their national product per capita is less than a tenth of Israel's, and their infrastructure is little developed. With the exception of the Jewish settlements, Israel has paid scant attention to the welfare of these lands under their control since 1967. Many Palestinians in the Occupied Territories formerly found work in Israel. Now, with strict imposed security measures, Palestinians find it almost impossible to get to their former job or even get around roadblocks from one city to another. The economy of the Palestinian Authority, never strong, is plunging. In Gaza, more than eighty percent of the population is unemployed. With high unemployment and a rapidly decreasing tax base, Palestinian Authority coffers are nearly dry.

Although the armed struggle of the Palestinians is costly, much of the cost of arms for the Intifadeh is borne by sympathizers in other countries. As I write, the Israelis have intercepted a ship in the Red Sea that was bound for a port in Gaza. The ship, captained by a Palestinian member of the Fatah organization, was carrying a large shipment of arms manufactured in Iran, financed privately by a Saudi 2002 citizen or citizens, and destined for the Palestinian Authority.

4

SYRIA AND THE GOLAN HEIGHTS

Syria is ready to establish normal relations with Israel in return for Israel's full withdrawal from the Golan.

Hafez Al-Assad,
late president of Syria at conference with
U.S. President Bill Clinton,
October 27, 1994

Syria wants Israel to return the Golan Heights, the area north and east of the Sea of Galilee (Lake Kinneret). The Golan is not included in the original 1947 UN partition plan, for it is Syrian territory. At the end of the first Arab/Israeli War, the Golan remains in Syrian hands. Across the border Israeli and Syrian troops continue to skirmish. Israelis covet the Golan and the farmland and water resources it represents. From there, in the years between 1948 and 1967, Syrian guns regularly shell Israeli settlements in Galilee.

1947

1948-
1967

In the northern town of Beit Sha'an, I speak with an Israeli woman who remembers the frequent nights in her childhood spent in terror, huddled in a reinforced basement while Syrian shells explode overhead.

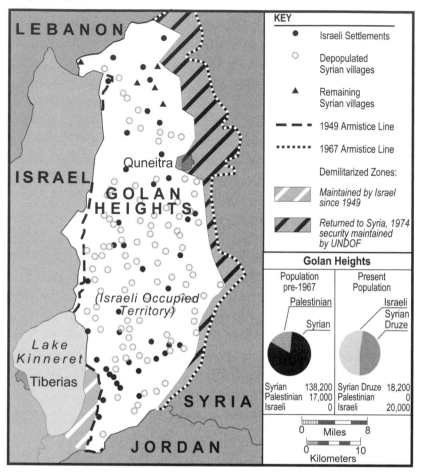

Map 9. The Golan Heights, depopulated villages, Israeli settlements and administrative areas.

Israel takes control of the Golan Heights in the 1967 War. It quickly dismantles Syrian gun emplacements and effectively ends the threat from that quarter. Then it begins the systematic destruction of Syrian villages, forcing their occupants to flee to other parts of Syria. Estimates of the number of Syrians displaced vary, from 70,000 (Israeli estimate) to 150,000 (Syrian estimate). Also fleeing to Syria are some 17,000 Palestinians, who now are refugees for the second time. The Syrian nationals are given temporary housing in apartments in and around Damascus. The Palestinians are housed in UN refugee camps, joining their compatriots who reached Syria in 1948.

1967

Photo 3. Eastern shore of Lake Kinneret (Sea of Galillee) from Hippos archaeological site.

One group of Syrian nationals who neither flee nor are forced out in 1967 are the Druze, of whom 18,000 continue to live in their Golan villages. The Druze are an Arab people who practice an offshoot of Islam.

Most of the Golan is now given over to commercial grazing and dairy enterprises conducted by some 20,000 Israeli setters who live either on kibbutzim (collective farms) or moshavs (cooperative farms). Israel now gets much of its beef and dairy products from the Golan.

In 1973 Syrians and Israeli armed forces clash once again over the Golan. The United Nations subsequently sets off a strip varying in width from six to fifty miles along the east side of the Golan, which has since been patrolled by some one thousand members of a United Nations Disengagement Observer Force. Israel vacates this territory but not before leveling the town of Quneitra, the former chief city of the Golan. Syria decides not to rebuild Quneitra but to leave it as evidence. The strip has since been resettled by some of the Syrian villagers who originally fled the Golan.

1973

37

Syria wants the Golan back. Its claim to the Golan extends to the northeast shore of Lake Kinneret, as recognized under the never-implemented 1947 UN partition plan. Many Israelis are willing to give back the Golan Heights if these heights are demilitarized and if the new border remains well away from Lake Kinneret. But further they refuse to go.

"No way," growls the Israeli taxi driver, as he tells me what he has heard on the evening's radio concerning Syria's demands. "Kinneret is ours, shore to shore." He will give his vote to whichever party vows to keep Israel intact.
During my travels, I traverse the beautiful Golan Heights area, as well as the land bordering Lake Kinneret. The view from the Golan toward snow-capped Mount Hermon to the north, the Jordan Valley below, and Lake Kinneret to the west is unforgettable. But the double rows of barbed wire fencing protecting the border and the concrete bases of pre-1967 Syrian gun emplacements convince me that a peace settlement in this area may still be a long way off.

Syria refuses to consider establishing diplomatic relations with Israel until the matter of the Golan Heights is settled. Meanwhile, Syria backs Lebanese Hezbullah guerrillas, who cross Israel's northern border to harass kibbutz settlements. It is beyond question that Syria is lending assistance to the Palestinian Authority. At this writing the refugee population in Syria has increased to nearly 500,000. Of these, nearly thirty percent remain in UN refugee camps. Although the remainder have become integrated within the Syrian economy, none have been offered Syrian citizenship.

5

PALESTINIAN REFUGEES

*Refugee camps are no longer the makeshift tented
structures of the early years, but 50 years on are densely-
packed and crowded fixed constructions. Consequences of
chronic density [are] poorer housing, greater physical and
mental health problems, increasingly poor study habits
among children, and a sense of powerlessness among the
population.*

Oxfam Report, March 1999

Between 1947 and 1949, about 750,000 Arabs leave their homes in Palestine, pushed out by the Jewish military and/or fleeing in panic, depending on the chronicler. They go mainly to the West Bank, then under control of Jordan, and to the Gaza Strip, Lebanon, and Syria. After the Six-Day War in 1967, another 300,000 Palestinians become refugees as they leave the West Bank for Jordan, unwilling to live under Israeli rule. Technically, a Refugee is someone who has been uprooted from his/her home. A Registered Refugee is one who has sought UN assistance. Today, more than a half century later, two-thirds of the dispersed Palestinians still remain Registered Refugees, uprooted and in need. Since 1948, the question of Palestinian refugees has been a core issue in Arab/Israeli relations. The refugees want to return home, to the land now ruled by Israel.

1947-
1949

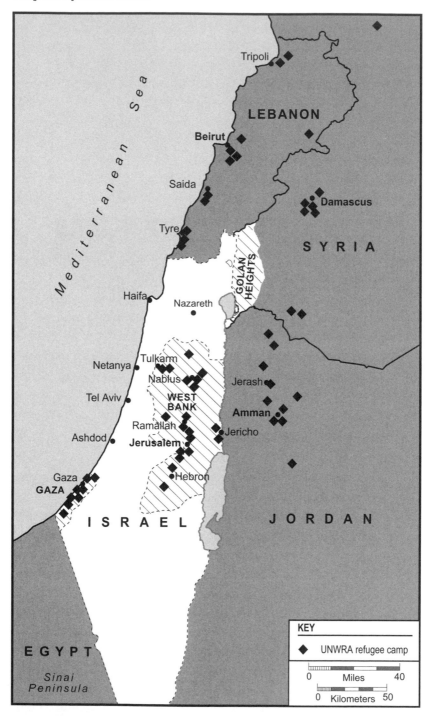

Map 10. Locations of UNWRA Palestinian refugee camps.

40

	Total Palestinians*	Palestinian Refugees**	Registered Refugees***	Refugees in Camps***
Jordan	2,494,100	1,865,900	1,570,200	280,200
West Bank	2,100,000	699,000	583,000	157,700
Gaza	1,200,000	820,700	824,600	452,200
Israel	1,188,700	258,750		
Syria	498,800	476,600	383,200	112,700
Lebanon	460,800	437,100	376,500	210,700
Saudi Arabia	295,300	295,300		
United States	218,100	185,400		
Persian Gulf States	143,500	149,900		
Egypt	52,300	43,400		
Libya	40,100	40,100		
Iraq	39,400	39,400		
Other Arab Countries	6,000	6,000		
Other Countries	177,700	236,100		
Total	7,727,289	5,553,650	3,737,500	1,213,500

* Palestinian Return Center, London, 1998. Updated in 2000 on basis of estimated 3.5% annual population growth rate.
** Palestinian Return Center, London, 2000. Refugees are those who have been uprooted from their homes
*** Public Information Office, UNRWA, Gaza, 2000. Registered Refugees are those who seek UN assistance.

Chart 1. International distribution of Palestinians.

Any final settlement between Israel and the Palestinian Authority must eventually deal with the Palestinian refugees who wish to return and have not accepted (or been offered) citizenship elsewhere. Yet, resettlement of Palestinian refugees is not currently on the negotiating table. The issue festers. And it concurs with the strategy of Israel's Arab neighbors, Jordan excepted. None of them has offered citizenship to the Palestinian refugees or contributed measurably to their well-being. It better serves their long-term policy that more than a million refugees remain wards of the UN, unsettled, dispirited, and angry, reminding the rest of the world that they have a right to return home.

What begins as a displaced population of three quarters of a million people in 1948 has now reached more than five and a half million, all of whom have an intense emotional claim on the land

41

they, their parents, or their grandparents left. Most have spent a lifetime consumed with one objective: to return "home."

This table shows that the largest number of refugees live in Jordan, Gaza, and the West Bank, with Lebanon and Syria also having sizeable numbers. The rest are spread throughout the Arab and Western worlds. The lucky few, the highly educated, have found professional niches in countries of Europe, North America, and the various Arab states.

Since 1948, the United Nations Relief and Works Agency (UNRWA) has been charged with providing at least minimal living accommodations for the refugees who require it. Even today one-third of all Registered Refugees (those who apply for aid) remain in UN camps. In the West Bank, it is one-fourth, and in Gaza, it is over fifty percent. In effect, the refugees living in camps are stateless, unable to leave, and unable to work. Jordan has offered citizenship to its Palestinian population, and some 600,000 have accepted. Hundreds of thousands of others have found a way into the Jordanian economy and are now refugees only in name. In Jordan, only fifteen percent of Registered Refugees remain in camps.

An independent Palestinian state, if and when it does emerge out of the Occupied Territories, will not solve the problem of the refugees in camps in Lebanon, Syria, and Jordan. The Palestinian state would be hard-pressed to find room for them. Israel does not want them back and has worked to keep resettlement out of any peace negotiations. (Palestinians, however, point out that there are portions of far northern Galilee where Israeli settlement is light and farming today is done by imported foreign workers. There is still room in Israel where Palestinians could be resettled, they say.) Meanwhile, in the crowded refugee camps, most Palestinian refugees still harbor the notion that someday a united Arab force will push Israel into the sea. At the least, they pray just to return home. Their children play soldier and fantasize themselves as avengers, and their young men, recruited by Palestinian extremist organizations, act out these fantasies.

Not all Palestinians are refugees. Some 1.2 million Palestinian Arabs live in Israel and are Israeli citizens. Of the 2.1 million Palestinians in the West Bank, nearly thirty-one percent are not refugees: They lived in the West Bank in 1948, and they live there today, although without the rights of Israeli citizens. The Gaza Strip is another story: Less than one-fourth of its 1.2 million people are native to Gaza. In Jordan, those who have accepted Jordanian citizenship are no longer classed as refugees.

6

PEOPLE OF THE HOLY LAND

*The wonderful hospitality, the authentic longing for Zion,
the naïve messianism are perhaps beautiful things to one
who loves such things, but for me they are not the symbols
that I want to see in the society [of western culture] that
my spiritual fathers and I fought to establish here.*

**Ammon Dankner, columnist for the
liberal Jerusalem newspaper Haaretz,
cited by David K. Shipler Arab and Jew**

*Immersed in the swirling countercurrents of competing
images of the Jew as alien, as superior, as illicit,
as powerful, the Arab [in Israel] learns
the special techniques of staying afloat.*

David K. Shipler, Arab and Jew

Various terms are used to categorize the people of the Holy Land: *Israeli, Jew, Arab, Palestinian, Jordanian, Bedouin.* To consider these terms with greater precision, here are some guidelines:

- All citizens of Israel are Israelis, and most Israelis are Jews.
- Almost all Jews have their cultural roots in Judaism. But many, probably most, would describe themselves as secular rather than religious.
- More than a million Israeli citizens are Palestinians.
- All Palestinians are Arabs. They or their ancestors presently live or formerly lived in what was once known as the Palestine Mandate, the heartland of the Holy Land.
- An Arab citizen of Israel is both an Israeli and a Palestinian.
- Most Palestinians are Muslims, but five percent or more are Christians.
- A Bedouin is someone with tribal affiliation who presently (or in the fairly recent past) lives in arid regions as a nomad.
- All Bedouins are Arabs, but most Arabs are not Bedouins.
- Jordanians are citizens of the country formed from the part of the British Mandate that was east of the Jordan River.
- Palestinians make up more than half the population of Jordan.
- Most native-born Jordanians have Bedouin heritage; most Palestinians do not.

Arab and Jew

Who is an Arab and who is a Jew? In ancient times, both came from the same Middle Eastern Semitic stock and used similar languages. By tradition, both are descended from a common ancestor, Abraham, with the Arab branch stemming from Abraham's firstborn, Ishmael, and the Jews from the second son, Isaac. The origin of this deeply ingrained tradition is covered in Part II. For now, it can be said that an Arab is easier to define than a Jew, for most Arabs speak Arabic as their mother tongue. (However, not all who speak Arabic as their mother tongue are Arabs, for many Jews and other non-Arabs in Arab countries grow up speaking Arabic as their first language as well.) Probably, but not necessarily, an Arab is a Muslim, for Islam claims the allegiance of more than ninety percent of all Arabs. His/her ancestors may or may not have been Bedouin nomads from the Arabian Desert, with a traditional way of life centering on animal husbandry.

Palestinians, who are Arabs, are the descendents of the various non-Jewish people who lived in the Holy Land for thousands of years past. In the latter years of the Roman Empire, most were Christian. Their ancestors were absorbed into Arab culture when the faith of Mohammed reached the Holy Land, beginning in the seventh century. Many, but not all, eventually adopted Islam. Most Palestinians do not have roots in the desert, but some do. Most Jordanians, by contrast (excluding the Palestinian newcomers), are but two or three generations away from their nomadic and tribal Bedouin past. Few Palestinians can name their tribal affiliation; most Jordanians can.

Unlike the Arab, a Jew is not defined as a Jew because of his/her mother tongue, for Jews now in Israel have come from more than 100 countries, including Arabic-speaking countries. Nor does he/she have to be a strict observer of Judaism to be an Israeli Jew, for many in Israel think of themselves as secular. Israeli Jews believe their cultural roots are in the Holy Land, and for this reason they choose to live there (or have come because they can no longer live in the land of their birth).

Because the cultural roots of Palestinian Arabs are also in the Holy Land and Palestinians were living in the Holy Land when twentieth-century Jewish immigration began, Jews in Israel must deal with the fact that they have displaced Palestinians. They also are aware that their own people were displaced in the Holy Land 2,000 years ago. Jews of ultra-nationalist or Orthodox religious persuasion feel their occupation (for them, re-occupation) of the Holy Land is destined and God's will; a radical minority are convinced that the occupation will not be complete and successful until all Palestinian Arabs are gone or subjugated. Israelis of more moderate or liberal views (a rapidly shrinking majority) feel that Jews and Palestinians can live together, in equity and justice, in the Holy Land and that Israeli policy should work toward that end.

Part II tells the story of ancient Israel that is meaningful to all Jews, observant or not. It also tells the story of the coming of Christianity and then Islam to the Holy Land—a story that has put indelible ethnic and cultural stamps on the land that Israel now controls.

Israelis

Of all the countries within the Holy Land, Israel has the most well-developed tourism program, as well as the majority of sites associated with the Bible. As a result, some visitors to the Holy Land perceive that the Holy Land and Israel are one and the same and that most people of the Holy Land are Hebrew-speaking followers of Judaism. But the Holy Land extends beyond Israel to include parts of the four countries on its border, all of whose people are Arabs. It is true that the great majority of Israel's six-million citizens are Jews and that almost all Israeli Jews learn to speak Hebrew, the resurrected ancient language that is now the *lingua franca* of Israel. But nearly one-fifth of Israeli citizens are Palestinians whose mother tongue is Arabic, whose children go to Arabic language schools, and who worship either as Muslims (the vast majority) or as Christians.

The first Christians were Jews, and today a small community of Messianic Jews combines both ancient Jewish traditions and Christian beliefs. Representatives of many branches of Christianity live in Israel and care for ancient or modern churches, seminaries, hospitals, and schools started by others of their faith in years past. Many of these institutions serve Arabs and Jews alike and provide venues where dialog can take place. Although most Christians strive to remain as neutral as possible, some tend to make common cause with the Palestinians, others with the Israelis.

Israel's Jewish population is ideologically fractured as they consider how to deal with the Palestinians they have displaced. Israelis are fiercely democratic, and the Knesset, Israel's parliament, is split into a score of political parties, representing the full range of opinion within the country. The ultra-conservative far-right, the religious and ultra-nationalist parties, never command a large segment of the electorate, but without their alliance, no party can gain a majority. The far-right currently controls the Knesset.

Tourists quickly learn to abandon any pre-existing stereotypes regarding Jews in Israel. Although Israel's Jews share a common religious heritage and now speak a common language, they are a blend of all the cultures and ethnic strands that immigration has introduced. To absorb its newcomers, Israel has had to blend cultural and genetic threads that Jews acquired in centuries of Diaspora in Asia, Africa, and Europe. Of Israel's 6 million people, about 4.8 million consider themselves to be Jews. A strong Semitic appearance has persevered through the centuries; nevertheless, Israeli Jews differ vastly in appearance. People seen on the streets of Jerusalem can range from a green-eyed, fair-skinned Slav whose Jewish ancestors might have come from the Russian steppes to a dark-skinned, black-eyed Ethiopian whose Jewish ancestors lived in highland East Africa.

Although small numbers of Jews lived in Palestine throughout the past two millennia, Jewish immigrants begin coming from Europe to Palestine in the latter part of the nineteenth century. The largest number of Jews in Israel come originally as refugees, uprooted and stateless. They come because they cannot live any longer in the land of their birth. Survivors of the Holocaust reach Israel in the late 1940s and 1950s. In the subsequent three decades, many Jews come to Israel from Arab countries, where their ancestors have lived for centuries. In the past two decades, the greatest migration has been from Russia. For most of these immigrants, their move to Israel is an act of desperation. Some Israelis, however, have voluntarily uprooted themselves, mostly from Britain, North America, and Australia, to be a part of the Jewish "in-gathering" and "nation-building" that has created the modern state of Israel.

Most Jews in Israel would agree that the main reason for Israel's existence is to provide a nation where Jews can work out their own destiny in their own country. This reasoning requires a country where the overwhelming percentage of the population is Jewish. At present slightly more than eighty percent of the population of Israel is Jewish. The low rate of natural increase of the Jewish population is similar to that of the world's industrial countries. But through immigration (most recently, from countries of the former Soviet Union), the annual rate of population increase is around 2.5 percent. The rate of natural increase among Israel's Palestinian population, by contrast, is 3.5 percent. This ratio guarantees that unless immigration is increased, the Palestinian citizens of Israel will form an ever larger proportion of the population. This situation underlies Israel's steadfast refusal to consider allowing Palestinian refugees the "right of return" to Israel that they seek. It also underlies Israel's continuing efforts to encourage Jews all over the world to make their home in Israel.

Immigrants to Israel form three broad groupings based on their geographical origin, and these groupings tend to mark their cultural outlook, the people with whom they associate, and the way they vote: the Ashkenazim, or Jews who come to Israel mainly from central and eastern Europe but also from North and South America, South Africa, and Australia; the Sephardim, who are forced from Spain and Portugal during the Inquisition and scatter throughout North African, Eastern Mediterranean, and Balkan lands; and Eastern, or Oriental Jews, who descend from ancient communities in Islamic lands of North Africa and the Middle East.

Most immigrants arrive with little or no knowledge of Hebrew. Once settled, they are no longer considered refugees but Israeli citizens. They learn Hebrew and are integrated into the life and economy of their new country. Children learn quickly in schools. For young people, mandatory service in the military is the great integrator. For adults, integration is not always so easy.

I am a guest in the home of a family of Jewish immigrants from England. The home is culturally familiar. There is a piano, and on it a Mozart sonata. The bookshelf holds volumes I too have read. Dinner features ham, for the family is not religiously observant. Their loyalty is to Israel, and they have come to help build this nation. After dinner, I join the family in attending the final-day festivities for their daughter's fourth-grade class. There is music, dancing, and recitation. But nothing is familiar—not the oriental minor key and half-tones of the songs the children sing, not the dances they perform, nor the recitations in Hebrew. Afterward, back at their home, I realize that the children are talking with each other in Hebrew, while the parents converse in English.

Communication between generations is stilted. In immigrating, the parents have retained much of their own culture, but their children are absorbing another. The parents must swallow their frustration, subverting it to their pride in their children's rapid assimilation. It is the poignant, bittersweet dilemma of all immigrants everywhere.

Many immigrants enter Israel with a good education, and Israelis value learning. Their universities and research institutes are excellent by international standards. Israelis are creative, hard-working, entrepreneurial, argumentative strivers. Life is fast-paced, and the economy reflects this input. Israel has an average gross national product per person above $16,000—greater than Spain's, less than Ireland's.

With the United States, Israelis have a kind of tempered love relationship, knowing that often they must bend to the wishes of their benefactor, but refusing to on occasion as well. They are beholden to the United States for financial aid, for peace-making efforts, and for support in the international arena. Israel receives far more United States foreign aid per person than any other country. Israelis depend heavily on their co-religionists in the United States for support of nongovernmental projects, and Jewish and Christian tourists from the United States form the backbone of what has been a thriving tourist industry, up until the present Intifadeh.

The majority of Israelis are Western in thought and culture, but an oriental strain is also present, evident especially in popular Israeli music. Israel's Jews may or may not be "religious," for Israelis tend to define themselves first by their cultural heritage and then, if they think it relevant (as most do), by their Jewish faith. They tolerate, not always patiently, their compatriots of the religious right.

By law, buses in Israel must stop running at sundown on Friday night in observance of the Jewish Sabbath and do not begin running again until sundown Saturday. Needing to get from Tel Aviv to Jerusalem on a Friday evening, I find that I am not alone in my frustration. People grumble, make wry jokes, and try to get where they must go, as I do, by waiting until one of a crowded fleet of privately owned minibuses has room for one more passenger.

Nearly one-fifth (nineteen percent) of Israeli citizens are Palestinians, whom the Israelis prefer to call Arabs. In 1948, only 130,000 Palestinians remain within Israel (out of an original population of nearly 900,000). Today, the Palestinian population in Israel has swollen to more than 1.2 million. Most are city dwellers, who cluster in East Jerusalem, in central and western Galilee around Nazareth, in Jaffa, and near Beersheba.

Below me, visible from Suleiman's Wall, is Jerusalem's Arab Quarter, occupying about one-third of the old walled city of Jerusalem. (The rest of the Old City is divided among the Christian, Jewish, and Armenian quarters.) The winding canopied streets of the Arab Quarter are thronging with tourists, drawn by the array of foods and handwork of a "different" culture. The Arab merchants in East Jerusalem suffer these days, as do so many others in Israel, because the tourists are staying away.

Israel's Arab citizens, who are Palestinians as well, have full democratic rights, including representation in the national assembly and access to all social services. Their children go to Arab-speaking public schools, and Arabic is Israel's official second language. But Israel's Palestinians tend to perceive themselves as second-class citizens, a barely tolerated minority, non-Jews in a Jewish state, exempted from military service because their loyalty is open to question.

Indeed, in this period of renewed Palestinian Intifadeh, the loyalty of Israel's Arab citizens is being severely tried. They are torn between conflicting values. They benefit from Israeli citizenship. They need the jobs that Israel's economy offers, jobs now unavailable to the Palestinians in the West Bank and Gaza, where roads into Israel are frequently barricaded. But they bear pent-up resentment for their own situation as well as for that of their fellow-Palestinians in exile. Do they support the Intifadeh, or do they resist or ignore it? Like most Palestinians everywhere, most Israeli Arabs favor a Palestinian state with Jerusalem as its capital. But if such a state comes into existence, they may choose to become citizens of both countries (as some Israeli citizens hold on to their American passports).

Palestinians

Palestinians are descended from the non-Jewish indigenous people of the Holy Land. For some, their roots go back thousands of years, for others, only hundreds. They are the people living in Palestine when Jewish settlers begin arriving in Israel in the late nineteenth century. Except for those who manage to retain their own homes in Israel, the West Bank, and Gaza, Palestinians are the people who are uprooted and lose their homes to the flood of Jewish refugees into Palestine in 1947 and 1948. The Palestinian Diaspora scatters the 750,000 Palestinians who flee or are pushed out, but most Palestinians still remain within the Holy Land, whether semi-settled or in refugee camps.

Today there are approximately eight million Palestinians, half of whom have official Registered Refugee status. By UN definition, they will retain that status until they are able to return home or are compensated for the home and land they, their parents or their grandparents lost. But more than half are not Registered Refugees, and they participate in the life of the country where they live. More than 1.2 million Palestinians, for example, live as citizens within Israel. The largest number of Palestinians, two-and-a-half million, now live in Jordan, where they make up sixty percent of the population. Those living in the West Bank number approximately 2.1 million. Another 1.2 million live in the Gaza Strip. As in the Gaza Strip, about eighty percent of the nearly one million Palestinians who live in Lebanon and Syria have Registered Refugee status.

Palestinians are a genetic mixture of all the peoples who have lived in the Holy Land for the past thousands of years. They are of the racial/linguistic family known as Semites, but their blood has strains from the Hittites, Persians, Greeks, Romans, Crusaders, and Turks, as well as Arabs. What defines Palestinians and makes them distinct from most Israelis is not their appearance but their language and the adherence of most to Islam. They are Sunnis, not Shi'ites, and as such are in accord with co-religionists in Egypt, Jordan, Syria, Iraq, and Saudi Arabia. They are not fanatic in their observance. They want nothing to do with the *sharia* (a civil government based on

Koranic law), and their women wear scarves but not veils. A small percent of Palestinians are Druze, an offshoot of Islam.

About fifty years ago, eight percent of Palestinians were Christian, some with roots going back to the earliest days of Christianity. Most Palestinian Christians today are Orthodox, of Greek, Syrian, Coptic, Armenian, or Russian variation. There are also Syrian Uniate Catholics, the Maronites and the Melkites, who are affiliated with Rome. And there are Palestinians who in the past century have adopted the faith of Protestant and Roman Catholic missionaries, educators, and health-care professionals who have set up churches, schools, and hospitals in Palestine. Christian Palestinians tend to be among the better educated, and when possible, many leave Palestine to seek new opportunities elsewhere. As a result, the Christian population is dwindling. It is now less than one percent of those who live in the West Bank and Gaza, and about thirteen percent of the Palestinians who are Israeli citizens. In other words, among displaced Palestinians (but not among those in Israel), Christians have left the Holy Land in droves. There are twice as many Palestinian Christians living in Dearborn, Michigan, than in Ramallah, and three-fourths of Bethlehem's Christians live away from their homeland. Among other factors, it is becoming increasingly uncomfortable to be a Christian in Palestinian lands, for as resistance hardens, it does so in militant Islamic terms. Christians who take no part in the resistance are often perceived by fellow Palestinians as Israeli sympathizers.

Palestinian Arab families tend to be large, with four or more children. Palestinians value family living and do not begrudge the time it takes to prepare traditional foods. Most Palestinians live in cities and towns. From earliest times, Palestinians have been both rural and urban. In cities, they have been skilled traders and craftsmen, and many are now professionals and highly educated. A decreasing number of Palestinians are farmers. In the countryside, those who follow traditional farming methods are finding that they cannot survive, and like farmers everywhere, they must either cease farming or increase their holdings and modernize. But their position is precarious, for they are not allowed to purchase additional land, and they run the risk of losing their existing land and olive groves to Israeli bulldozers; further, they are denied access to irrigation water.

Many quit farming. But when they move to urban areas, they find that chances for employment are bleak.

A few Palestinian farmers wear a garb much like that worn twenty centuries ago. But most Palestinians long ago abandoned this traditional style of clothing in favor of Western dress. Although many Palestinians—including their leader, Yasser Arafat—wear the *kaffiyeh* headdress that marks a nomadic Bedouin tribesman, less than one percent of Palestinian Arabs are nomadic.

In the West Bank, I have seen an Arab in long brown robes and kaffiyeh plowing uneven furrows behind a mule, a scene reminiscent of Biblical times. But I have also seen Arabs in blue jeans using modern equipment for irrigating farms that resemble those of nearby Israeli kibbutzim. (Clearly some Palestinians are able to arrange water rights.) I remember Palestinian construction workers on commercial projects in Jerusalem. They were wheel-barrow-pushers and hod-carriers who probably at that time made the daily trip to work from a Palestinian town in the West Bank, not far outside the city, but now are restrained by roadblocks and interrogation. I remember, too, the well-spoken Palestinian who led me to a dining room table in a Tel Aviv hotel and the Palestinian clerk in Bethlehem who spoke perfect English and assisted me as I made a purchase.

Palestinians in the Holy Land are teachers, students, shopkeepers, accountants, plumbers, farmers, computer programmers, doctors, librarians, and frustrated and unemployed refugee camp dwellers. They are united only in this: Palestinians must have their own sovereign country, with Jerusalem as its capital.

People of Surrounding Countries

Like the Palestinians, the people who live in the countries on Israel's border speak Arabic and are overwhelmingly Muslim. Yet, in all of these lands, and particularly in Lebanon, there is also an ancient Christian presence. Most of the people of Lebanon and Syria, and some Jordanians, carry in their blood a blend of all the peoples who in the past traveled or settled along the Fertile Crescent, or occupied the Trans-Jordan plateau country. But most native-born Jordanians feel their roots are far closer to the desert than those of the Lebanese and probably even the Syrians, who themselves have a goodly portion of desert from which to draw inspiration.

The average Jordanian (excluding Palestinians) thinks of himself as a Bedouin, and he can name the desert tribe with which he is linked. However, if he lives in a city or town and engages in urban life, he is a Bedouin only by remote tribal affiliation. One can see Bedouin encampments, with their black coarsely woven goat-hair tents open to leeward, in all the drier parts of the Holy Land, but they are especially prevalent in Jordan and the Sinai Peninsula. *In Jordan, I have seen many Bedouin tents with pick-up trucks parked nearby. In part, the trucks are used to take the children to school.* Once used to a money economy, few Bedouins return to a nomadic way of life, but Bedouin encampments offer housing that is far less expensive than apartments in the cities.

The Bedouins of Jordan and the Sinai Peninsula have learned to profit from services to tourists. Led by a young Bedouin, I descend on camelback from the top of the Moab Plateau, near Mount Nebo, to the shores of the Dead Sea 3,000 feet below. Another time, I take tea in a Bedouin encampment within Wadi Rum at the southern tip of Jordan. Although my host family has a rudimentary complement of animals, they also have three pick-up trucks they use to transport tourists around the spectacular formations of Wadi Rum. In Petra, the "rose-red city of the [Jordanian] desert," it is Bedouin merchants, camped nearby who monopolize the trinket trade as well as the camel rides. In the sere landscape of the Sinai, a Bedouin family, who surely can get little sustenance from a land without vegetation, offers me tea and freshly baked bread.

The rapidly expanding capital city of Amman has grown from 60,000 when the British Trans-Jordan Mandate ended in 1946 and the Hashemite Kingdom of Jordan became a sovereign country to its present size of a million and a half. It now sprawls in light gray concrete sameness across all six of its hills.

I have exchanged ideas with Jordanian scholars and bartered with Arab merchants in noisy commercial quarters. I have listened to an Orthodox priest in a northern Jordanian city, proud of the heritage he is helping to keep alive. In the port city of Aqaba, where Jordan sends and receives its water-borne freight, I register the pride of a museum-keeper as he shows me his display of Bedouin tribal knives and other paraphernalia.

Along the coast of the Sinai Peninsula, I have seen the results of poor planning and overbuilding as Egyptian developers sought to cash in on a craze for coral-reef diving that never materialized. I sense that their efforts are doomed to become concrete derelicts on the narrow stretch between the mountains and the Gulf of Aqaba.

Though the people of the countries surrounding Israel are overwhelmingly Arab, Muslim, and supportive of the Palestinian cause, they are entrepreneurs, too, and practical. Most think that association with Israel will pay off, and in an ideal world, commerce always does. Already it has for the Jordanians, whose income from tourism has risen measurably since Israelis have been allowed to cross their border.

Since 1994, Jordan and Israel have had diplomatic relations. Jordan has absorbed most of its Palestinian population as citizens. Since 1979, the year of the Camp David Accord, Egypt has been at peace with Israel. Although at that time Israel returned the Sinai Peninsula, it did not relinquish the Gaza Strip, to which thousands of Palestinians fled in 1948 only to be frustrated after 1967 when again they ended up in Israeli territory.

Lebanon and Syria continue to oppose Israel, refusing to acknowledge either its existence or its right to exist. They use the Palestinian refugees, still languishing in UN refugee camps, the Israeli invasion of Lebanon in 1982, and the subsequent Israeli complicity in attacks on two Palestinian refugee camps as justification for guerilla raids in Israel and the support they give to Arafat. Refugee camps in Lebanon and Syria are a breeding ground for resentment and a training ground for Hezbullah militants. The *Hezbullah*, an organiation of Islamic extremists, is financed largely by Iran but directed by Syria. Iran's support comes because Hezbullah represents the Shi'ite Muslim community in Lebanon, and Iranians overwhelmingly are Shi'ites. Hezbullah, like its counterpart militant Islamic organizations in the Palestinian Authority, provides needed social services for the Shi'ite community, but they also are committed to the total demise of Israel. They attract frustrated young men in the same way that Hamas and the Islamic Jihad do in Palestine. Indeed, the three organizations are frequently in league.

Palestinian refugees in the UN camps in Lebanon want their former lands back, in addition to the houses and shops they once occupied, and they agitate. Many feel that Yasser Arafat has betrayed them, for the UN Resolution he is promoting as a basis for settlement in Palestine makes no provision for them. In the summer of 2000, Israel withdraws its troops from southern Lebanon, troops that originally invaded Lebanon in 1982 to prevent cross-border Hezbullah incursions. For a time, the border has been quiet, but Israel remains wary of its northern neighbors, and with good reason. Syria, which holds Lebanon almost as a fiefdom, claims that it cannot promise to restrain Hezbullah militants. Meanwhile, Hezbullah recruits have been appearing in the ranks of Hamas and the Islamic Jihad.

I have no recent experiences to report from the lands beyond Israel's northern border. In Lebanon in 1958, I crouch behind sandbags at the airport as the country is being torn apart by factionalism. In those days—before Camp David—the only way one can get into Tel Aviv from Cairo, 200 miles distant, is to fly first to Beirut, then to Cyprus, and finally into Israel. Today, it is still not possible to travel between Israel and Lebanon or between Israel and Syria. Not so many years ago, I am ready to spend a month in Syria, flying directly from the United States, when at the last minute the offer is withdrawn; security cannot be guaranteed.

Should peace ever come between Israel and its neighbors, a rich dividend for all parties will be the tourism that could well encompass the entire Holy Land. Meanwhile, both Lebanon and Syria promote tourism, and with good reason. Both countries have countless sites no less valuable than those in Israel to the historian, the archaeologist, and the pilgrim. Tyre and Sidon (Sayda), for example, are in Lebanon, and Antioch and Damascus are in Syria. Greek and Roman ruins abound.

Further coverage of the lands surrounding Israel appears in Chapter 24.

7

A LONGING FOR PEACE

*I went to Arafat in order to tell him that in spite of
everything there are still many in Israel who will not let
despair destroy the hope of peace. It is incumbent on all
who believe in the cause of a just peace to work together.*

Shulamit Aloni (Recipient of the Israel Prize for Human Rights), January 20, 2002

In Jordan, I am sharing bread, cheese, and oranges with my cab driver in a gray-green grove of old and twisted olive trees. The setting is timeless and placid, and he is optimistic that peace in the region is just around the corner. "The Egyptians have done it, and we have done it. Lebanon and Syria will be settled soon," he states with conviction.

Almost all people in the Holy Land and on its borders long for peace. When informal dialog takes place between moderate Israelis and Palestinians, all agree that provocation and retaliation must end. They also agree that the Jewish settlements in the West Bank and Gaza must be abandoned. But they cannot agree on Jerusalem. Pope John Paul II goes to Israel to ask all sides to give and to plead especially for those Palestinians who are stateless and impoverished. But in the nearly two years since his visit, the situation has only worsened despite strong peace efforts from both the Clinton and Bush administrations.

Israelis often refer to their land as Canaan, the Promised Land of the Exodus from Egypt more than 3,200 years ago. The Canaanites disappeared from history. It is doubtful that they were totally wiped out in the battles with the Hebrews. Perhaps through intermarriage many were absorbed by the Hebrews and other conquerors. Or perhaps those who remained fled to the coast, merged with the Philistines, and lost their identity in Assyrian captivity. The Palestinians have no intention of going the way of the Canaanites. And the Israelis have no intention of leaving Palestine. This is likely to be the toughest dilemma of our new century, one that now figures into the International War on Terrorism. Most Israelis and Palestinians desperately want an end to violence, but all feel that justice—and the God of their fathers—is on their side.

PART II
THE PAST AS
PROLOGUE:
From Abraham
to Arafat

It is in the past that the tensions of the Holy Land today are rooted. History is unavoidable in the Holy Land. Every tell, every pile of ancient columns, every church, indeed every pilgrimage site nudges the traveler to grope for an understanding of the past, to form a working chronology on which to pin one's journey.

What follows is the story of the people and events of this ancient land. The earliest part of the story cannot be called history, for its sources are oral tradition. Hundreds of years separate some events from their written narratives, and the chroniclers do not always agree. Nevertheless, the accounts as they appear in the Hebrew Scriptures (the Old Testament of Christians) underlie the world's three monotheistic faiths: Judaism, Christianity, and Islam. The chronology is rough, and much of it remains in dispute. For dates, I use the widely accepted BCE (Before the Common Era) and CE. Where dates are approximate, the symbol "ca" is appended.

8

THE PATRIARCHS

"The whole land of Canaan, where you are now an alien,
I will give as an everlasting possession to you and your
descendants after you; and I will be their God."
Genesis 17:8

"Your name will no longer be Jacob, but Israel."
Genesis 32:28

The archaeological record of settlement in Palestine goes back at least 10,000 years. However, my interest in probing for roots of conflict begins with the story of Abraham, as told in the Book of Genesis.

Abraham

CA. 1850 BCE

Nearly four millennia ago, Abraham, a man of means and owner of many flocks and herds, is living in the Sumerian city-state of Ur on the Euphrates River in lower Mesopotamia.

With his family, servants, and flocks, along with those of his father and his nephew Lot, Abraham leaves Ur and travels to ancestral lands in Haran, in the region known as Padan Aram. Haran is about halfway along the Fertile Crescent between Mesopotamia and the Mediterranean in what is now southeastern Turkey. In Haran, a

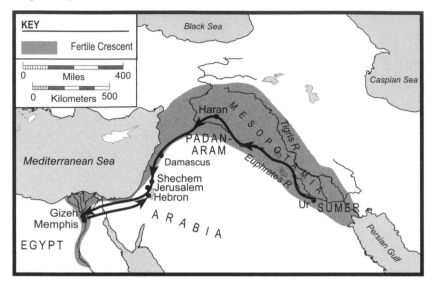

Map 11. The journey of Abraham.

Sumerian city-state like Ur, Abraham and his family prosper. There his father dies.

God tells Abraham to migrate to the land at the eastern end of the Mediterranean Sea. There he will become the father of a great nation. Traveling with his nephew Lot, their wives, servants, and flocks, he leaves behind the comfortable life he has known in Ur and Haran and becomes a nomad.

He travels the ancient Fertile Crescent route, keeping his flocks north of the desert. Eventually, he reaches the hilly land at the eastern end of the Mediterranean Sea, the land God has promised him. The land has been settled for thousands of years. It has a Bronze Age culture. Early empires from Mesopotamia and Anatolia, and local kings as well, have warred over it. The Hittites have passed through on their way to Egypt, and a few have stayed to claim land. Abraham stops first at a settlement called Shechem within the central hill country, the site of the present town of Nablus. He continues slowly to the south, but there is drought in the land. With Lot, Abraham escapes the threat of famine by going for a time into northern Egypt. He later returns and settles with his family and flocks in the vicinity of Hebron, near the northern reaches of the Negev Desert. Lot and

his family and flocks settle near the urban environment of Sodom
and Gomorrah, cities at the southern end of the Dead Sea.

*The arid land I see in the vicinity of Hebron is now blooming because of
irrigation. For Abraham, it was grazing land and probably received
more rainfall than now. Because Abraham settled near Hebron and
was buried nearby, Muslims consider the town a sacred site. Most of the
town is administered by the Palestinian Authority. But Israel has used
Hebron as one of many resettlement sites for immigrants. In today's
Hebron, the atmosphere is often charged.*

Ishmael, Isaac, and the Rock of Sacrifice

Three generations of Abraham's descendents can be named by CA. 1800
Jews, Christians, and Muslims the world over, because Abraham is BCE
the father alike of Judaism, Christianity, and Islam. Although Abraham
and his wife Sarah are childless and Sarah is long past childbearing
age, God tells Abraham that Sarah will have a son who will make
him the father of a mighty nation. God will give this nation the land
of Canaan as their heritage; in turn, God will require circumcision as
a sign of the covenant. It happens as God promises: Sarah gives birth
to Isaac. Meanwhile, Abraham has an older son named Ishmael by an
Egyptian servant woman named Hagar. God promises that Ishmael,
too, will be the father of a great nation. Out of favor with Sarah,
Hagar and Ishmael flee southward into the Negev Desert. Ishmael
grows up, takes an Egyptian wife, and becomes the father of the
Arab nation. (Twenty-four centuries later, the Jewish community in
Mecca and Medina passes on to Mohammed other traditions: that
Abraham goes to visit Ishmael in Mecca and that together he and his
son build the Kaabah, the huge cube-shaped monument set with a
sacred black meteorite that centers Islamic worship in Mecca.)
As he concentrates his hope on Isaac, Abraham's faith is severely
tested when God requires that he sacrifice his son. Father and son
walk for three days from Hebron to Mount Moriah, where Abraham
erects an altar. He trusses Isaac and has a knife in his hand when, at
the last moment, an angel stays him. Abraham has proven his faith in
God, and Isaac lives. Mount Moriah becomes the Temple Mount in

Solomon's time, with the Temple built over the site of Abraham's altar. Muslims revere the same site, where they believe Ishmael, not Isaac, is trussed for sacrifice. Today, the site lies under the spectacular golden Dome of the Rock in Jerusalem on the raised natural platform that Muslims call Al-Haram al-Sharif (The Noble Sanctuary). Jerusalem is Islam's third most holy city, after Mecca and Medina.

The Dome of the Rock, which dates from the early eighth century CE, must be one of the world's most beautiful buildings, totally pleasing in symmetry. At the opposite side of the great platform stands the Al-Aqsa Mosque. It is one of the world's largest. During the feast of Id, following Ramadan, the mosque holds at least as many Muslims as the crowds of Jews who once assembled in the courtyard of the Temple that Solomon built on this site. I am gratified to be allowed inside the mosque, required only to remove my shoes. No insistence, even, that I cover my head. I can only assume that Muslim leaders here want people to understand that they, too, have a valid claim on the Holy Land.

Esau and Jacob

CA. 1750 BCE   Isaac grows up to father two sons, Esau and Jacob. With the connivance of his mother, Jacob, the younger son, cheats Esau out of his inheritance. Esau moves to Edom, the semi-arid plateau country to the east that is now part of Jordan.

The plateau is cut by deep, dry gashes where it meets the Jordan Valley, but on the upland surface, I see crops growing without irrigation in soil that seems to be easily worked.

Esau prospers in Edom and has flocks of sheep. In time, he forgives Jacob his trickery. Jacob goes to the far-off oasis of Haran to find a wife. He works twenty years for his uncle Laban, is tricked into marrying his cousin Leah, later wins her more attractive sister Rachel, then returns to settle near his father in the northern Negev. God favors Jacob and calls him *Israel,* meaning "to strive with God and prevail." Jacob fathers twelve sons, of whom only the youngest two, Joseph and Benjamin, are by Rachel. Joseph is Jacob's favorite.

9

THE EXODUS

The Lord said, "I have indeed seen
the misery of my people in Egypt...
So I have come down to rescue them
from the hand of the Egyptians
and to bring them up out of that land into a good and
spacious land, a land flowing with milk and honey..."

Exodus 3:7,8

CA. 1700 BCE

Jacob's twelve sons, the first Israelites, begin the lineage of the Twelve Tribes of Israel. Their saga is told in the books of Genesis and Exodus. The brothers are herdsmen. Jealous of Joseph, whom their father favors, they sell him to Egyptian slavers, and they give him up for dead. In Egypt, however, Joseph eventually comes into Pharaoh's service and is placed in charge of grain supplies. Facing famine in their semi-arid grazing lands and hearing of food in Egypt, the brothers go to the Nile Valley. Joseph makes himself known to them and arranges for his brothers to get provisions.

The Israelites in Egypt

CA. 1700- 1300 BCE

Protected by a benign Pharaoh, who may himself have been of foreign blood, Joseph's brothers and their father, Jacob, begin to live

71

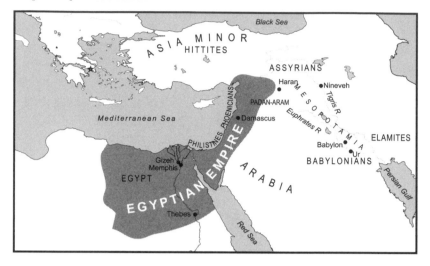

Map 12. The Egyptian Empire, ca. 1450 BCE.

with their flocks in the land known as Goshen in the eastern part of the Nile Delta. Their numerous descendents remain in Egypt for several hundred years, eventually becoming slaves working on the grandiose construction projects of less-tolerant pharaohs. They pick up the name of *Hebrews* (probably a pejorative term) from a word that means *foreigners,* or *swarthy ones.*

Eqyptian Conquests

CA. 1450
BCE

    While the Hebrews are laboring in Egypt, the Egyptians—with iron-age technology learned from their imperial rivals the Hittites— invade and conquer the hill country homeland of the patriarchs, the adjacent coastlands, the hill country to the east of the Jordan River, and probably parts of Syria. Egyptian governors rule in the towns of the region, and Egyptian armies are garrisoned there to hold off invaders. A period of peace and commerce in the region follows, and the Egyptians develop trade links with the wealthy and technically advancing peoples of the eastern Mediterranean islands.

    Egyptian rule is challenged by the arrival of the so-called *Sea Peoples,* including the Philistines, who occupy the coastlands. (Historians conjecture that the Sea Peoples may have been the Minoans, whom the Greeks defeat on Crete.) At first, Egypt manages to keep the Philistines at bay, but eventually the invaders become strong enough to defeat the Egyptians. For hundreds of years, the Philistines occupy the coastal plain, and with their knowledge of iron-working and other advanced technology, they pose a threat to other peoples of the region.

Today, the Gaza Strip, the ancient port city of Jaffa, and the commercial center of Tel Aviv are located in the coastal plain once occupied by the Philistines. Tel Aviv is a modern city. It has beautiful beaches and is a good place for travelers to rendezvous. However, it is of only minor interest to the pilgrim because it was never occupied by the Israelites in ancient times. It throbs with the pace of the New Israel. In the north in Netanya, a world-class electronics industry is developing. On the beaches, tall hotels house both Israeli sun worshippers and tourists at the beginning and end of their journeys. In relation to both ancient and modern Jerusalem, Tel Aviv and its environs are still like the land of the Philistines: brash, outward-looking, technologically superior, but seemingly without depth of spirit. But now I am ahead of the story.

Moses

CA. 1350 BCE

In Egypt, where the Hebrews are enslaved, God chooses Moses to be their champion. Rescued as an infant by Pharaoh's daughter and given an Egyptian name, Moses grows up in Pharaoh's service. He fears retribution for slaying a guard who is beating Hebrew slaves and flees to the desert of Midian—the southern and driest part of what is now Jordan—spilling over into Israel's Negev.

In Midian, Moses becomes a shepherd. While he is with his sheep and goats, God speaks to him from a burning bush (by tradition, near Mount Sinai, which would indicate that Moses did a good deal of wandering with his flocks). He commands him to lead the Hebrews out of slavery. Moses returns to Egypt. With the help of divinely imposed plagues, he persuades Pharaoh (probably Ramses II) to "let my people go." He then leads the Israelite tribes away from Pharaoh's army, across the Sea of Reeds—the swampy area to the north of the Red Sea—and into the Sinai Desert. The pursuing soldiers are drowned.

The story of the escape, known as the Exodus, is still written largely and symbolically in the hearts of Jews everywhere. The feast of Passover commemorates the event when the angel of death, sent by God to kill all the first-born sons in Egypt, passes over the dwellings of the Israelites, which have been marked with the blood of a slaughtered lamb. Passover is one of the holy days of the Jewish calendar. It is celebrated wherever Jews congregate but most meaningfully in Jerusalem. (During what Christians now call Holy Week, Jesus and his disciples are in Jerusalem, crowded with visitors at the time of the Passover. The Supper they celebrate together is the traditional commemorative Seder.)

CA. 1300
BCE

No Other God

The Israelites flee southward into the Sinai Peninsula. There on a high peak known variously as Mount Horeb, Mount Sinai, or Jebel Musa (the Mount of Moses), God speaks directly to Moses. He tells Moses to lead the Israelites into the Promised Land, Canaan, where they will multiply and become a great people. Above all, the Israelites are to worship no other god but God. Moses descends the mountain and assembles the Israelites to tell them what he has heard. They must worship only God. Then he goes back up the mountain. But in an age of universal polytheism, the Israelites are not yet monotheists. They believe that other gods exist, and they are all too ready to worship any local god who might do them good. Moses goes a second time to the mountain, and this time he receives the Ten Commandments, inscribed on two stone tablets. Meanwhile, the Israelite tribes encamped at the base of the mountain build and begin to worship a golden calf. When he returns from the mountain, Moses sees the golden calf and becomes so angry that he breaks the stone tablets. The Israelites repent.

Once again, Moses returns to the mountain, where God inscribes new stone tablets. He makes a covenant with Moses and his people. He will give them the Promised Land, leading them in battles against the Canaanites, but they in turn are to remain faithful to him. God gives Moses the complex laws governing religious observances and social amity that the descendents of Jacob are henceforth to observe.

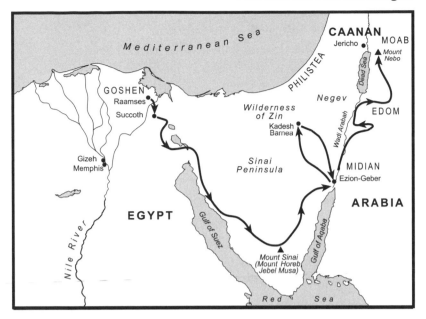

Map 13. Exodus of the Israelites, ca. 1300-1260 BCE.

The tablets and the record of the laws by which the Israelites shall live are placed in a structure called the Ark of the Covenant, which the wanderers carry with them.

The commandments that Moses receives on Mount Sinai do not immediately change the Israelites into monotheists. The process takes centuries, during which the Israelites are as ready to adopt the gods of the people among whom they live as they are to remain faithful to the One God. But the covenant that God issues on Mount Sinai, pledging that Israel shall be his people and demanding faithfulness in return, is the lodestar to which the Israelites return time and again. They are repeatedly nudged by prophets who call down God's wrath on those who stray.

Years of Wandering

CA. 1300-1260 BCE

Moses sends Joshua and Caleb north to spy out the land of Canaan, and they return to tell the people that the land they saw is fertile. But other spies of Moses report that the Canaanites are strong and well armed. The Israelites complain. They are afraid of the

Canaanites, who have picked up iron-age technology from the Egyptians and Philistines and with whom they will have to do battle. Indeed, the Canaanites are a far more sophisticated people than the Israelites. The Canaanites are farmers and town dwellers and not nomadic herders. For their doubts and other sins of faithlessness, God decrees that none of the generation that led the people out of Egypt, including Moses, will live to set foot on the Promised Land.

It takes forty years of wandering before the older generation dies off. Their wanderings are first in the Sinai Peninsula, then in the lower reaches of the adjacent Negev Desert, and finally on the plateaus of Midian and Edom to the east. There they must fight the local peoples, some of them the descendents of Esau. During all this time, God sees that they get sufficient food and water. At last, they reach the better-watered Moab plateau, north of Edom, and engage in the first of many battles with one of the local peoples, the Ammonites, whose chief center is Rabbath Ammon (now the site of Jordan's capital city, Amman). Then they descend from the plateau to camp on the eastern bank of the Jordan River.

The View from Mount Nebo

CA. 1260
BCE

Moses dies before the Israelites can enter Canaan, but on Mt. Nebo, a hilltop in Moab, to the east of the Dead Sea, he is given a glimpse of the lower Jordan Valley and the future that awaits the people he has led. The land called Moab (together with Edom and Midian to the south) occupies a dissected plateau rising sheer to 3,000 feet above the Jordan Valley and the Dead Sea. A similar dissected plateau rises to the west of the Jordan, crowned by the city of Jerusalem. The Jordan River flows between these two plateaus in a geological trough, a rift valley that actually extends from north of the Sea of Galilee southward to encompass the Dead Sea, the Wadi Arabah, the gulfs of Aqaba and Suez, and the Red Sea. (In Africa, this trough continues into the Great Rift Valley.)

The Jordan River flows southward out of the Sea of Galilee to empty into the Dead Sea, the lowest spot on earth. The portion of the Promised Land that Moses sees is a lush garden on the west bank

Photo 4. Amman, the fast-growing capital of Jordan.

of the Jordan, hot and immensely fertile and dominated by the city of Jericho (which even then occupies a site that is 6,000 years old).

From Amman, I travel thirty miles west to climb the same heights that Moses did. I cannot see Jericho through the haze of pollution, but I can make out the Dead Sea far below. The Franciscan order maintains the site, and a church on the location dates to Byzantine time. On the day I am at Mount Nebo, all is being readied for the visit of Pope John Paul II the following day.

Trailing the Israelites

I am intrigued by Amman, a city that has exploded with growth since it was named the new capital of Trans-Jordan, one of the Arab states that emerged at the end of World War II. Then it was little more than a village. Now it has more than a million occupants living in gray-white, flat-roofed limestone buildings of nearly uniform three and four-story height spread out among six hills. The center of Amman occupies an ancient site. Even today the city takes its name from the Ammonites, a nomadic people descended from Lot's youngest daughter—the people

Photo 5. The ancient rock-hewn tombs of Petra.

against whom the Israelites are pitted, time and again, in the Biblical accounts. I see no evidence of Ammonite occupancy in archaeological digs, but plenty of Roman ruins testify to the former importance of this trade route city. The Greeks named it Philadelphia, but the presence of "Amman" on contemporaneous tomb inscriptions suggests that the name never took hold.

From Amman, I head south and follow the ancient route of conquerors and traders called the Kings' Highway. The narrow but well-paved asphalt road generally hews to the plateau surface, but twice it must descend from the plateau, winding precipitously down into the wadis that cut into and drain the plateau, before going up again. I begin in the land once known as Moab and head southward through ancient Edom and the stark desert of ancient Midian until I reach the spectacular ruins of Petra.

Petra is worth any effort it takes to reach it. Here, from the second century BCE to the second century CE, the Nabatean trade empire maintains its security and its rock-hewn tombs at the end of a stark and narrow mile-long entranceway known as the Siq. Its unique tombs are a syncretic synthesis of Greek, Roman, and Egyptian architectural features. Most imposing is the great tomb misnamed "The Treasury,"

Photo 6. The Gulf of Aqaba from the resort city of Eilat.

suddenly revealed in pink-hued grandeur where the narrow Siq opens onto a wide causeway. I am shocked by the great increase in the numbers of tourists, and hotels to accommodate them, in the six years since I was last in Petra. Jordan has obviously given Petra highest priority in tourism, and it should, for tourism is now the number-one source of income for Jordan.

Many of the tourists in Petra are from Israel, welcome now as the result of the Jordan/Israel peace treaty of 1994. Many others, as I, are following a standard Holy Land tour route that includes not only Israel but also Amman, Mount Nebo, Petra, the port cities of Aqaba (Jordan) and Eilat (Israel) at the head of the Gulf of Aqaba, and St. Catherine's Monastery at the foot of Mount Sinai in Egypt's Sinai Peninsula. I rush through Aqaba, but I have seen it previously and find it a pleasant and rather quiet resort town as well as a seaport. Eilat is another story. It is Israel's Caribbean playground. Here Israelis of all classes, from wealthy to itinerant, can let their hair down on a boardwalk that resembles Coney Island in its heyday and in nearby five-star luxury hotels where all food is kosher.

Through the Gulf of Aqaba, both Israel and Jordan receive petroleum and other products. The port facilities in both Aqaba and Eilat are well developed. Aqaba is Jordan's only link with the sea, and both a high-speed desert highway and a railroad head north from there to Amman. Possessed of several Mediterranean ports, Israel is not totally dependent on Eilat, but Eilat facilitates its trade with Asia. In 1956, when Egypt blockaded the straits of Tiran, at the south end of the Gulf of Aqaba, the Israelis were desperate, for they counted on this sea route to get petroleum. The 1956 war between Israel and Egypt resulted in Egypt's temporary loss of the Sinai Peninsula.

The Gulf of Aqaba has some of the world's most beautiful coral beds, and scuba diving attracts visitors to both Aqaba and Eilat. Diving may be even better from the shores of the Sinai Peninsula, but I wouldn't have known it from the sad condition of the half-built hotels that line the narrow coastal plain of the peninsula. Egypt's most popular resort now is the one the Israelis developed at the southern tip of the Sinai, at Sharm el Sheik.

There can be no desolation so absolute as that which confronts the traveler in the Sinai. Peaks are sharply etched, devoid of vegetation, defiant. But the road is smooth, and at length I reach the base of Mount Sinai, the highest peak in a roughly dissected, rocky, and extremely arid region. On a nearby and slightly lower peak is St. Catherine's Monastery, probably the oldest continuously occupied monastery on earth, guarding the traditional site where Moses received the Ten Commandments. Portions of the monastery walls expose stone and mortar construction, preserved in the desert dryness, that dates back more than 1,500 years. In one vault, an eerie seated mummy, clothed in ecclesiastical robes, preserves the body of a revered monk from long ago. Nearby is a cache of monks' skulls that has been accumulating for many centuries. The monastery's present complement of black-robed, bearded Orthodox monks is less than two dozen, and these few have to cope with the swarms of tourists who now come during the three hours, twice a week, that entrance to the monastery is allowed. Because of the crowds, I am prevented from entering the library filled with ancient manuscripts, where the oldest known copy of the Bible—the Codex Sinaiticus, dating to the third century CE—was discovered a century ago. Portions of this priceless document are now in museums in St. Petersburg, Berlin, and London; nevertheless, I was looking forward to simply experiencing the monastery's ancient library. The footpath from the road to the monastery leads past

Photo 7. St. Catherine's Monastery, near Mt. Sinai.

a wall, over which I can see a monk watering a garden. There is nothing else green in all of the Sinai, it seems, but here at St. Catherine's the monks are able to grow figs and grapes. The almond trees are in bloom. Reentering Israel, I head north along the Wadi Arabah, the exceedingly dry rift valley that descends gradually northward from the Gulf of Aqaba to the shores of the Dead Sea, 1,200 feet below sea level. On either side of the Wadi is a harsh, rugged land, sculpted by wind and deeply eroded. Springs sustain a few bushes in the transverse wadis, but there is no surface water. South of the Dead Sea, I see road signs leading toward desert areas called Paran and Zin, wilderness areas named in Exodus where the Israelites camped. Near the southern end of the now-shrinking Dead Sea, I am shown the supposed site of the destroyed cities of Sodom and Gomorrah, where Lot's wife, looking backward on the flaming cities, turns into a pillar of salt.

There is reason to believe that the traditions associated with Genesis and Exodus took place at a time when the whole desert and semi-arid region received more rainfall than now. This could explain the traditional site of the destroyed pleasure-loving ancient cities, formerly covered by shallow waters at the southern end of the Dead Sea but now exposed as mineralized desert. It could also help to explain how tribal peoples numbering in the tens of thousands could be sustained during their desert wanderings, manna notwithstanding. Today, the white droppings of insects living on a desert bush are collected by nomadic peoples for food, and the collected droppings are called "manna." At the very least, there must have been springs in the days of the Exodus, for even now I see occasional flashes of green in wadi cuts.

As the Dead Sea shrinks, possibly from climate change but certainly because of the withdrawal of irrigation water from the Jordan River, both the Jordanians and the Israelis are exploiting the rich mineral salts that are being exposed. On each side, a thriving industrial complex turns out not only agricultural chemicals but also bath salts, facial masks, and cosmetic products that are sold all over the world. The Dead Sea has also spawned a spa industry, drawing people who come to bathe in the mineral-rich and exceptionally buoyant waters. One look at the mud-covered bathers emerging from the water convinces me to forgo the experience.

The Torah

The story of the Patriarchs and the epic of the Exodus are passed on by the Hebrews from one generation to the next mostly as oral tradition, for only gradually do the Hebrews produce scribes. The earliest written fragments of the Exodus possibly date from the tenth century BCE, but not until the latter part of the sixth century are various versions of the epic compiled by anonymous priestly scribes, whose interest in part is in validating the role of the priests. Scholars can detect at least four sources interwoven into the record that finally emerges. Two of these probably date from the tenth or ninth centuries, and two from the seventh and sixth centuries. The writings are inscribed as the Books of Genesis, Exodus, Leviticus, Numbers, and Deuteronomy. These five books form the Jewish Torah and also the first books of the Christian Old Testament, the Pentateuch. The stories, repeated around campfires and in caravanserais, are probably a source from which—more than a thousand years later—Mohammed, an overland trader from Arabia, acquires many of the ideas that eventually are written in the Quran. Most importantly, they are the world's first codification of monotheism, the overriding concept shared alike by all groups who come as pilgrims to the Holy Land.

10

THE PROMISED LAND

*And now, Israel, take notice of the laws and customs that I
teach you today,
and observe them, that you may…
enter and take possession of the land that Yahweh,
the God of your fathers,
is giving you.*

Deuteronomy 4:1

The Israelite epic continues in the Promised Land, the land of
Canaan. Canaan, by Moses' designation in the Book of
Numbers, includes all the land that is now thought of as the
Holy Land: from the Mediterranean Sea to and beyond the Jordan
River, and from the slopes of Mount Hermon and the Golan Heights
in the northeast to the Dead Sea in the south. The people of Canaan
are a mixture of all who have passed along the Fertile Crescent in
thousands of years past and found the land suitable for their crops or
flocks. They are polytheists. They worship the gods brought from
Mesopotamia, and to these some have added the gods of the Hittites
and the Egyptians. They live within a number of small contending
kingdoms, whose rulers maintain armies. These are the people, the
territories, and the rulers whom the nomadic Israelite tribes must
subdue.

CA. 1700
BCE

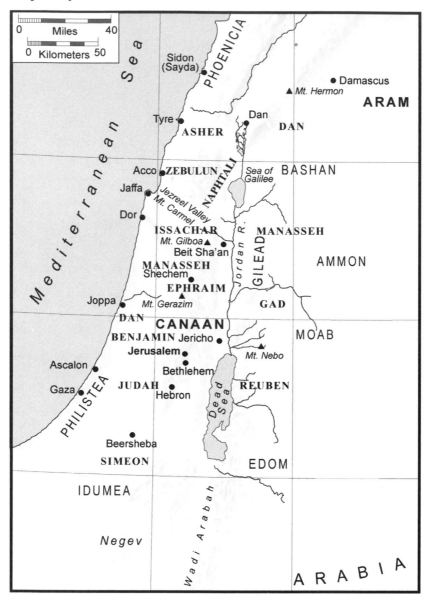

Map 14. The tribes of Israel in Canaan, ca. 1100 BCE.

CA. 1260-
1060
BCE

Battling the Canaanites

Led by Joshua, warriors among the tribes cross the Jordan River near the northern end of the Dead Sea and attack Jericho. Eventually Jericho falls, and for the next 200 years the twelve tribes of Israel fight to claim the portions of the land of Canaan that have been allotted to each. God has promised the Israelites that they shall rule over all the land "from Dan (in the far northeast) to Beersheba (in the Negev)." Two of the tribes remain east of the Jordan, seven are apportioned the northern and central part of Canaan, and three occupy the southern hills. The largest of the tribes, Judah, dominates the south. The battles between the Israelites and the Canaanites, as described in the Book of Joshua, are bloody, and the Israelites seldom give quarter. What is depicted as a relentless conquest is probably a gradual displacement, sometimes punctuated with battles, but more often leading to a cultural blending. The southern coastal area controlled by the Philistines does not yield, nor does that of the Phoenicians on the coast north of Philistine territory. The lands bordering the Mediterranean Sea remain a festering threat to the Israelites, who settle mostly in the hill country east of the coastal plain.

Tribal Contention

CA. 1200-1030 BCE

Tribal judges preside over the various Hebrew settlements, and prophets attempt, often in vain, to keep the people loyal to their God and to Mosaic law. But surrounded by Canaanites, and probably intermarrying with them, many of the Israelites forget their heritage. In addition, the Israelite tribes are contentious. The northern tribes refuse to cooperate with Judah, or even with each other. Not until the end of the eleventh century are the Israelite tribes sufficiently unified to face an enemy in concert.

Saul

CA. 1020-1000 BCE

Saul makes the first efforts toward unification from 1020-1000, but he violates the rules of holy war by taking prisoners and booty. For this, the prophet Samuel tells him that God will spurn him. Saul leads the Israelites in a fight against the Philistines for control of the strategic Jezreel Valley, the routeway to the Mediterranean. The Philistines overwhelm his troops, slay his sons in front of his eyes, then pierce him with arrows. Saul falls on his own sword. This occurs on Mount Gilboa, near the ancient (and modern) city of Beit Sha'an.

Deep in the diggings of the Beit Sha'an tell, I see the remnants of what probably was a Philistine wall, to which the victors fastened the bodies of Saul and his sons. From the tell, I can see Mount Gilboa rising above the valley to the northwest, a hilltop that any army would most assuredly need to control. I will come back to Beit Sha'an later in this narrative.

11

KINGDOMS AND POWER

Wherever David went, Yahweh gave him victory. David ruled over all Israel, administering law and justice to all his people.

2 Samuel 8:14,15

As Saul is in the north trying to unify the Israelites, the Philistines go on the attack. They approach the southern hill country of Judea and threaten to overwhelm the Israelites there. The Israelites have reason to be afraid, for the Philistines are well-armed with forged weapons and hammered shields. David, the shepherd boy anointed by the prophet Samuel to be Saul's successor, confronts the giant Philistine warrior Goliath and slays him by using only a slingshot. The Philistines withdraw—for by agreement the match would determine the battle—and David's reputation is established.

CA.1020 BCE

David

After Saul's death, David takes on the mantle of leadership. He wins victories both to the west against the Philistines on the coastal plain and to the east against the Ammonites and others on the plateau of Moab. He sends the Hittite soldier Uriah, husband of Bathsheba, whom he covets, to certain death in an assault on the walls of Rabbath Ammon. In Canaan, he defends and makes secure the territories of the Hebrew tribes. Under David, the Israelites are now unified for the first time since they entered Canaan.

For the capital of his hard-won kingdom, David chooses the ancient site of Jerusalem, a site that for the previous thousand years has served as the leading city of the Jebusites, one of the Canaanite tribes. Surrounded by forested slopes on the salubrious, well-watered plateau that rises above the hot, humid, and fertile Jordan Valley. He builds a wall to enclose and protect his city. On the stones of a Jebusite foundation, David builds his palace. There he brings the Ark of the Covenant, containing the laws given by God to Moses in the Sinai.

In Jerusalem, I am shown the site of David's palace, which is adjacent to the Temple Mount. Archaeologists have established a layer of stones built on a bronze-age foundation that may be the base level of David's palace lying on a Jebusite foundation.

Solomon

Solomon, David's son and successor, brings power and wealth to the united kingdom. His territory encompasses all the land from north of Damascus to the Gulf of Aqaba, and from the Mediterranean Sea to the plateau of Moab and beyond, possibly to Mesopotamia. Wealthy from trade and the booty of conquest, Solomon builds a spectacular temple. He chooses a perfect site near David's palace in Jerusalem, on the high and nearly flat area that the Israelites know as Mount Moriah, the Mount of Sacrifice. Ever since Solomon built his temple there, the site has been known to Jews and Christians as Temple Mount. Solomon buys cedar from the mountains of Lebanon, secured through Phoenician-controlled Tyre, and he employs Phoenician craftsmen to carve it. Solomon's Temple follows prescribed measurements given by God to Moses in the Sinai. At the highest point, the Holy of Holies, Solomon enshrines the Ark of the Covenant. He builds a protective wall to encompass his enlarged city. Tradition has it that Solomon is visited by the Queen of Sheba (probably present-day Yemen in southwestern Arabia or possibly Ethiopia).

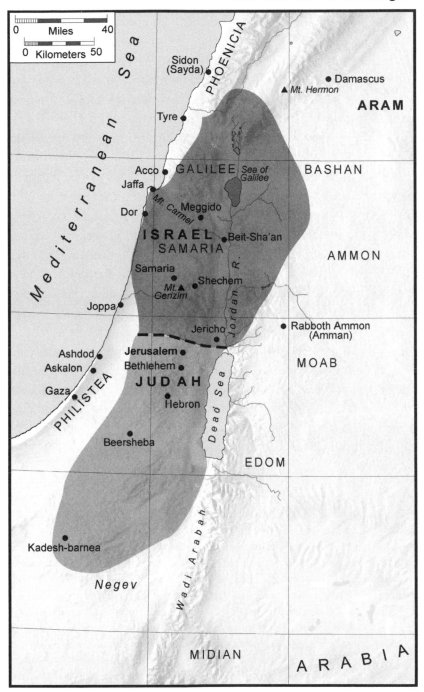

Map 15. The northern and southern kingdoms, ca. 800 BCE

Divided Kingdoms

The unification of the Israelites ends with Solomon's death. To build his empire and his Temple, Solomon has required harsh labor and heavy taxes from the people of his kingdom. When his son and successor promises even harsher measures, the ten northern tribes revolt. There are now two kingdoms, one in the north and one in the south.

CA. 928-721 BCE

Not until the second century BCE will the Jews of Israel again be unified under one king, and then only for a hundred years. The southern kingdom known as Judah, from the name of its largest tribe, is the smaller and less fertile of the two. However, it contains Jerusalem, the focus of Hebrew consciousness.* On the east, it reaches to the Jordan River (and sometimes beyond). On the south, it goes into the northern Negev Desert. On the west, where its hilly slopes descend, it is bordered by the Philistine-held coastal plain. The northern kingdom, called Israel, has a moist and verdant northern area where the waters coming off Mount Hermon pour out in springs that mingle and flow into the Sea of Galilee. It also has most of the fertile Jordan River lowlands, and a central hill and valley region that reaches to the sea in the long ridge known as Mount Carmel. The boundary between the two kingdoms runs through the dry and sparsely populated central hill country, later known as Samaria.

---

*How do the Twelve Tribes, and later the Ten Lost Tribes, come to be numbered? Jacob has twelve sons, whose descendents, formed into separate tribes, return from Egypt to settle in Canaan. The descendents of Levi are to be priests and thus are not to be allotted land. The descendents of the sons of Joseph – Ephraim and Manasseh – are given status as separate tribes eligible for separate territorial allotments. Of the twelve tribes who gain territory in Canaan, nine are in the north and three – Judah, Benjamin, and Simeon – are in the south. Simeon's tribe receives no land of its own but is given the desert portion of Judah's allotment. When the tribes, united under David and Solomon, split to form two kingdoms after the death of Solomon (ca 900 BCE), Judah and Benjamin are the two tribes named as comprising the southern kingdom, hereafter named Judah. By this time, Simeon as a tribal entity has disappeared. In 721 BCE, the Assyrians conquer and disperse the nine northern tribes. Together with the tribe of Simeon, they become known in history as the Ten Lost Tribes.

For the next two centuries, a series of kings rule in the two kingdoms. Often the kingdoms are at war with bordering peoples, and sometimes with each other. Kings and people alike are often profligate and are as likely as not to take up with the gods of the peoples against whom they do battle and with whom they sometimes intermarry. Prophets move among the kingdoms, foretelling their doom and the destruction of Solomon's Temple. This is the period of the prophets Amos, Hosea, Elijah and Elisha, Isaiah, Jeremiah, Micah, and Nathan. On Mount Carmel, the forested ridge that extends from the hills of Samaria westward to the Mediterranean, Elijah demonstrates that the One God has power and Baal, the god of the Caananites, is powerless. But still the Israelites are faithless more often than faithful.

12

IN THE WAKE OF EMPIRES

*In the nineteenth year of Nebuchadnezzar king of
Babylon, Nebuzaradan…an officer of the king
…entered Jerusalem.
He burned down the Temple of Yahweh,
the royal palace and all the houses in Jerusalem…
[He] deported the…population
[except for] some of
the humbler country peoples…"*

2 Kings 25:9-12

CA. 72I
BCE

What about the Canaanites, the indigenous people who lose the battles fought for the Promised Land? The Canaanites, who leave no written record, are partially wiped out by the advancing Israelite tribes. Cultural intermixing is attested to by the prophets' continual tirades against the Israelites for taking up with the gods of the Canaanites. The archaeological record suggests that some of the defeated Canaanites flee to the coastal plain, intermarry with the Philistines, and in 721 BCE are taken captive by the Assyrians. After this, the Canaanites, along with the Philistines, disappear from the stage of history. The Phoenicians on the coast likewise yield to the Assyrians, but by this time the focus of Phoenician power has shifted westward to Carthage, Sicily, and Spain.

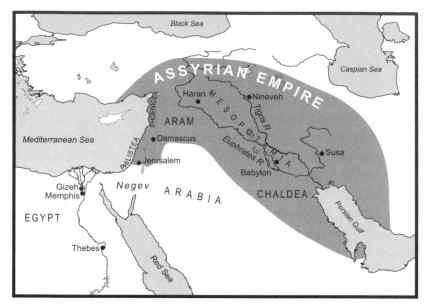

Map 16. The Assyrian Empire, ca. 700 BCE.

The Lost Tribes and the Samaritans

CA. 721-586 BCE

The conquest of the Assyrians dooms the northern tribes that occupy the kingdom of Israel. It is their misfortune to occupy coveted lands on the trade route between Egypt and Mesopotamia. The Assyrian invaders torch their cities and carry off many of their people into slavery, dispersing them eastward among the far-flung settlements of the Assyrian Empire. Those who survive in their lands of exile eventually blend in to their new surroundings, and history hears no more of the so-called *Lost Tribes*. In their homelands, the Assyrians displace the conquered Israelites with those conquered elsewhere. The newcomers bring their own gods, but they also make an effort to worship the God of the Israelites who are left behind and with whom they intermarry. From the new blend of peoples and religions, a separate group evolves in the hilly lands of central Palestine, a group called the Samaritans. The Judeans never accept the Samaritans as legitimate. They dispute their understanding of the Judaic law, and they dispute the separate Temple they build on Mount Gerazim near ancient Shechem. (Today the land of the Samaritans is the West Bank, the territory of the Palestinian Authority.)

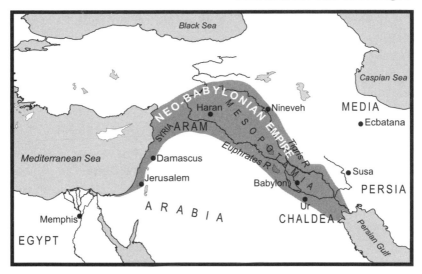

Map 17. The Neo-Babylonian (Chaldean) Empire, ca. 600 BCE.

The Babylonian Captivity

Judah, less strategically located than Israel, manages to strike a bargain with Assyria and for the next hundred and fifty years becomes a vassal state. But by the beginning of the sixth century, the Chaldeans, whose chief city is Babylon in Mesopotamia, have conquered the Assyrians, and in 597 they conquer Jerusalem. They deport thousands of Judeans to Babylon, on the banks of the Euphrates River. They are selective, however. They take only the professionals, priests, craftsmen, and the wealthy.

CA. 597-586 BCE

In 586, the Chaldeans return to Jerusalem, raze the city, and destroy Solomon's Temple, as the Prophets had predicted. They carry off all the residents of Jerusalem to captivity, leaving only country folk to till the soil. The Book of Jeremiah, written in Jerusalem at this time, chronicles the misery of those left behind, with Temple destroyed and countryside a wasteland.

To escape exile, some of the Jews flee into Egypt, both to upper Egypt and to the area that later becomes Alexandria. The people of Judah are now split into three groups: those in Babylonian exile, who are literate and leave a record; those who flee to Egypt and probably never return; and those left behind in Judea, the farmers and herdsmen who must face famine and desolation. It is thought that Jeremiah dies in Egypt.

In Babylon the exiles weep. They realize now how precious is their heritage. Unlike the scattered northern exiles, the Judeans in the Babylonian Captivity stay together and draw strength from each other. Exile strengthens them in their worship of God. Over and over again, they retell the legends of their past, and the priests and scribes labor to pull together a written record. Although the earliest writer of Psalms—devotional poems meant to be sung—is David, it is clear that some of the Psalms are set four hundred years later in the period of exile. Most scholars now think that the Psalms known as the exilic and post-exilic Psalms are actually poetic evocations written as late as the third century BCE. The Book of Daniel is likewise set in the period of exile but is probably not composed until the mid-second century. For Jews, the exile is a watershed experience.

CA. 586-538 BCE

The Persian Empire

CA. 539 BCE

The Babylonian Captivity lasts some fifty years. The Persians defeat the Chaldeans, and the next year the enlightened Persian ruler, Cyrus—in awe of the powerful god of the Judeans who saves his wise men in the lion's den and in the fiery furnace—commands his followers not only to return to Judah but also to rebuild their temple in Jerusalem. Not all of the exiles wish to return, however. The defeated Chaldean Empire extends eastward to the Indus and north to encompass the territory gained from the Assyrians. The Persians not only take over all this territory but also proceed to enlarge it, building the most powerful and best-administered Empire the world has yet known.

Many of the Jews in exile, seeing opportunity, scatter throughout this vast Empire, living in cities and towns and becoming merchants and administrators. They fare well. But they do not forget their heritage or lose their identity. Even today there are still a waning number of Jews in Iraq and Iran whose ancestry can be traced back to the Babylonian Captivity.

CA. 539-330 BCE

In Beit Sha'an, I talk with a cab driver who came to Israel as a boy when his family left Baghdad. He knows Arabic as fluently as Hebrew.

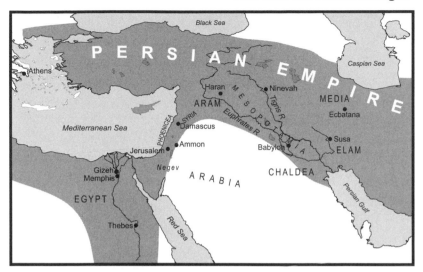

Map 18. The Persian Empire, ca. 450 BCE.

On the Silk Road in China, I learn of Jewish traders who for a thousand years and more were a link between China and the cities of the Middle East. In the old Chinese capital city of Kaifeng, Jews establish a thriving merchant community, of which nothing is left today.

Most of the Jewish community in Egypt, like that in Babylon, does not return, forming part of a growing Jewish presence both in upper Egypt and the cities of the Delta. Later, this community plays a prominent role in Alexandria.

My visit to Israel coincides with the two-day Feast of Purim, celebrated by Jews all over the world in memory of the Jewish Queen Esther, whose story is told in the Book of Esther, written in the second century. As the favorite of a Persian ruler in Susa (the new capital of the Empire), Esther is able to save her people from the cunning and wicked Persian minister Haman. From this story, we realize that although the Jews settle in diverse communities throughout the Babylonian/Persian realm, they remain a separate people. In Israel, the celebration of Purim resembles a combination of Christmas (the giving of presents) and Mardi Gras (masked costumed revelers dancing in the streets and lavish private parties). Purim is especially fun for Israeli children, who get to dress in costume. I remember a Hassidic father in a long black coat smiling

97

indulgently at his two costumed children as they wait to join in the dancing.

Return of the Exiles

Ordered to return home by Cyrus, a portion of the exiles begins to filter back in 538. They settle in Jerusalem or elsewhere in Judea, and some make new homes in the northern territory that later comes to be known as Galilee. But they want little to do with the dry central hill country of the Samaritans, for they consider the Samaritans tainted.

CA. 538 BCE

The period of captivity has had a linguistic effect: In Babylon and Persia, the Israelites learned to speak and write Aramaic, the trade language used within the Persian Empire. They bring back Aramaic as a common tongue, and gradually Hebrew becomes only a liturgical language. Aramaic, like Hebrew, is a Semitic language but with significant differences from Hebrew, so the two languages are not mutually understood.

Temple and Torah

In Jerusalem, now part of the Persian Empire, the Jews rebuild the Temple that the Babylonians destroyed. The task is finished by the year 515. To help the returned exiles remember their heritage and to reinforce the role of the priesthood, Jewish priests and scribes codify the partly oral, partly written traditions in the Torah. Ever since, these traditions have enabled Jews to retain their identity, regardless of where displacements have set them down.

CA. 515 BCE

Is it possible that the people of the Ten Lost Tribes would have retained their identity had they also had access to a written record? Surely it has been the threat of assimilation that has given an urgency to the work of Jewish scholars through the centuries and has spurred Jewish families to be faithful in their observance of Jewish rites and traditions.

In addition to the Torah, the compilations of the sixth, fifth, and fourth century BCE scribes include the poetry of David and other psalmists, the wise sayings ascribed to Solomon, the teachings of the prophets, and the record of activities in Israel after the return from captivity. As a group, these writings are assembled as the Hebrew Scriptures. Much later, when early Christian scholars consider the authenticity of the books that become the Bible, the writings of the Hebrew Scriptures are accepted as the Old Testament.

Jews and Christians alike have spent millions of hours and billions of words trying to understand, piece together, ascribe, and decode the writings of the Old Testament. Among practicing Jews there can be no more honored profession than that of the Torah scholar.

In Jerusalem, unlike in Tel Aviv, I see hundreds of men and boys, with sallow faces, side curls, black hats, and black overcoats, who are members of an ultra-conservative Jewish sect known as the Hassidim. The men devote their entire adult life to the study of Scripture and Scripture commentaries. Their observance of Deuteronomic law is strict to the letter. They are the most numerous among those praying at the Western Wall just inside Jerusalem's Old City. They sway back and forth as they read their prayers, bewailing the fate of their twice-destroyed Temple. They refuse army service but do alternative service. They are an extremely conservative political minority, and in the Knesset, Israel's parliament, they influence the far-right groups that hold the swing vote, which means no political party can rule without their consent. It is the Hassidic vote that has succeeded in halting all bus traffic throughout Israel between sundown Friday and sundown Saturday. Most Israelis, who tend to be either less-religious or totally secular, would like to see the Hassidim disappear. But they will not, and they are growing relatively more numerous because their birthrate is high.

I befriend an Israeli teacher named Esther. She is distraught, having just come from a meeting with her 18-year-old daughter. The daughter has committed herself to Hassidic teachings, is studying in a religious school for females run by the Hassidim, and is doing alternative military service by working in a school for autistic children. Someday she fully expects to be the wife of a Hassidic scholar. My friend knows what that will mean: Her daughter will have as many children as God provides; meanwhile, she will have to work to support the family while her

Photo 8. Hassadim praying at the Western Wall.

husband carries on his scholar's duties. She knows that the government provides partial support for Hassidic families, but she knows too that many Israelis see the Hassidim as parasites because of this. Her daughter will be forever marginalized, forever harried. (I am reminded of "Fiddler on the Roof" set in czarist Russia in a Hassidic village.) Esther is an observant Jew; her husband wears a skullcap. When I am in their car driving between Beit Sha'an and Jerusalem, he offers a prayer aloud for our safe journey. But neither of them is in sympathy with the Hassidim.

Israel under Persian Rule

The two centuries of Persian rule in Palestine are largely benign, and the Jews prosper. But they live among polytheistic peoples, and some intermarry with them, diluting faith and tradition. The Persian rulers take great interest in the religions of their subjects, and Ezra and Nehemiah, in the service of the Persian king, are detailed to Jerusalem, where in the middle of the fifth century they work to CA. 440 purify Judaism. Marriages between Jew and non-Jew are now BCE forbidden. The accounts of their efforts (in the Books of Ezra and Nehemiah) make it clear that the essential features of Judaism, born of reflections during the Babylonian Captivity and the subsequent compilations of the scribes, date from this post-exilic period. In general, this is a period of strong personal piety and strict corporate worship. The Jewish community has the Torah, and Judaism has come of age. The Jews engage in trade and crafts in addition to farming. Using Aramaic, they put aside as archaic the Hebrew tongue in which the scribes are writing. By the fourth century BCE, the Torah is available in Aramaic translation.

CA. 350 BCE

13

GREEKS AND ROMANS

*I do not separate people, as do the narrow-minded, into
Greeks and barbarians.
I am not interested in the origin or race of citizens.
I only distinguish them on the basis of their virtue.*

Alexander the Great

*On the west side of the Dead Sea, but out of range of the
noxious exhalations of the coast, is the solitary tribe of the
Essenes.*

Pliny the Elder, Natural History

T he Persian Empire comes to an end in the fourth century when Alexander the Macedonian defeats the Persians and establishes a new world order—that of Greek, or Hellenic, culture. In 332, Alexander's armies march through Palestine on their way to Egypt, putting an end to Persian rule there. CA. 332 BCE

The Legacy of Alexander

Upon Alexander's death in Mesopotamia in 323, his vast Empire—including the Jewish homeland—is divided among his generals. In this way, the Jews come under Greek rule, first of the Ptolemys from Egypt and later of the Seleucids from Syria. Colonies CA. 323-167 BCE

103

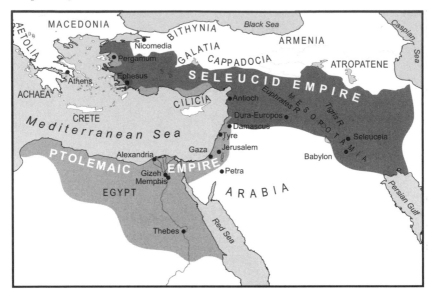

Map 19. The successors of Alexander the Great, the Ptolemaic and Seleucid Empires, ca. 250 BCE.

of Greek settlements appear, and many Jews living among them adopt Greek names and Greek ways. The Greeks settle returned soldiers in their colonies, and the soldiers crave Greek products and Greek entertainment.

A number of Greek trading towns occupy the trade routes from Damascus southward toward the Nabatean capital at Petra and from the Jordan Valley westward to the sea. Most of these Greek towns are east of the Jordan River. The most prominent among them is Philadelphia, now Amman, named for a Ptolemaic ruler. Under the Greeks, Beit Sha'an, the city guarding the Jezreel Valley, comes to be known as Scythopolis, after the Scythian mercenaries who have settled there. This is the beginning of the semi-self-governing league of cities that is later to be known collectively as the Decapolis. The Decapolis cities are Greek; most of the Jews who live there are hellenized. They provide the skilled labor, such as carpentry, weaving, and glass making, to build and furnish the Greek cities. Elsewhere in Judea and Galilee, the less-educated Jews resist Greek culture and remain as pastoralists and farmers.

Most educated Jews are literate in Greek in addition to Aramaic and a smattering of liturgical Hebrew. As Jews become hellenized, some also become secularized. To counter this, priests and scholars work to preserve the forms of traditional Hebrew worship. At the far end of the spectrum, reform groups arise, and their members live apart from the Jews of the cities or the Temple in reaction to what they feel is a departure from Mosaic Law. In the caves of the northern Negev Desert, their scribes record their activities on vellum and transcribe copies of the Torah.

The Essenes and the Dead Sea Scrolls

Sometime in the second century BCE, a group of dissidents called the Essenes decides to secure their scrolls in large clay jars deep within the cave they use for meetings. More than two thousand years later, in the caves of Qumran, an illiterate Bedouin boy finds scrolls of parchment in clay jars. The year is 1948. He takes them to his father, who fortunately decides to sell them instead of using them to start a fire. In this way, scholars eventually acquire the first of a trove of Dead Sea Scrolls that are subsequently found in a number of caves near Qumran, fronting the northwestern shore of the Dead Sea. CA. 120 BCE

In forty years of carefully piecing together fragments of the Dead Sea Scrolls, scholars have learned much about Judaism and the life of Jewish people two hundred years before the birth of Christ.

I spend some time in the impressive Museum of the Scrolls in Jerusalem learning about the Essenes and seeing actual fragments of the scrolls. Understandably, the most precious scroll, an almost intact transcription of the Book of Isaiah, can be viewed only as a copy. Both Jewish and Christian scholars continue their search for ancient manuscripts, for the canon of both the Hebrew Scriptures and the Old and New Testaments is based only on copies of copies, and on translated versions at that. Thus, the Dead Sea Scrolls are a world treasure. One only wonders how many manuscripts of the past have been used to start fires.

The Maccabees

By the second century, the Ptolemys have been superseded in Palestine by the Seleucids, who rule from Syria to the north. A harsh

Seleucid ruler desecrates the Temple and tries to force the Jews to abandon their form of worship. The Jews revolt in 167. They are led by brothers from the Hasmonean house, who become known as the Maccabees (meaning *hammers*). The Maccabeean revolt and the century of strife-torn self-rule that follows produce one great ruler, Judas Maccabeus, and a series of ineffectual ones, all Jewish priests with Greek names. This period is known as the Hasmonean Kingdom. In this period, numbers of Jews move into the fertile northern region known as Galilee.

CA. 167-163 BCE

Once belonging to the Canaanites, then wrested away by the Hebrews, Galilee falls to the Assyrians in the eighth century BCE, subsequently to the Persians, and is first ravaged then neglected under the Seleucid Greeks. By the beginning of the first century BCE, Galilee, under Hasmonean protection, again has a strongly Jewish population. Later, the region of Galilee figures prominently both in the Christian Gospels as the site of Jesus' ministry and as a refuge for Jews who are banished by the Romans from Jerusalem after 70 CE.

The Septuagint and the Apocrypha

CA. 200-50 BCE

The record of the Jews in the years after the return from captivity in Babylon is sketchy. It is told, in part, in writings known collectively as The Apocrypha. The Apocryphal books first appear in the Septuagint, the Greek translation from the Hebrew ordered by Ptolemy and supposedly completed in Alexandria by seventy Jewish scholars. A date of around 200 BCE can be given for the Septuagint, with many subsequent additions and revisions during the following century and a half. The Books of Maccabees, which tell the story of the Jewish revolt from Seleucid rule and the subsequent century of Jewish rule, are written much later than the original Septuagint. Jewish scholars are united concerning the Apocryphal writings. They accept them as valuable historical documents but without canonical status. Most of the Apocrypha appears in the Catholic Biblical canon, but Protestants (other than Anglicans) generally reject its canonical status on grounds that the Apocryphal books are not a part of the original Hebrew Scriptures. Part of the Old Testament canon or not, the Apocryphal writings are valuable for what they tell of the 400-year

Map 20. The Hasmonean Kingdom, ca. 100 BCE.

period before Roman rule begins. They reflect the struggle of the Jewish people to maintain their faith and way of life under foreign rule and in the face of alien Persian and Hellenic cultures.

CA. 15
BCE
The Beginning of Roman Rule: Herod the Great

The legions of the Roman general Pompey have little trouble conquering the Hasmoneans, whose strict Jewish observances (for example, circumcision ordered for all males under their jurisdiction) have alienated not only the Greeks of Palestine but many Jews also. In 63, Pompey declares Palestine a Roman province and attaches it to Syria (the remnant of the Seleucid Empire, which Rome has already conquered). He gives the Decapolis trade cities limited autonomy, including the right to coin money; nevertheless, he awards some of the cities as booty to favorites. He also decides that the best way to rule is to turn over responsibility to a trusted local. Herod, a prosperous Jew with roots in the northern Negev province of Idumea, ingratiates himself with Rome and wins Pompey's commission. Herod (called the Great) rules Palestine as an absolute monarch, and with the tribute he exacts, embarks on a huge building spree so that he will leave a legacy and the Romans will be impressed. He enlarges and refurbishes the Temple in Jerusalem to be grander than it has ever been before. He builds theaters and baths in cities that he controls. He awards two of the Decapolis cities, Gadara and Hippos, to his son.

CA. 6-4
BCE
Herod dies in 6 or 4 BCE (the record is contradictory); thereafter, the Romans rule Palestine directly. Rome appoints a series of legates to rule in Palestine. By 25 CE the name of the legate is Pontius Pilate. None are more pleased at Roman rule than the citizens of the Decapolis cities that have been given to Herod's son. Roman rule is welcome because the Romans in the eastern province speak Greek, enjoy Greek entertainment, and treat their provinces fairly rather than capriciously, as had been the case under Herod.

14

SOURCES AND EVIDENCE

*...I am Cyrus, King of the world. When I entered
Babylon...I did not allow anyone to terrorize the land...I
kept in view the needs of the people and all its sanctuaries
to promote their well-being...I put an end to their
misfortune.*

*Cuneiform inscription on a clay cylinder
discovered in 1879, now in The British Museum*

After 63 BCE, the history of Palestine becomes a little less
conjecture and a little more corroborated by written accounts,
and somewhat easier to trace through coins and other
archaeological finds. However, for the years before Rome, there are
certain known dates around which Biblical accounts, based almost
entirely on oral tradition, can be pinned.

Corroboration and Discrepancies

We know with precision the dates of Egyptian dynasties and
the periods of rule by the Assyrian, Chaldean, and Persian Empires,
the Ptolemys, the Seleucids, and the Hasmoneans. Although the Bible
records events that occur in time and place, it is not primarily a work
of history, but rather an account of the relationship of humans to
God under historic circumstances. Imprecision and contradiction

become apparent when its various writers are compared, or when named rulers or dates fail to concur with known history. Archaeologists hoping to find corroborative evidence for the Biblical narrative have been digging in Palestine for two hundred years, and they are slowly piecing together the past. There is a good deal of corroboration when it comes to place names but precious little regarding persons.

However, there are also frustrating discrepancies between the Biblical accounts and the archaeological record. Careful digging in the 10,000-year-old site of Jericho, for example, has thus far yielded no evidence of the battle fought by Joshua when the Jews first entered the Promised Land. There is likewise no clear-cut archaeological evidence of the kingdoms of David and Solomon. (The dig that could yield evidence can never be done, for the site of Solomon's Temple is now occupied by Islam's sacred Dome of the Rock. In recent years, Palestinians in charge of the Haram al-Sharif have been removing material from under the Dome and depositing it in a quarry outside the city. Israelis suspect that the diggers are deliberately trying to destroy any evidence that might eventually give Jews a legitimate historical claim to Jerusalem. Israelis have attempted to tunnel under the Dome, but they have been stopped by Palestinians, who claim that their efforts not only trespass but also physically undermine the stability of the Dome.)

Evidence of the Roman period of rule is widespread in the Holy Land, but most Roman ruins date from the high period of Roman building after 100 CE, not from the time of Christ. Thus, they give no definitive record of the appearance of the Holy Land at the time of the Gospel accounts. Even Jerusalem is almost totally rebuilt early in the second century.

It is not likely that the politically unimportant people who accompany Jesus would have left inscriptions. However, on a stone plaque unearthed in Caesarea, the port city that Herod builds for the Romans as their capital and names after the emperor, I see a commemorative stone plaque on which is clearly inscribed in Latin the name of the Roman legate Pilatus.

110

That Jesus actually lived and taught in Palestine has strong place-name corroboration and is also mentioned in the accounts of the Jewish/Roman historian Josephus, who writes in the seventh decade of the first century. I will speak more of Josephus in a later chapter.

The Gospel Record

The first four books of the New Testament, known as the Gospels, are the chief source for what we know of the life of Jesus. From the Gospels, we learn that a Jewish Galilean named Jesus is born in Bethlehem, grows up in Nazareth, teaches chiefly in Galilee, gathers followers who believe him to be the Messiah, is condemned to a criminal's death, rises again, and ascends into heaven. The Gospels are called Matthew, Mark, Luke, and John, but none of the Gospels names its author. These names come to us via tradition and inference. There is little doubt that all of the Gospel writers are Jewish. By tradition, Matthew and John are Jesus' disciples, and Mark and Luke are the same as the Mark and Luke named in the Book of Acts. But of the Gospel writers, collectively known as the Four Evangelists, only John gives internal evidence that he has first-person knowledge of Jesus. All the Gospel authors write some decades after the Ascension, at a time when it is becoming apparent that the events of the life of Christ must be set down in a systematic fashion, among other reasons to avoid controversy occasioned by contradictory hearsay. Internal evidence indicates that they have access to collections of Jesus' sayings that have been written down from oral tradition, but these primary sources are now lost.

Matthew gives the longest, most complete account of Jesus' life and teachings. He takes pains to present Jesus as God's fulfillment of Old Testament prophecies, as the promised Messiah or Savior. Probably he writes while living in a Jewish community (some scholars suggest Antioch) outside Palestine. As a Jew, Matthew would have spoken Aramaic, but he writes in labored Greek. He has access to the Gospel of Mark, as well as to a source that is inferred but has disappeared. The Gospel of Matthew is written sometime between 80 and 90 CE.

Mark, by tradition (uncorroborated by modern scholarship), is the son of a woman from Jerusalem named Mary, at whose house the earliest Christians meet. Thus, he may have been an early believer but not one of the twelve disciples. If so, he may well have taken his account from first-person sources. Tradition places him among the Seventy whom Jesus commissions to spread his gospel. There is a John Mark who accompanies Paul on many of his travels and is with Peter in Rome. But Mark is a common name in the Roman Empire, and the two Marks may be separate individuals. Mark writes his Gospel in Greek from somewhere outside Palestine (his knowledge of Palestinian geography is faulty) to an audience that is probably not Jewish. His Greek is neither polished nor literary, but straightforward. It is not his mother tongue. Because of a reference to the destruction of the Temple, the date is probably 70 CE or shortly after. His is the earliest of the Gospels.

Little is known about the author of the Gospel of Luke. There is a tradition that Luke is a physician, but scholars now dispute this. It is clear that the author of Luke is an educated man and writes fluently in Greek. He knows the Septuagint. He also knows the Gospel of Mark, which he uses as a source. He probably uses other written sources now lost, for his Gospel contains a good deal of material not found in either Matthew or Mark. Like Mark, he too may have spoken with first-person witnesses. Luke the Evangelist is undoubtedly the author of the Acts of the Apostles, which follows the four Gospels in the New Testament and tells of the early spread of Christianity. But the author of the Gospel of Luke and the Acts of the Apostles may or may not have been the Luke who was with Paul during his two years of imprisonment in Caesarea, from 58 to 60 CE. His narrative of the Book of Acts ends with Paul's imprisonment in Rome. Most scholars date the Gospel of Luke and the Book of Acts sometime between 80 and 85 CE and agree that they are a single two-part narrative. Because of their sources and their similarities, the Gospels of Matthew, Mark, and Luke are known as the Synoptic Gospels.

The Gospel of John is quite different from the other three. It gives the fullest account of Jesus' trial, crucifixion, and resurrection, but it lacks the familiar parables of the other three Gospels. John writes as a Jew to Jewish Christian communities. It is not certain that John is familiar with the other three Gospels, and he may have used an entirely different source. The Gospel of John cannot be dated with precision, but tradition places it toward the end of the first century. Probably the version that has come down to us is completed at that time, although the self-described "beloved disciple," who is with Christ during his ministry, may have narrated or recorded his account much earlier. John the beloved disciple is an untutored fisherman and probably speaks Greek as well as Aramaic, but he is not a man of letters. John the Evangelist writes in fluent Greek. For this reason, many scholars think that late in the first century an unnamed scribe edits the version of the Gospel of John that becomes part of the New Testament canon. The writer of the Gospel of John is probably also the author of the three letters (1 John, 2 John, and 3 John) that are part of the New Testament canon, but he is not the writer of the Book of Revelation. There are two contradicting traditions concerning John's later years. By one tradition, he is an early martyr. By the other, he becomes the leader of a Christian community in Ephesus in Asia Minor where he brings Mary, the mother of Jesus. By this tradition, both John and Mary live to die of old age.

The house where Mary supposedly lived is preserved to this day on the outskirts of Ephesus. It was one of the places I visited when in Turkey some years ago. I viewed the site with a great deal of skepticism, for it is substantial and does not appear to be of sufficient age to be authentic. But I did not at the time (and do not now) doubt the possibility that in their latter years John and Mary could have lived in Ephesus.

15

JESUS CHRIST

Now there was about this time Jesus, a wise man, if it be lawful to call him a man; for he was a doer of wonderful works...He drew over to him both many of the Jews and many of the Gentiles. He was [the] Christ...And the tribe of Christians, so named from him, are not extinct at this day.

Flavius Josephus,
Antiquities of the Jews, Book 18, Chapter 3

The people that walked in darkness have seen a great light; on those who live in a land of deep shadow a light has shown...For there is a child born for us, a son given to us, and dominion is laid on his shoulders.

Isaiah 9: 1,6

The Four Evangelists are familiar with the Hebrew Scriptures, and they assume their readers are also. They make frequent reference to the Prophets of old, particularly Isaiah, who in the eight century BCE foretells the coming of a messiah, a savior for the Jewish people. Isaiah's prophesies resonate in Roman Palestine no less than under the rule of the Assyrians and subsequent conquerors. The Jews look for a messiah who will lift their yoke.

Matthew, Mark, Luke, and John present Jesus Christ (*Jesus* is the Greek form of *Joshua*, a Hebrew name meaning *savior*; *Christ* is the Greek word for *Messiah*) as the fulfillment of Old Testament prophecy, but not as the militant savior in the tradition of King David for which the Jewish community has longed. Jesus is presented as the Son of God, as preacher and healer, as redeemer through the ultimate sacrifice, as one resurrected from death to life, and as ascended Lord who bids his followers to spread the Good News. Some of the Jews who meet him or learn of him believe that he is indeed the Messiah. Others reject him as an imposter and insist that their messiah has yet to come. From the nucleus of Jewish believers, the movement later to be called Christianity is born.

In the Gospel accounts, details of time and place are often of less importance than events and their significance. Nevertheless, from comparing the four Gospels, it is possible to piece together a chronology and tie it to places where events occurred. That Jesus actually lived and taught in Palestine has strong place-name corroboration and is also mentioned in the accounts of the Jewish/ Roman historian Josephus, who writes in the seventh decade of the first century.

Birth

In the Gospel account, fulfillment of prophecy begins with the visit of the angel Gabriel to Mary, a virgin engaged to Joseph, a carpenter. Mary learns that she will conceive and bear a son who will save his people. Both she and Joseph can trace their lineage to King David, and the prophets have said that a Messiah will come from the house of David.

In Nazareth, I visit the Church of the Annunciation, purporting to be on the site where Mary learns from the angel Gabriel that she is to become the mother of Jesus. The Church, a site overseen by Franciscans, contains recently installed modern murals from all over the world depicting the Annunciation.

116

According to the Gospel of Luke, Jesus of Nazareth is born while Herod is still king, so the actual date of his birth may be anytime between 7 and 4. Mary and Joseph travel to Bethlehem in Judea (Joseph's birthplace) to be counted in the imperial census ordered by Caesar Augustus. The town is crowded, and the only quarters the couple can find are in a stable, probably located within a cave. There Jesus is born.

CA. 7-4 BCE

My visit to Bethlehem is one day after the Pope's visit, and Bethlehem is teeming with young people from all over the world—especially young Roman Catholics—who have come to hear a Mass the Pope will give on the Mount of the Beatitudes in Galilee the following day. Today is their day to see Bethlehem. The lines to the Church of the Nativity are long and slow moving, and the young pilgrims while away the time by singing folk songs in scores of languages and joining in folk dances. Eventually, I abandon the attempt to get into the Church of the Nativity, which is overseen by Orthodox groups, and go instead to an adjacent and fairly recently constructed Franciscan church, where the Roman rite is broadcast around the world every year on Christmas Eve. Below this church are grottos, and here I can get an idea of the stable quarters that the Holy Family occupied. Stables, I learn, were often situated in caves; hence, the site is probably much closer to the original in feel than the embellished site at the Church of the Nativity.

Learning that a young child, to whom wise men come to pay tribute, may someday be a threat to his rule, Herod orders all males under the age of two to be executed. Forewarned in a dream, Joseph takes his family into Egypt, where they live for an indeterminate period, certainly until after Herod dies.

Early Years

Jesus grows up in his family's home in Nazareth, in the northern province of Galilee. Probably his family's roots in Galilee are not deep, for Joseph was born far to the south in Bethlehem. Both Mary and Joseph are Judeans, now resettled in the north.

CA. 5-8 CE

117

Luke records that when Jesus is twelve, he journeys with his family to the Temple in Jerusalem, engages in discourse with scholars in the Temple, and gives his parents anxious moments when they find he is not among the group of people returning to Nazareth. They return to the Temple and find him there. From then until about the age of thirty, nothing is known of Jesus' early life. Tradition assumes Jesus learns the carpenter's trade from his father Joseph. Nazareth, a small town, is only four miles away from the thriving city of Sepphoris, where (as revealed by recent archaeology) many well-to-do Greek-speaking Jews live. A carpenter of Nazareth could have found much in Sepphoris to keep him busy. If indeed his work takes him to Sepphoris, Jesus would undoubtedly come to know Greek as well as his native Aramaic. The Hebrew he knows is from his study of Scripture.

Baptism, Ministry, and Travels

CA. 24-

29 CE   At about age thirty, Jesus begins the teaching and travels that are chronicled in the four Gospels. One of the first events recorded is his selection as a reader in the synagogue in Nazareth, an honor that could only have been bestowed on someone who is deemed worthy and who reads Hebrew flawlessly.

Walking through a busy Arab bazaar in Nazareth, I arrive at a small Christian church that sits on the site of an ancient synagogue and has been restored to be as faithful as possible to original construction. Like so many places I visit, the event might have occurred there.

At the beginning of his ministry, Jesus is baptized by John the Baptist, his contemporary and the son of his mother's cousin, who may have been a member of the Essenes sect and who has been traveling the country preaching and prophesying. The baptism takes place at the southern end of the Jordan River, near where it empties into the Dead Sea. At this time, the Jordan holds far more water than at present, for most of its flow is now tapped for irrigation, and little reaches the Dead Sea.

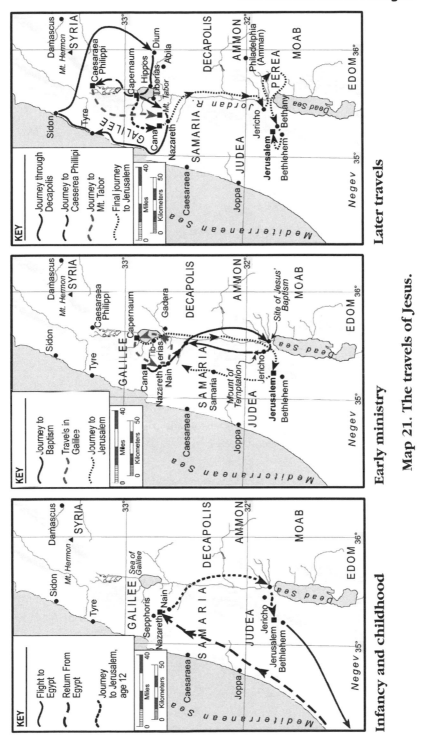

Later travels

Early ministry

Map 21. The travels of Jesus.

Infancy and childhood

Whether the baptism site was on the east bank or the west bank of the river is now under contention. The west bank has long been a cherished pilgrimage site, where busloads of believers, especially from North America, come to renew their baptismal vows as they immerse themselves in Jordan River waters. The site is usually crowded. My bus drives nearby but does not stop at the site, and I am not disappointed.

Recently, Jordan has found what it considers to be indisputable evidence that the baptism of Jesus takes place on the eastern (or Jordanian) bank of the river. Indeed the account in the Gospel of John speaks of a site "beyond the Jordan," which implies the east bank. Jordan times the site dedication to coincide with the Pope's visit to Jordan. Preparation of accommodations at the new site has been the number-one use for limited Jordanian tourist funds in 1999-2000. It appears as if Jordan and Israel are in for a protracted skirmish over which is the real site. The stakes in tourism are not to be belittled. The course of the river has probably shifted several times in the past two thousand years, so both claims, or neither, may have validity.

Following his baptism, Jesus stays for forty days in what Matthew and Luke call "the wilderness." The Gospel writers do not locate the wilderness, and probably do not need to, for the experience that Jesus has there—resisting repeated temptations by the devil and being strengthened thereby—need not be site-specific.

Nevertheless, when I read this account, I recall the Judean Desert, the dry and sharply dissected region that lies between the Jordan Valley and the western plateau. The Judean Desert is in a rain shadow, cut off from the moisture-bearing winds that blow inland from the Mediterranean Sea. As I go by bus north from Jerusalem to Beit Sha'an, I am struck by the contrast between the semi-arid but wooded plateau where Jerusalem sits and the desolate appearance of much of the Judean Desert. By contrast, the Jordan Valley, which can only be reached via the desert descent, is lush and green from irrigation. The Valley is now heavily settled, both by Israelis, Israeli farmers and their Palestinian neighbors. I try to picture the Jordan Valley as it must have been when Jesus was tempted in the wilderness or when he walked there on journeys between Galilee and Jerusalem. The furrows in the fields must have been like irregular ones I see, and the Arab farmers urging their donkeys would have been garbed similarly to those I see walking behind their animals.

After this period of preparation, Jesus goes north again into the Galilee region and is invited to a wedding feast given by his mother's friend. The event occurs in Cana, a village to the north of Nazareth. There he performs his first miracle, turning water into wine.

Cana is a challenge to the pilgrim. There are three churches there, of three different persuasions, each claiming to occupy the site of the miracle. I am taken into a church maintained by the Roman Catholic Franciscans. Aesthetically, the church is pleasing. But the dilemma persists, and in the end precise location makes no difference.

Jesus adopts as his home base the fishing village of Capernaum, on the north shore of the Sea of Galilee, to which he returns from each of his journeys.

There he recruits his disciples, several of whom are fishermen. During the course of his ministry, Jesus performs miracles connected with the Sea of Galilee: He walks on water, he multiplies the catch, he calms raging winds, and he turns two fish into enough to feed 5,000 people. He crosses the sea to the "land of the Gadarenes" on the southeast, where he heals a man raging with madness. And he enters Galilee by way of the Decapolis, which means he must return to Capernaum by sea. Matthew, Mark, and John call this body of water the Sea of Galilee, Luke calls it the Lake of Gennesaret, and during Jesus' time the Romans called it the Lake of Tiberias. The name on Israeli maps is Lake Kinneret.

From the shores of Tiberius, once the Roman administrative city on the west shore of the lake and now a resort town, I board an oversized boat that purports to model an ancient fishing vessel. Later, in a kibbutz on the western shore of the Sea of Galilee, I see a small boat recently recovered from deep mud along the shore. According to carbon dating imaging, it has been underwater for about 2,000 years. The site is now a national park, and the boat, having been carefully treated by impregnation with

Photo 9. The northern shore of the Sea of Galilee.

a preservative, is handsomely displayed. As I see this small boat, I am inclined to think it is more like the one in which Peter and Andrew fished and Jesus took sail for the opposite shore.

The larger boat that I am in pulls away from the shore for a two-hour quiet time of reflection. From the center of the Sea of Galilee, I can see the hills that nearly surround it, quite low and gentle to the north and higher to the east than to the west. To the north, I can see the hillsides where Jesus preached to the "multitudes," where he told parables, and where the Lord's Prayer was first spoken. To the south is the outlet of the lake into the Jordan River. A guide points southeastward, in the direction of the ancient Decapolis sites of Gadara and Hippos, both of which I hope to see later at close range. Gadara is in Jordan. Hippos is adjacent to the Golan Heights, territory claimed by Syria but controlled by Israel. The Golan territory that borders on the north west shore of the Sea of Galilee remains the sticking point in the negotiations between Israel and Syria over the return of the Golan.

When I reach the northern shore, I find the site of ancient Capernaum covered with churches, and it is here that I am shown the foundations of a house that tradition says is the house of the brothers Peter and Andrew, Jesus' first disciples. A church with foundations dating to the

122

second century is adjacent to the site. The Mount of the Beatitudes is nearby. It is not a mount but a gently sloping hillside. I am disappointed because it is not possible to sit on its grassy slopes as listeners once did. Today, barbed wire fences off these slopes. All sitting must now be done in churches or in adjacent courtyards. Nevertheless, the significance of the Beatitudes and the Lord's Prayer remains, even if heard from a bench instead of a hillside.

A week after my visit to the Mount of the Beatitudes, the barbed wire must have been removed temporarily, for the grassy slopes hold thousands of young pilgrims, those whom I see in Bethlehem and many thousands more, who gather at this site to hear the Pope say Mass. Nearly eighty years old and infirm, the Pope does not spare himself as he travels this week on his personal pilgrimage to sites in the Holy Land. Protecting the Pope yet allowing him access to all the places he wishes to visit presents the Israelis with the greatest crowd control and security challenge they have ever faced. I am impressed with how smoothly all seems to be going.

During his ministry, Jesus makes the 80-mile journey to Jerusalem several times, probably traveling one way through the dry hill country of Samaria and the other along the Jordan Valley.

To reach Jerusalem from the Jordan Valley, he must go through Jericho, then turn westward, reaching the plateau by crossing the dry and dusty Judean Desert. In Bethany, on the outskirts of Jerusalem, he is befriended by Mary and Martha and their brother Lazarus, with whom he often stays. Mary washes the dust from his feet. Martha bustles about preparing the meal. On one occasion, the Gospel narrates that Jesus raises Lazarus to life after he has been four days dead.

I visit Bethany, now an Arab town within the Palestinian Authority. The traditional site of the tomb of Lazarus is barely accessible, down a steep flight of stone steps leading to a tiny room that may or may not be a tomb. At the entrance, merchants are out in force, selling postcards and Holy Land souvenirs.

At the beginning of the third year of his ministry, Jesus journeys to the ancient but still active Mediterranean ports of Tyre and Sidon, gateway to Lebanon. On his return, he makes a side trip through the Decapolis region, east of the Jordan.

The Gospels do not give a reason for this itinerary, but we can map it. The road to the Mediterranean leads through Magdela and Nazareth, westward along the north face of the Mt. Carmel ridge to the site of present-day Haifa (then Ptolemais), and then north along the coast to the ancient Phoenician ports of Tyre and Sidon, which are under Roman jurisdiction. It doesn't make sense for Jesus to take the long way home "by way of the Decapolis" unless he has a mission there. But nothing more is said.

Later in the trip, I manage to visit both of the Decapolis sites where his return might have been facilitated. Most authorities take for granted that he passes through the larger and more famous site, Gadara, and enters the lake from this place. But the deep Yarmouk Valley, tributary to the Jordan, cuts between Gadara and the lake, making access exceedingly difficult. The Gospels speak of an earlier visit that Jesus makes to the "land of the Gadarenes," but I conclude that this earlier visit is not to Gadara itself but to that part of the region of Gadara that is tangent to the lake. I engage a taxi driver to take me to the undeveloped archaeological site of Hippos, high above the east shore of the lake, and I conclude that it is through Hippos and not Gadara that Jesus probably returns. At the foot of the fairly steep but direct slope from Hippos, a boat could moor, taking Jesus back to Capernaum. This, of course, is conjecture, but I feel fortunate to have seen the ruins of Hippos, which will soon be developed as an official archaeological site.

At another time, Jesus and his disciples travel north to the Roman resort city of Caesarea Philippi, whose present-day name of Banias is an Arab adaptation of the Greek "Panias". The Greeks had dedicated this site to the nature god Pan. It is in Caesarea Philippi that Peter first acknowledges the divinity of Jesus, "son of the living God."

Because I sense how precious water is in much of Israel, it is gratifying to find it here in abundance, as as well in the entire Hula lake district, a marshy region that collects the waters flowing off Mount Hermon and

124

sends them southward to the Sea of Galilee. The entire area north of the Sea of Galilee is verdant and fertile, and heavily cultivated. (Later I learn that many of the workmen in this agricultural area are paid laborers from countries other than Israel.) To the north and east is Syria, and to the immediate east is the Golan Heights. In Banias school children are on holiday, and I see a group of attractive teenage girls, very dark, who giggle as they pass. They grant my request to take their picture, and when I remark that they seem happy, one replies, "We have to be; we have no place else to go." My guide tells me that they are Ethiopian Jews, who are proving to be the most difficult to acculturate of all the in-gathered peoples. (I can't help but realize that one part of their difficulty may be racism.)

West of Banias, I stop at a kibbutz equipped with guesthouses, a lovely place with flowing water and wildflowers and plenty of grassy areas. Here, in a spring at the edge of the kibbutz, I witness a baptism in a very private ceremony performed not in the Jordan River but on the grassy banks of one of its many sources.

Jerusalem

On his final journey—coinciding with the days before the feast of the Passover—Jesus, together with his disciples and a host of followers, makes his way from Capernaum to Jerusalem. They travel southward down the east side of the Jordan River Valley, cross to Jericho, then climb the dry Judean hills to reach Bethany. Dusty from the last phase of the trip, Jesus rests here and probably is tended by his friends Mary and Martha. He asks his disciples to secure a donkey for him. Riding the donkey, he then goes on to the Mount of Olives (a hill, not a mountain, overlooking Jerusalem), descends the steep path to the bottom of the hill, crosses the Kidron Brook, and enters the city through one of its gates.

I descend the Mount of Olives by the same route, moving from the brilliantly domed Russian Orthodox church at the top to the Garden of P‍ASSOVER *Gethsemane at the bottom. Had I continued on foot, I would have* W‍EEK *followed Jesus' route as he entered the city. But I take an easier way, by bus and then foot, to reach the Temple Mount.*

Jerusalem is crowded at this Passover season. Jews have come from near and far to celebrate. By this time, Jesus is well known, and crowds accompany his journey through the city to the Temple Mount. They carry palm branches and shout, "*Hosanna!,*" following Hebrew processional tradition that by this time is more than five hundred years old. My Israeli guide translates Hosanna as a Hebrew word meaning *Lord Save Us.* The crowd does not say, "Lord Save Us from Roman Tyranny," but they can imply it. People in the crowd, chafing under Roman rule, are looking to Jesus, the Messiah, to lead them in revolt. During the coming days, they learn (to the disappointment of most) that Jesus is indeed leading the way, but to a different and apolitical goal.

Jesus spends the first days of Passover week preaching and teaching in the Temple. He foretells the coming destruction of the Temple, a prediction not likely to endear him either to the priests or the gathered crowd.

The Temple Mount today bears little resemblance to its appearance during the time of Christ. Later, I see a scale model of the Temple that Herod built, and I form a pretty good idea of the layout: an outer courtyard where merchants sell animals for sacrifice, and trinkets as well, an inner courtyard where worshippers gather, and a restricted High Altar area (now enclosed within the Dome of the Rock).

In the outer courtyard, Jesus rails against the money changers. At night, he and his disciples return to the Mount of Olives, where they probably sleep in temporary quarters set up to accommodate the Passover visitors.

Trial, Death, Resurrection, and Ascension

On the fifth night of this Passover week, Jesus sends his disciples to secure a room where they can celebrate the Seder together. The exact site of this room has several claimants.

I visit one Norman-style site, probably built by Crusaders, that is impressive but hardly evocative of first-century Jerusalem.

126

Then Jesus crosses the Kidron Brook to the Garden of Gethsemane at the foot of the Mount of Olives.

Gethsemane means oil press, and most certainly in Jesus' time, the production from the trees on the Mount of Olives was carried down slope to be pressed into oil. Now, however, there is no olive press, but only very old olive trees in a tranquil setting. Next to the garden is one of the most beautiful churches I've seen in the Holy Land, capped with multiple small domes. It is a recent Franciscan undertaking, with frescos contributed by artists from all over the world.

In the quiet garden Jesus prays, but his disciples cannot resist sleep. At length, Jesus is taken by a detail of priests and soldiers who escort him first to the house of Annas, formerly the high priest, and then to that of his son-in-law, Caiaphas, who now holds the office. Caiaphas considers Jesus a heretic and a troublemaker, but he wants the Romans to deal with him because the religious courts do not mete out death sentences to dissenters.

The monks in an Armenian monastery claim to have uncovered the site of the house of Caiaphas, and a grizzled attendant beckons me past the monastery gate to see it. He speaks no English, but puts forth one word, "Caiaphas." We go down several layers, climbing over debris, until we reach digs that could certainly have been the house of a dignitary from the ancient past. I'm ready to accept the claim, and I thank him, only to learn later that two other sites make claim to the house of Caiaphas. The Armenians have been in Jerusalem almost from the beginning of Christian pilgrimage, and Armenian Christianity is among the oldest. But through the centuries, the Ottoman Turks, the Georgians, and the Russians, let alone the Greeks and other Orthodox groups in Jerusalem, have made things so difficult for the Armenians that they have built their own fortress within a fortress. To reach the Armenian section, I had to climb a steep hill, and by luck I stumbled on the open gate and the friendly attendant.

Ordinarily, one would not need to use such a difficult entrance into the Old City, but I manage to visit Jerusalem on the Sunday that the Pope has chosen to say Mass at the Church of the Holy Sepulchre. The

Pope wishes to reflect and pray in this most holy site in Christendom, and thanks to the strict crowd control of the Israeli army and the Jerusalem police, he gets his wish.

Without access to television or English newspapers, I am blithely unaware of the press of crowds that await me. For security, all gates are blocked. A soldier tells me that if I climb the hill into the Armenian section I can get through the walls. He is right. Proceeding into the Old City, I do not see the Pope, who is heavily escorted through a gate that is secure. But I see a group of invited and colorfully garbed clerics, representing all branches of Christendom, marching in slow cadence through the city streets on the way to the Church of the Holy Sepulchre. Because it is Sunday, I attend services in the oldest protestant church in Jerusalem, an Anglican church only two blocks away, served by a priest with the name of Neil Cohen. His English Jewish heritage is obvious, and his church has sent him here to minister to Christian Jews. His congregation is eclectic; a Chinese woman who is living in Jerusalem to study Hebrew guides me there.

PASSOVER
WEEK
DAY 6

From the religious courts, Jesus is remanded to Pontius Pilate, who rules ordinarily from the port city of Caesarea but is on an official visit to Jerusalem. Pilate probably anticipates trouble from the crowds gathered for the Passover season. He stays in the Antonia Fortress, adjacent to and overlooking the Temple Mount. Pilate questions Jesus, finds no fault in him, and is pleased to learn that he is a Galilean. That puts him in the jurisdiction of Herod Antipas, the ruler of Galilee and the trans-Jordan province of Perea, the same Herod who earlier executed John the Baptist. Herod also is in Jerusalem for the Passover. Pilate sends Jesus to Herod, and Herod is delighted. He has heard about Jesus but never met him; perhaps he can get Jesus to perform a miracle. But Jesus remains totally silent in Herod's presence. His soldiers taunt him, then send him back to Pilate. Pilate confronts the Jewish leaders and the crowd. He tells them that both he and Herod have examined Jesus, and there is no basis to charge him. But the crowd is insistent, calling on Pilate to crucify Jesus. To mollify the crowd, Pilate orders Jesus scourged, and his soldiers mock him with a crown of thorns.

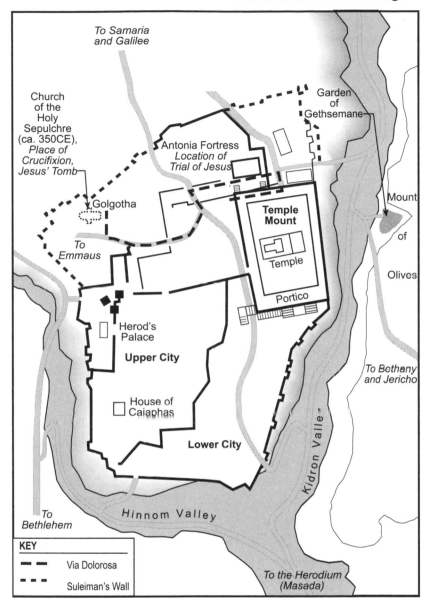

To Samaria
and Galilee

Church
of the
Holy
Sepulchre
(ca. 350CE),
*Place of
Crucifixion,
Jesus' Tomb*

Garden
of
Gethsemane

Antonia Fortress
*Location of
Trial of Jesus*

Golgotha

Mount

**Temple
Mount**

To
Emmaus

Temple

of

Olives

Portico

Herod's
Palace

Upper City

To Bethany
and Jericho

House of
Caiaphas

Kidron Valley

Lower City

To
Bethlehem

Hinnom Valley

KEY

– – Via Dolorosa

- - - Suleiman's Wall

To the Herodium
(Masada)

Map 22. Jerusalem at the time of Christ.

Pilate questions Jesus, finds him guiltless of treason, but orders
him scourged anyway.

*The Antonia Fortress has long since disappeared, but in the bowels of its
former site, I am shown marks etched in stone where Roman soldiers
once amused themselves with a last-man-out game, with chits or tokens*

representing prisoners. The prisoner represented by the losing chit is scourged and mocked. Although Jerusalem as a whole has changed from the way it looked in Jesus' time, there is no reason to believe that the Antonia Fortress is greatly altered.

From a balcony, Pilate shows the scourged Jesus to the crowd (*Ecce Homo!*), hoping to avoid the decision he is reluctant to make. When he realizes he has no alternative, considering the mood of the crowd, he washes his hands symbolically to relieve himself of guilt, then condemns the prisoner to be crucified.

From the courtyard of the Antonia Fortress, Jesus starts his last journey, carrying his cross, along a route now labeled the Via Dolorosa. Most pilgrims wish to pause reflectively at each of the stops, or Stations of the Cross, representing events that take place on the horrific journey. Some of the events are chronicled in the Gospels but others are backed only by tradition.

With the press of people who come to the Holy Land this week because the Pope is here, as well as others who, like I, schedule the trip well in advance without knowing of the papal visit, the Via Dolorosa is hardly a reflective experience.

PASSOVER
WEEK
DAY 7

For Jesus, the painful, humiliating procession ends in an abandoned stone quarry called Golgotha, the place outside the city walls where criminals are crucified. There Jesus endures the agonizing death that is the Roman method of execution. A wealthy Jew, Joseph of Arimathaea, offers his nearby tomb as a burial place, and this is where the body of Jesus is laid. A heavy stone is rolled across the entrance to the tomb, and soldiers are put on guard. The next day is the Sabbath, when no activity can take place. But early on the morning

EASTER

of the third day after burial, women who come to anoint the body of Jesus, Mary of Magdala, Mary the mother of Jesus, and others, find the stone rolled away and the tomb empty. Angels appear to them, to tell them "He is not here, He has risen." They hasten to tell others. Peter comes to the tomb and also finds it empty. Here Christianity gains its core: a crucified savior who, as the Son of God, rises from the dead.

Photo 10. The Via Dolorosa crowded with tourists.

The places of crucifixion, burial, and resurrection are now enclosed within the enlarged Old City as rebuilt by the Romans in the second century and defined by Suleiman's Wall, erected in the sixteenth century. These sites are incorporated within the sprawling, massive, indescribable complex of columns, great arches, chapels, and reliquaries collectively called the Church of the Holy Sepulchre. On the day I visit the Church of the Holy Sepulchre, my first day in Jerusalem, the crowds are so thick that I almost suffocate. I leave with only one impression I wish to remember: a tomb, quite hidden and little marked, that supposedly is the family tomb of Joseph of Arimathaea. This is not billed as the burial place of Christ. Had it been, I would never have been able to get near it.

FORTY
DAYS
LATER

131

During the forty days Jesus remains on earth after his resurrection, he appears to many people, most notably to Mary of Magdala on Easter morning, to travelers on the road to Emmaus, and to his disciples, either on the shores of the Sea of Galilee or in a house in Jerusalem (the Gospel accounts vary).

I note the site of Emmaus on the drive from Jerusalem to Tel Aviv. It lies at a place where the hills meet the coastal plain. The area appears to be extremely fertile and fairly prosperous, as it must have been at the time of Christ. Jesus' ascension, witnessed by his disciples, takes place on the Mount of Olives.

I am troubled by the inconsistencies in the Gospel accounts of where the disciples are to meet Jesus following the resurrection and where the ascension takes place. Matthew says they are to hasten to Galilee, where he will show himself, but Galilee is a good eighty miles away through difficult hill country. By fast public bus, it takes me the better part of three hours. Mark says nothing on the subject. Luke and John indicate that Jesus appears to the disciples in Jerusalem, but John also recounts a later appearance on the Sea of Galilee. Matthew has the ascension taking place on a hill in Galilee. Mark does not give a place but says the event happens while the disciples are gathered with Jesus around a table. Luke says the ascension takes place outside Jerusalem, "near Bethany," which he confirms in Acts as the Mount of Olives. John does not mention the ascension. I know I should let such inconsistencies alone, but I am too place-oriented to avoid such musings. Here is one of so many bits of evidence that dates and places in the Bible are of only minor concern to the writers. What is important to the writers are the events themselves and their significance. Clearly, the Bible cannot be read as strict history, and its geography is often sketchy. Nevertheless, its time/place framework is intact, even if the details are not.

16

THE NEW FAITH SPREADS

Jesus the Jewish prophet…was executed by the Romans in a manner so hideous that his followers could never forget it…[But] their small Palestinian sect grew into a movement that spread like scattered seeds through the Roman world…

Thomas Cahill, *Desire of the Everlasting Hills*

In the case of those who were denounced to me as Christians…I first interrogated these; those who confessed I interrogated a second and a third time, threatening them with punishment; those who persisted I ordered executed…There were others possessed of the same folly; but because they were Roman citizens, I signed an order for them to be transferred to Rome.

Pliny the Younger, Governor (111-113 CE) of Pontus/Bithynia [in what is now Turkey] to the Emperor Trajan, Letters 10.96-97

Just before his ascension, Jesus proclaims what Christians have since called *The Great Commission*. His followers are to go into all the world to tell everyone the Good News, to "make disciples of all nations," and to baptize them into the new faith. In other words, Christianity is to be a missionary religion, spread by its followers.

Pentecost

FIFTY
DAYS
LATER

Ten days after the ascension, the disciples are gathered in Jerusalem. There they receive a sign, a tongue of flame resting on the head of each disciple, signifying that they have indeed been chosen to spread the Good News. To this end, they are now able to speak in several languages. They begin to tell of Jesus and of their experiences with him to the Jews who are in Jerusalem at this time of year, on pilgrimage from many parts of the Mediterranean world for Pentecost. Pentecost, originally a "first fruits" harvest festival (for the harvest of winter wheat), has by this time come to mean for the Jews the celebration of the Mosaic law given by God on Mount Sinai fifty days after the first Passover. The term is Greek, the festival ancient. Jewish Christians begin to give new significance to the meaning of Pentecost, coming as it does fifty days after Easter. As the Jewish pilgrims return home, the news spreads. Meanwhile, the new religion—perceived at the time as a variant or reform of Judaism— takes root first in Jerusalem.

Paul

Gradually, the disciples and their followers understand that their mission is not only to fellow Jews but also to Greeks, Romans, and all others. The word spreads, as new ideas will. At first, the spread is slow, impeded at every turn by Jewish ecclesiastical leaders, of whom Paul—a devout Jew and Roman citizen from Tarsus, on the southern coast of what is now Turkey—is one. Paul tries to identify and wipe out the followers of the new faith. On one such mission, he travels north to Damascus, the northernmost of the Decapolis cities. But on the road to Damascus, Paul is felled by a blinding light, encounters Christ in a vision, and is himself converted.

CA. 45-67
CE

Paul changes from a persecutor of those who follow the new faith to an inspired proponent and missionary. The first believers are

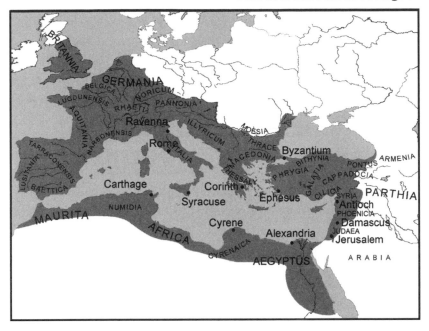

Map 23. The Roman Empire, ca. 40 CE.

from the Jewish community, not only in Jerusalem but throughout the eastern Mediterranean and Rome. But the perception of Christianity as a religion distinct from Judaism grows, especially as the new faith takes root in Asia Minor among both Jews and non-Jews.

Paul and other missionaries travel with relative ease along Roman roads and in Roman shipping lanes. They establish communities of new believers as they go, not only in such Greek cities as Ephesus, Corinth, and Philippi, but also in Rome. Eventually, some of the early missionaries pay for their faith with their lives, for as the number of Christians grows, the Romans perceive that Christians are not merely a nuisance but a threat to their own state religion. Paul is held prisoner for two years at Caesarea, the Roman port city and administrative center in Palestine. He is sent to Rome for trial, is shipwrecked on the island of Malta, touches at Syracuse in Sicily, then remains for two years under house arrest as a prisoner in Rome. Finally, he is set free for lack of evidence. By tradition, he meets death during the persecutions of Nero in 67 CE.

The Pax Romana

CA. 50-
200
CE

The Book of Acts (The Acts of the Apostles), written by the same author as the Gospel of Luke, tells the story of the early spread of Christianity. Most of the other books of the New Testament, other than the four Gospels, are letters from Paul and other early missionaries to various Christian communities in the Greek-speaking world. In addition to the places documented in the New Testament, tradition places the early spread of Christianity as far as India, Ethiopia, Spain, Britain, and to wherever Roman legions are posted. Given the stability and intercourse facilitated by the *Pax Romana,* none of these traditions can be easily dismissed. Wherever Christianity spreads, Jerusalem and Palestine begin to take on almost a sacred aspect, a holy destination, where pilgrims can "walk where Jesus walked."

17

SITES OF PILGRIMAGE

Thanks to Constantine's mother,
the Christian tradition today has as many holy sites and
shrines in Israel as do the Jews and Muslims combined.
To be sure, some of the sites which Helena pointed out
were already considered holy shrines commemorating
specific events in Jesus' life. Helena...
lent a great deal of legitimacy to the original traditions;
no one was arguing with the mother of the emperor of
Rome.

David E. Lipman, Gates to Jewish Heritage

I am able to visit most of the sites associated with the life and ministry of Jesus, with the exception of Tyre and Sidon, which are in Lebanon. At first, I am deeply skeptical of the authenticity of the sites. But the more I learn, the more I have reason to believe that most of the sites of pilgrimage actually do mark places at or quite near to where Gospel events occurred.

Aside from the New Testament accounts and the ever-growing archaeological record, pilgrims owe their understanding of life in Palestine in the first century BCE to the Jewish historian Flavius Josephus, who writes in the seventh decade of that century. Josephus mentions Jesus, but his is the only historical source to do so, and he is not interested in pinpointing sites connected with Jesus' life. So

137

the authentication of the sites must rest on tradition. Is tradition reliable?

I come to believe that it probably is.

330 CE

Most of the sites that Christian pilgrims visit, sites connected with the life of Jesus, begin to be places of pilgrimage within a hundred years or less of Jesus' death and resurrection. The Acts of the Apostles and the letters of Paul bear witness to the growing number of people who are willing to identify themselves as Christians. Certainly less than three generations separate the events from the desire of the devout to visit these sites. Oral tradition may thus be considered fairly reliable.

Later, when Helena, mother of the first christian Roman Emperor, Constantine, comes to the Holy Land in the early fourth century to arrange for the building of churches on the sites, she and her advisors take as much care as possible to authenticate the sites. Helena commissions the Church of the Holy Sepulchre to be built on the site of Jesus' crucifixion and tomb. Although it is almost totally destroyed by a Muslim caliph in the eleventh century, Helena's church is rebuilt by Crusaders a century later and greatly renovated in the nineteenth century. Its basic Byzantine architectural features persist but with gothic and neo-gothic overlays. Today, like most heavily visited sites in the Holy Land, the site of the Church of the Holy Sepulchre is backed by long and unbroken tradition of pilgrimage.

It is recorded that the execution and burial take place outside the city wall. How, then, can the massive, sprawling Church of the Holy Sepulchre within the Old City of Jerusalem possibly contain the authentic sites? That is the problem that Oxford archaeologist Kathleen Kenyon attempts to solve. She knows that the Jerusalem of the first century is smaller than the area of the present walled city. After exhaustive research, she finds evidence of a quarry where executions take place and of tombs nearby hewn into the face of the quarry. She authenticates that the Church of the Holy Sepulchre is indeed located on this site. Roman Catholic and Orthodox scholars, and most Protestant scholars as well, accept this finding. However, on a hill outside the present city wall, in a spot that seems to fit all preconceptions, a group of English Protestants maintains a garden

Photo 11. The Church of the Holy Sepulchre.

and an ancient tomb. A guide points to a nearby hill site as the place of crucifixion. Some tourists prefer to think that this quiet site, not the impossibly complex and—yes—gaudy Church of the Holy Sepulchre, is where they should concentrate their devotions.

Covered with churches, the pilgrimage sites now bear almost no resemblance to how they must have appeared in Jesus' time. I find that it helps to refresh my hazy knowledge of Palestine in Roman times and to have a map at hand at all times. In this way, I can try to reconstruct in my mind the sites and the people associated with them as they appeared when Jesus walked in Palestine. I had expected to be repelled by the proliferation of structures that everywhere commemorate, and in a sense desecrate, the sites. I find instead that I can respect the fervor and piety of those who erected these churches of so many different styles, representing such varied liturgical traditions and aesthetic values. My twenty-first-century aesthetics would tear it all down and try to restore it to its original appearance. But who am I to impose my values on those pilgrims of the past who came to memorialize the pilgrimage sites, all in their own way?

18

The Jewish Revolts and the Diaspora

So he gave order to the soldiers
both to burn and plunder the city...
They slew those whom they overtook without
and set fire to the houses
whither the Jews had fled,
and burnt every soul in them.

Flavius Josephus,
Antiquities of the Jews, Book 20

These Jews have penetrated to every city,
and it would not be easy to find a single place
in the inhabited world which
has not received this race.

Strabo, Geography

History is fortunate to have the accounts of Josephus. 66-73
A leader of the Jewish revolt that starts in Caesarea CE
and spreads to Galilee in the year 66, Josephus is
captured the following year. He determines that the revolt is
a lost cause and ill-advised, and casts his lot with Rome. Of
priestly heritage, Josephus now devotes his life to making
Jewish traditions comprehensible to the Graeco-Roman world.

For the remainder of the Jewish revolt, he stays on the scene as an interpreter, ingratiating himself with the Roman authorities.

Destruction of the Temple

70 CE

Josephus chronicles the Roman destruction of the second Temple in 70 CE. This Temple is the one the Jews rebuild in 515 BCE after they return from captivity in Babylon. The second Temple is erected on the site of the Temple that Solomon built. Herod's modifications toward the end of the first century BCE greatly enlarge the second Temple, increasing the size of the platform and extending the Temple edifice. Although the Romans raze the Temple, they leave the massive retaining walls standing. They also leave standing a portion of the wall that extends beyond the western side of the Temple Mount. This remnant is known as the Western Wall. Today, Jewish pilgrims come from all over the world to pray in front of it, some silently, some chanting aloud, as they sway back and forth bewailing the fate of their twice-destroyed Temple. Israeli soldiers come here as well, linking arms as they lean against the wall in grim resolution that "this shall not happen again."

As I approach the platform of the Haram al-Sharif, I have to climb steps that ascend the still visible and still massive Herodian retaining wall. At the Western Wall, and from a respectful distance, I train my camera on two men whose hands hold Scripture and who sway back and forth as they pray aloud. I sense the intensity of their emotion.

Masada

70-73 CE

Josephus gives an account of how a small band of Jewish zealots captures the imperial fortress of Masada, west of the Dead Sea, and defies the Romans for an additional three years. The fortress of Masada is being partially restored, enough so that visitors can get an idea of how extensive it is and how difficult to access. Strongly built by the Romans both to withstand a siege and to serve as a comfortable retreat for the proconsul, Masada sits on a flat-topped knoll high above the Dead Sea. The zealots capture the massive fortress at a time when the Romans are concentrating their efforts elsewhere. The zealots still have adequate food and water when, three years later, the Romans finally complete a ramp that gives them entrance to the fortress. The night before the Romans enter, the defenders choose suicide rather than submit to capture. Today, Israeli Jews, whose religion forbids suicide, are ambivalent about the Masada heroes. Although young soldiers in training are taken to the fortress to internalize the heroism of the first century Jewish defenders, the final suicidal act is not condoned.

A narrow path aptly called "the snake" gains entrance to the fortress by a steep 1,500-foot climb of switchbacks. While in control of Masada, the Romans bring in all supplies over this tortuous route. Fortunately, an aerial tramway affords tourists a much easier route. Foolishly, I descend by the snake. The view is spectacular, across the turquoise Dead Sea and toward the haze-filtered cliffs of the Jordan plateau to the east. But because I am concentrating so strongly on braking my legs and urging unused muscles forward, I have no time or inclination for photography. The descent takes a half hour, the most precipitous half hour of my life. For the next several days, my thigh muscles complain incessantly. I retain a sense of accomplishment nevertheless.

After the Jewish revolt, the Romans send Josephus to Rome to write history. He writes several multiple-volume works. One, *The Jewish War*, is an account of the revolt, prefaced with a brief survey of the previous two hundred years of Jewish history, all of it extra-Biblical. A second, *The Antiquities of the Jews*, records in considerable detail the history of the Jews in what is now known as the first century of the Common Era. Throughout, Josephus blames the Jewish revolt on a fanatical minority. Ill-conceived the revolt may have been, but it takes the Roman legions seven years to put

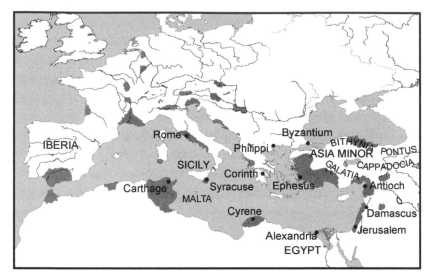

Map 24. The spread of Christianity by 200 CE.

it down. After the destruction of the Temple, the Romans expect no more trouble from their unruly Jewish subjects.

Judaism and Christianity in First Century Palestine

37-100 CE

In the lifetime of Jesus and during the rest of the first century, the Jewish community in the Holy Land is divided between traditionalists, who still wait for a promised Messiah, and Messianists, the followers of Jesus. To the scholars of organized Judaism who treasure their monotheism, Jesus' claim to be the Son of God is an abomination. Not all Jewish traditionalists oppose the Messianists, however, and for a time both worship together in the synagogues.

During the Jewish Revolt, attitudes begin to harden. The Messianists in Jerusalem take no part in the revolt, and they flee Jerusalem for more tolerant communities in the north. Angry with the Messianists for deserting their cause and deprived of their beloved Temple, Jewish scholars begin to rethink the nature of their heritage. What does it mean to be a Jew? The Messiah is still awaited. Those who consider Jesus as the Messiah are misguided. Jewish scholars eventually decide that they cannot worship together with the followers of Christ, and they expel Messianic Jews from their synagogues. From this time on, Jewish Christians worship chiefly in home-based communities, for the concept of a church as a structure does not yet exist. Before the end of the first century, Judaism and Christianity have split irrevocably. Matthew, Mark, and Luke write before the split; John's Gospel is completed after. It is significant that only John names the Jews specifically as being responsible for the crucifixion of Jesus. In subsequent centuries, the account in the Gospel of John, taken literally by Christian zealots, will bring untold grief to Jews.

The Bar Kokba Revolt   132 CE

Toward the beginning of the second century, the Romans decide to rebuild Jerusalem. The desecration of the Temple Mount, with statues of the emperor as a Roman god, provokes one last Jewish revolt in 132. After this revolt, known as the Bar Kokba Revolt, Jews are forbidden to set foot in Jerusalem and Judea.

Talmud and Mishnah from Galilee   100-300 CE

The remaining Jews now live chiefly in Galilee, the northern province. There, over the next two centuries, the Jews and the Romans develop a *modus vivendi*: The Jews promise to obey Roman law, and the Romans agree to consider their religion legitimate. This is a period of rich scholarship among the rabbis of Tiberias and Sepphoris. A collation of rabbinical studies of the Torah, known as the *Talmud,* and commentaries on Jewish law, known as the *Mishnah,* emerge from this period.

Diaspora

After the fall of Jerusalem in 70 and the Bar Kokba Revolt in 132, the Romans take thousands of Jewish captives back to Rome and to other cities in the Empire. Many other

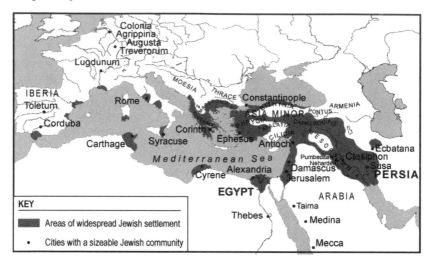

Map 25. The Jewish Diaspora, ca. 200 CE.

Jews subsequently flee in terror, leaving the Holy Land forever. As we have seen, this is not the first Jewish *Diaspora* (a word that can mean both the "scattering" of a people and, collectively, all the places where they settle). Already there are Jewish colonies in many cities of the Roman world, and the emigrants seek safety among their fellow Jews outside Palestine. Some join their co-religionists in Mesopotamia, descendants of the Jews who remained in Babylon instead of returning to Judea. Others go to Arabia, Egypt, the farther reaches of northern Africa, Spain, Greece, and the Italian Peninsula. Still others go to the northern fringes of the Roman Empire, where they carve out a new life amid Germanic and Slavic peoples.

If the Jews merge with the local population (and some do), history hears no more of them. But in most parts of the Diaspora, the Jews maintain themselves as a separate people. Many are skilled and educated and readily find a place in the economies of foreign lands. Gradually, the Jewish settlers blend their tongue and many of their customs with those of their neighbors. Religious leaders (rabbis, or teachers) in each community keep the knowledge of the ancient Hebrew texts alive. In western lands, the Jews in the Diaspora follow the Torah in the Septuagint version and subsequent vernacular translations. By the sixth century, Jewish scholars in the Holy Land have assembled all the Hebrew and Aramaic writings, from the Torah through the second century books of Daniel and Esther, into a codified whole, known as the Masoritic Text, that sets the canon and standardizes the arrangement of the Hebrew Scriptures. By this time, too, the Christians have accepted the various writings in the Hebrew Scriptures as the Old Testament.

Under most Roman emperors, the Jews of the Diaspora are allowed to practice their religion without harassment. Wherever they go, however, they look to Jerusalem as their spiritual homeland, and they voluntarily tax themselves to send money back to the Holy Land. Before 70 CE, the tax goes to maintain the Temple in Jerusalem. After, it helps to maintain rabbinical leadership and scholarship among the remnant of Jews left in the Holy Land.

The Romans designate a new name for the region that the Jews consider their homeland. Henceforth, it is to be known as *Palestine*, a name coined from the now-defunct "Philistine" and designed to break any tie to Jewish occupancy forever. The people who live in Roman Palestine are an eclectic people, descendents of all who have occupied or traded in the region in past times: remnant Jews, Arabs, Nabateans, Romans, Greeks, Phoenicians, Persians, Scythians, Egyptians, Chaldeans, Canaanites, and others—all the peoples attracted through the centuries to the lands at the western end of the Fertile Crescent.

19

The High Point of Empire

*[The Decapolis] cities were centers of Greek culture
in an area predominantly populated by Semitic peoples
such as Jews, Arameans and Nabataeans.
[From ancient historical sources]
...we can learn a great deal
about the relationship between the
Greek population of the
Decapolis cities such as Hippos
and the Jewish population,
which was dispersed in the townlets and villages
along the shores of the Sea of Galilee
and on nearby Golan Heights.*

**Arthur Segal, Head,
University of Haifa Hippos-Sussita Project, 2000**

R oman occupation of the Holy Land reaches its zenith in the second and third centuries CE. It is a time of rapid urban growth and city planning with a main street, or *cardo,* intersected at right angles (wherever the topography allows) by a side street, or *decumanus.* Columns line the streets, supporting a roof beneath which merchants conduct every manner of business. A temple sits on the highest place, dedicated to whichever god the city adopts as its protector.

100-300
CE

149

Roman Construction

Roman architects and engineers display dazzling feats of construction, craftsmen beautify public places by covering stone with white marble, and mosaic artists create pictures out of tiny stone fragments in an array of colors. There is provision for entertainment, with theaters for plays, amphitheaters for bloody spectacles, and aqueducts to bring water from distant springs for public and private baths.

My first encounter with Roman construction is in the ancient port city of Caesarea, where a long aqueduct designed to bring water from Mount Carmel is still standing. So also is a theater, formed of limestone from a nearby hillside. Later, in the Decapolis cities that I visit, I see spectacular ruins, some partially reconstructed. They speak to the wealthy, commercially thriving, and thoroughly hedonistic society that exists in Palestine at the height of Roman occupation.

The Decapolis Cities

During the first and early second centuries, *the Decapolis* is a regional name widely accepted within Roman Palestine. It is a loosely defined league of cities but not an official governmental unit. The Decapolis consists of ten or more cities (depending on the source) that occupy prime sites on trade arteries. In later years of the Empire, the cities exist as separate entities, not as members of a league of cities and not as part of a definable region. All but one of the cities are located east of the Jordan River. Most of the sites are in Jordan, two are in Israel, and two are in Syria (including Damascus).

On a previous trip to Jordan, I visit two Decapolis sites: Philadelphia (now Amman) and Gerasa (now Jerash) on the high road from Damascus to Philadelphia. Jerash is being magnificently restored as a United Nations Heritage Site. On this Holy Land journey, I visit five more Decapolis sites, three in Jordan and two in Israel:

Photo 12. Restored colonnade on the site of ancient Gerasa (Jerash).

- Pella in Jordan, just east of the Jordan River. Pella is now undergoing extensive excavation and restoration. The Jewish community in Pella sheltered early Jewish Christians when the Romans razed Jerusalem in 70 CE.

- Scythopolis (once and now again Beit Sha'an), the ancient site in Israel that controls the Jezreel Valley passageway between the Jordan River Valley and Mediterranean seaports. It is the only Decapolis site lying west of the Jordan River.

- Gadara, the focus of much current archaeological activity, occupying the most spectacular site of all. From a hilltop in northern Jordan, it overlooks the deep gash of the Yarmouk River Valley, where today the borders of Jordan, Syria, and Israel are tangent.

- Abila (east of Gadara, also in Jordan), where archaeology is still in its early stages, but a few standing columns speak to the buildings they once supported.

- Hippos, high on a hill overlooking the Sea of Galilee from the east and almost pristine in its grass-covered piles of toppled columns. Once fortified but now totally abandoned, Hippos is only now beginning to be developed as an archaeological site.

Photo 13. Columns in Hippos toppled by earthquakes.

At each of these sites, I see fallen columns, areas that were once marketplaces, and streets paved with stone. In all, I can trace a cardo, and in most, I can also see the intersecting pattern of cardo and decumanus that represents the Roman sense of urban order.

Jerusalem Rebuilt and Renamed

In the second century, Jerusalem is thoroughly rebuilt as a Roman city. It takes the Romans three years to put down the Bar Kokba Revolt and settle the city sufficiently so that building can begin. The new Roman city is named Aelia Capitolina, but this name does not outlast Roman suzerainty. Most of the layout of the present Old City of Jerusalem is derived from the Roman street grid overlaid on the pre-existing city in the second century. Streets intersect rather than wind. Today, Israeli soldiers stand guard at these intersections.

As I walk through the streets of the Old City, I can recognize the original Roman layout. Near the Jaffa Gate, the entrance to the Christian Quarter, stands a fortress-like building known as the Citadel, whose original construction dates from Hasmonian times. Herod the Great uses it as his palace. Through the centuries all of Jerusalem's rulers have a hand in changing and enlarging it. The stone Citadel has now been converted into one of the most effective museums I have ever seen. It chronicles the history of Jerusalem from the time of David to the present, leading me from one chamber of the old palace/fortress to another, up and down stairs on three or four levels, and past gardens enlivened this Centennial year with glass sculpture of all colors, shapes, and sizes from the workshop of the American glassmaker Chihuly. Fortunately, I see this museum on my last day in the Holy Land, giving me a good opportunity to process what I have been experiencing.

Two severe earthquakes shake the region of the Decapolis and Jerusalem in the sixth and eighth centuries. Afterward, much of the glorious work of the Roman builders lies in ruins.

20

The Byzantines

Starting in the reign of Constantine the Great, practically every site of biblical fame became, as we would say today, a tourist attraction. From every corner of the Christian world people poured into Palestine: some as transient pilgrims, others on a longer-term basis. Monasteries of every nationality sprang up like mushrooms in the desert next to the Dead Sea.

Cyril Mango, Byzantium, the New Rome

As Rome weakens from incursions of Germanic tribes and Roman rule faces repeated threats from the east, the emperor Constantine moves his capital to Byzantium, the ancient Greek city situated across the Hellespont (the Bosporus) from Asia Minor. He renames the city Constantinople. In the year 315, Constantine converts to Christianity. Historians have given the term *Byzantine* to the era inaugurated by Constantine, in which the Roman Empire becomes Christian and rule is centered in Constantinople. In Palestine, this era lasts about three hundred years. 315-638 CE

Before Constantine, the Christian imprint on Palestine occurs gradually and surreptitiously. After, Christianity becomes the state religion. The Byzantines continue life much as before, enjoying theaters and baths, importing the luxuries that come over the trade routes, but eschewing the grisly amphitheater entertainment.

155

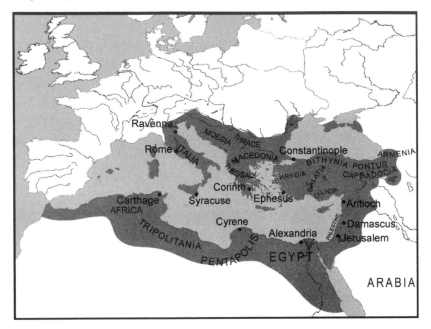

Map 26. Byzantine Empire, ca. 600 CE.

Where before it is dangerous to openly practice Christianity, now the onus is on those who still retain pagan rites.

Byzantine Christians leave many rich traces in ecclesiastical architecture in both Jordan and Israel. In some cases, Greek and Roman temples are converted to Christian basilicas. In other cases, temples are torn down, and their stones are used to build new churches. The floors of the churches are richly adorned with mosaics, and these, more than the temples, have survived the devastation of earthquakes.

500 CE

The Madaba Map

In Madaba, a Jordanian town halfway between Amman and Mount Nebo, a modern church has been built to incorporate within its nave an impressive mosaic map of the entire known world, from the Nile River to Mesopotamia. The mosaic map was lost under rubble for nearly 1,500 years. Unfortunately, much of this map was torn up by unknowing workmen as they excavated the site. However, the greatest gem remains intact: In the center

156

HΑΓΙΑΠΟΛΙCΙΕΡΟΥCΑΛΗΜ

Photo 14. Fragment of the Madaba mosaic map, showing Jerusalem.

of the map (which took more than a million tiny cut stones to complete) is a detailed plan of the city of Jerusalem.

From this source more than any other, people today can get a good idea of what Jerusalem looked like at the time the map was created. The Madaba Map is an invaluable world treasure.

In Madaba, I visit a workshop where young artists are attempting with much success to learn and employ the art of creating mosaics.

The Byzantine Record

In Byzantine times, most of the Decapolis cities, as well as the cities west of the Jordan River, are ecclesiastical sees, with bishops, basilicas, and scores of smaller churches. Roman temples disappear as their stones are recycled.

So feverish is the church building that on a former visit in Jerash, I can identify the mosaic floors of three separate churches within a 2-block area.

157

The Byzantine era is a difficult time for the Holy Land's Jews. Official government policy requires that all subjects adopt the Christian creed. In effect, Jews are required to convert. Some do, some retain their Jewish faith in secret, and some leave, adding to the Diaspora. By the year 350 CE, thirty-five years after Constantine adopts Christianity, it is estimated that ninety-five percent of all Jews are living outside the Holy Land.

By the beginning of the seventh century, Rome is no more, and even Constantinople is overextended. There is not enough tax revenue to keep up the roads that tie the Empire together, and there are not enough funds to rebuild after the devastation of the earthquake in the mid-sixth century. Many urban areas, including the Decapolis cities (Damascus and Amman excepted), gradually slip into obscurity.

21
The Coming of Islam

True piety is this: to believe in Al-lah,
and the Last Day, the angels, the Book, and the Prophets,
to give of one's substance, however cherished,
to kinsmen, and orphans, the needy, the traveler, beggars,
and to ransom the slave,
to perform the prayer,
to pay the alms.

The Quran, Sura II: 170-175

Surely they that believe, and those of Jewry, and the
Christians...
whoso believes in Al-lah and the Last Day,
and works righteousness...
no fear shall be on them, neither shall they sorrow

The Quran, Sura II: 59

In all of the years covered by the Biblical account and the Roman years afterward, the Arabian Peninsula exists as an almost silent backdrop to the events taking place in Palestine. Arabs are of the same Semitic stock as Jews. Traditionally, Arabs take their beginning from Abraham's first son, Ishmael. Biblical mention of Arabia is rare and often vague, for the Biblical writers seem to consider all of the desert to the south and east as "Arabia" and most desert dwellers as nomadic herders. Both Esau and Moses, who flee to Midian (which lies within the Arabian Desert), spend time as herders.

Trade Routes in Ancient Arabia

200 BCE-

200 CE   Fragrant frankincense and myrrh from the Hadramaut—the southern coastal area of the Peninsula, now within the countries of Oman and Yemen—are valued in the Holy Land and figure strongly in trade between the two regions. Early traders use a route along the moist Hejaz, the mountainous western region of the Arabian Peninsula. Solomon receives a famous wealthy visitor from Sheba (now a part of Yemen), who rules in the higher and wetter southwestern portion of the Peninsula. Another tradition, however, places the home of the Queen of Sheba in Ethiopia. Whether from Yemen or Ethiopia, the Queen of Sheba would have traveled at least part of the way on this ancient trade route.

From the second century BCE to the first century CE, and thereafter as part of the Roman Empire, the prosperous trading kingdom of Nabatea operates from the almost impregnable fortress of the capital city of Petra in the northern reaches of the Arabian Desert. From Petra, the Nabateans can control the trade that passes both north and south, and westward to Egypt as well. The Nabateans are farmers as well as traders, and in the desert they use irrigation practices that the Israelis imitate in the Negev two thousand years later. Although the Romans conquer the Nabateans, they continue to value their skills and knowledge as traders. Archaeologists digging in Decapolis cities often find Nabatean coins as well as images of Nabatean Gods.

Hiking in the desert south of Petra, in the area known as Wadi Rum, I come upon ancient rock art, crude but recognizable representations of camels and donkeys. The beasts have mounds on their backs, presumably goods, and underneath are messages in an incised script that bears little resemblance to Arabic. I am told the script is not Nabatean but is much older. The desert's mysteries await decoding.

160

The Arabians and Their Gods

At the beginning of the seventh century CE, most of the people of the Arabian Peninsula are not traders, however, but oasis farmers or nomadic desert dwellers. Most are Bedouin tribesmen, desperately poor, superstitious, and constrained by the tradition of blood feuds. They fear and try to placate a host of local gods of whom the most prominent is al-Lah. Al-Lah is the god of Mecca, the trading city on the east coast of the Peninsula. He is worshipped at the Kaabah, a huge black cube that houses a large meteorite. The Kaabah has been a shrine in Mecca since ancient times. Devotees of al-Lah come to this shrine to make pilgrimage, circling the Kabaah ritually. But al-Lah is not *the* god of the Arabs, only one of many. Each tribe has its own god. As yet, the Arab nomads have developed no theology, no sense that they are a god-inspired people. And they have never been unified.

In Mecca, Medina, and other towns in Arabia, new ideas reach the Peninsula along the trade routes. There are small communities of both Christians and Jews in these cities, foreigners who worship one all-powerful God. Although urban Arabs show little inclination to adopt the strangers' ways of thinking, they are not unaware of monotheism.

Mohammed

570-632
CE

Mohammed is born into this milieu in the year 570. He loses his father when he is two and his mother when he is ten. An uncle raises him. His tribe was once desert-poor, but now they have come to Mecca, are engaged in trade, and are thriving. Like other groups who live in Mecca, Mohammed's tribe has become dissolute with prosperity. Mohammed, who grows up to be a contemplative young man, realizes that his fellow tribesmen will come to no good if they continue in their ways. He worries about this but has no answer, no way of speaking truth to his tribe. Mohammed marries the widow of a rich merchant, fifteen years his senior, and with her wealth he can now engage in trade himself.

Mohammed gains some familiarity with the Jewish and Christian faiths. He learns of Abraham, Moses, and Jesus, and of the God who once spoke powerfully to both the Jews and the Christians. How and where he learns of Judaism and Christianity is not clear. The most likely way would be through encounters with Christians and Jews in Mecca. But he is often away on trading ventures. His travels take him northward into the land of the Byzantines, and there, too, he could gain fragments of Judaism and Christianity. On the way, he could encounter Arab tribes on the fringes of the Byzantine empire who have converted to these faiths. Mohammed can neither read nor write, so as one who must rely on memory, he hones this facility. In long, lonely hours on the trail and in month-long retreats in a cave at the base of Mount Hira, a few miles north of Mecca, he contemplates the ideas of monotheism and contrasts them with the dissolute ways of his fellow Arabs under polytheistic worship.

Mohammed longs for a God who will speak directly to the Arabs, as the God of the Hebrews and the Christians once spoke to the people of Palestine. In his fortieth year, in the cave at the base of Mount Hira, where he has retreated, Mohammed is visited by the angel Gabriel. Gabriel tells him that there is one God only and gives him many other messages that he must "Write!" He retains the messages in memory, but according to an early tradition, he fears for his sanity. He goes home to tell his wife, Khadija, what has happened, and she reassures him: He is a good and righteous man, and it is al-Lah who has spoken to him. Over the next twenty-two years, Mohammed's angelic visitor comes again and again in dreams, and Mohammed narrates to scribes what the angel tells him.

610-632 CE

What the scribes write reflect considerable knowledge of Jewish and Christian tradition. Mohammed refers to Adam and Abraham, Ishmael and Isaac, Jacob, Moses, David, Solomon, Mary, and Jesus. All but Mary, the mother of Jesus, are prophets, forerunners of the final revelations, that Mohammed believes he receives directly from al-Lah through Gabriel. "He has sent down upon thee the Book with the truth, confirming what was before it, and he sent down the Torah and the Gospel aforetime, as guidance to the people." (Sura III, 3)

Eventually, these writings become the Quran, a compact

162

collection of 114 individual Suras, or revelations, that together are shorter than the New Testament. In the Suras, al-Lah tells the Arabs how they shall live, how they shall worship, how they shall conduct business, how they shall treat one another, how they shall treat other "People of the Book," and how they shall treat unbelievers. Mohammed sees himself as the final prophet of al-Lah.

622 CE

The Hegira

From the outset, Mohammed's wife believes in his visions and in his mission. So also do a small group of his immediate family and followers. He begins preaching. But the people of Mecca want nothing to do with his new religion. Fights ensue, and Mohammed fears for his life. In the year 622, Mohammed and his small group of followers flee to Medina, an oasis city about 200 miles to the north. The flight is termed the *Hegira*, and Islam dates its calendar from that year.

In Medina, Mohammed meets with a group of Jewish leaders and attempts to join his new faith with theirs; in fact, he directs the believers in al-Lah, who Mohammed now deems the One and Only God, to bow toward Jerusalem, following Jewish custom. Then he learns from the Jews a local tradition that Abraham's son Ishmael was taken directly to Mecca and that Abraham came to Mecca to help his son build the Kaabah. When the Jews fail to recognize Mohammed as a prophet or to equate al-Lah with the God of their fathers, Mohammed directs his followers to bow toward the Kaabah instead. Now he has what he needs: Ishmael and the Kaabah tradition give Mohammed a strictly Arab connection. Al-Lah is universal, but through Mohammed's revelations, it is the Arabs who are elected to bring him to the world and the Arab language the medium by which the knowledge shall be conveyed. With these new understandings, Mohammed gains more followers in Medina, defeats armies sent out from Mecca, eradicates the Jewish community, then rallies his followers to return to Mecca and defeat the unbelievers there. Before his death in 632, Mohammed has joined all the Arab tribes of the Peninsula into a new unity, a unity based on faith in al-Lah, the

632 CE

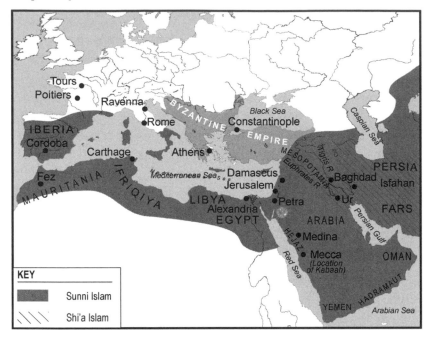

Map 27. Islamic and Byzantine lands, 850 CE.

One God, and allegiance to Mohammed, his Prophet. One of the last revelations Mohammed receives is, "Know ye that every Muslim is a brother unto every other Muslim, and that ye are now one brotherhood."

The Pillars of Islam

Borrowing from the stories contained in Jewish and Christian Scripture but with elements closely keyed to his Arab desert experience, Mohammed gives his followers a new and strict code for living and a new sense of self-worth. The Quran calls their faith *Islam*, which means *submission*. To be a Muslim, a member of the body of Islam, one must say in Arabic, "I bear witness that there is no God but al-Lah, and that Mohammed is his Messenger." This is the first requirement, or pillar, of the faithful. There are four others: to pray five times daily, turning toward the Kaabah in Mecca; to give to the poor; to take no food or drink from sunup to sundown during the month of Ramadan; and to make a pilgrimage, a *Hajj*, to Mecca. This last requirement need happen only once in a lifetime, and only if the believer is physically able to do so.

The Quran teaches that the One God has been from eternity and has been revealed gradually by the prophets. Mohammed has been given the final and complete revelation. Jews and Christians have also been given knowledge of the One God, but they have fallen from purity of worship. By saying that Jesus the Prophet is the Son of God, Christians are blasphemers. But Jews and Christians are, nevertheless, People of the Book, people to whom the One God has been revealed.

The Night Visit to Jerusalem

A tradition called *The Night Visit* holds that early during Mohammed's revelations, before the Hegira to Medina, the angel Gabriel takes Mohammed from Mecca to Jerusalem to the site where Ishmael (Isaac in Christian tradition) was once offered for sacrifice. From this place, Mohammed ascends briefly to heaven. There he meets Abraham, Isaac, Moses, Jesus, and other prophets. He returns to earth with new understanding and new empowerment. His wife later reports that he never leaves his bed during The Night Visit. Some Muslims accept that the event was a vision. Others believe that The Night Visit was corporeal. Whether bodily or a vision, the tradition magnifies the significance of the Jerusalem site for all Muslims. But Jerusalem is not the most holy site in Islam. This is reserved for Mecca. It is toward the Kaabah in Mecca that every Muslim all over the world prays, and it is to Mecca that Muslims make their pilgrimage, following a tradition that among Arabs is far older than Mohammed.

The Spread of Islam

The certainties of their new faith energize the Arabs, and the Quran urges them to make converts. The Arab tribes, desert-hardened, begin to unite and move out, westward into northern Africa, northward into the Holy Land and beyond, and southward into Yemen. Like Christianity, Islam becomes a missionary religion, its spread an act of piety, a Jihad. *Jihad*, the Arabic word for Holy

War, means *to struggle*. (Its meaning can refer also to a believer's inner struggle for self-improvement, the meaning moderate Muslims choose today.) Before the century is over, the followers of Islam have crossed into Spain to the west and reached the Silk Road to the east. Where converts do not readily accede, the Bringers of Islam use the sword. But to the Christians and Jews they conquer, they give special status as People of the Book. The followers of the Torah and the Bible may keep their faith, but they must pay a special tax. From the beginning, Muslims are ambivalent about Christians and Jews.

Mohammed's death in 632 precipitates a struggle for leadership. The one who is elected to succeed him is Abu Bakr, a close friend and follower, who becomes the first caliph, or leader. But many believe that Mohammed would have wanted his son-in-law, Ali ibn Ali Talib, to be his successor. Loyalty to Ali eventually leads to a split in Islam that never heals. Sunnis are those who align with Abu Bakr; Shi'ites are those who feel the choice should have gone to Ali. The split is political, not doctrinal, but it is reinforced later when Sunni partisans murder Mohammed's grandson, Husayn ibn Ali. The Shi'ites today are found mainly in Iran.

In the century after Mohammed's death, people who knew him, or even who receive second-hand or third-hand information about his life, recount what they know of the Prophet's life and of his sayings other than those revealed in the Quran. A collection of these sayings and traditions concerning his life becomes a treasured text of Islam known as the *Hadith*.

Islam in the Holy Land

In the Holy Land, Byzantine ways gradually become fused with those of Islam. The only real battle fought for control of Palestine occurs in the Yarmouk Valley near Gadara in 638. The Arabs win decisively over the Byzantines, and gradually the new religion of Islam begins to prevail in the Holy Land. In Jerusalem, before the end of the century, early Arab rulers build the magnificent Dome of the Rock on what was the site of the Jewish

Temple more than 500 years earlier. Its architecture is Byzantine. This is the spot where Ishmael (not Isaac, according to Muslims) is offered for sacrifice, and where Mohammed ascends into heaven (in a vision or actually, depending on the believer). It is Islam's third holiest site, after Mecca and Medina. At about the same time, Arab rulers build the Al-Aqsa Mosque opposite the Dome of the Rock on the Haram al-Sharif. From this time on, the flattened hilltop is Islamic.

661-909 CE

Christians, Muslims, and Jews live side by side in the Holy Land at first, recognizing their common heritage in the Old Testament patriarchs and respecting each other's holy places. Christians and Jews have to pay taxes, while Muslims are exempt. Otherwise, there is no overt persecution. Gradually, many Christians and Jews are absorbed into the Muslim Arab milieu but without overt coercion. This is true both under the Omayyad caliphs (661-750), who have their capital in Damascus, and the Abbassid caliphs (750-909), who rule from Baghdad. The principal change is that under the Abbassids, the Holy Land sinks into neglect, and even Damascus becomes a backwater.

Islamic Civilization

Arabic, the language of the Quran, is a holy language, so the Quran is not to be translated. (Indeed, modern translated versions cannot capture the power or even the precise intent of the Arabic, say scholars.) Believers not fortunate enough to have Arabic as their native tongue but instead speak Persian, Aramaic, or a hundred other tongues, must devote years of their youth to memorizing the Quran in Arabic. Schools, called *madrasas*, are set up all over the Islamic world for this purpose. The schools also appear in the Holy Land, giving such an education only to qualified believers. The sons of Christians and Jews do not qualify, so they must count on their own dwindling religious communities to pass on knowledge.

In their capitals, the caliphs encourage the decorative arts, almost always based on geometric patterns and words from the Quran. Intricate variations of the Arabic script are inscribed on stone, wood, ceramics, and tile. Like Jewish religious art, but unlike Christian art, Islamic art does not include the human figure.

As Islam spreads into lands of Greek and Persian learning, its followers come to include mathematicians, poets, philosophers, and artists. Learned scholars, often Jewish or Christian, translate the writings of the Greeks and Romans into Arabic (thus helping to preserve them). In Muslim lands, Jews become merchants and bankers for Muslim clients, whose religion constrains them from earning interest.

Like all faiths, Islam can be interpreted in a number of ways and is sometimes used to back up pre-existing customs. The Quran does not marginalize women, for example, and only for Mohammed's wives does it require the veil. But as Islam is securing its place in the wider world, its adherents adopt the customs of the Persians, Byzantines, and Jews of the time, who require that women wear the veil and be secluded. Much later, Western civilization shakes off these restrictions, but much of Islam still retains them.

The Crusaders

*This royal city [Jerusalem] situated at the center of the
earth, is now held captive by the enemies of Christ
and is subjected, by those who do not know God,
to the worship of the heathen.
She seeks, therefore, and desires to be liberated
and ceases not to implore you to come to her aid.*

**Pope Urban II,
to the assembled Frankish nobles
at Clermont, 1095 CE**

*The presence of the crusader states in the Near East for
almost two centuries certainly destabilized Muslim power,
and therefore hindered unification into a single Islamic
state.*

Thomas Madden, *The Impact of the Crusades*

U p to this time, Christian pilgrims continue to visit the
holy sites in Jerusalem, and their journeys and
destinations are respected. Jews, likewise, visit a
remnant of the Temple at the Western Wall. But when Muslim
rule becomes tyrannical under fanatic Fatimid caliphs from
Egypt (909-1171), historic churches are destroyed and
Christian pilgrimage is thwarted. Europe's rulers, both clergy
and lay, begin to prepare for a war to recover the Holy Land.

909-1171
CE

169

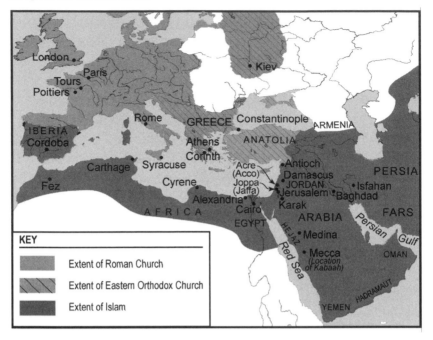

Map 28. Europe and the Middle East at the time of the Crusades.

Reclaiming Lost Territory

732 CE

The effort to fight the Muslims in the Holy Land is termed a *Crusade* by the Christians. Geographically, the idea of a Holy Land Crusade is a far reach for Europeans of this time, but its motivation is not unique. A Holy Land Crusade simply adds another front to an ongoing struggle to recover territory that Christians have lost to the Muslims. The first victory is at Poitiers, just south of Tours, where the Franks halt further Islamic penetration into Europe in 732 CE. By the time of the First Crusade, the Muslims have been ousted from northwestern Spain and the 500-year *Reconquista* to recover the entire Iberian Peninsula has begun.

The weakening Byzantine Empire has a precarious hold on southeastern Europe and the Anatolian Peninsula, but by this time there is little cooperation between the churches in Rome and in Constantinople. When the Crusaders march through Anatolia, they treat the Byzantines poorly, at times as the enemy, further

170

weakening not only the eastern Christian Empire but also the ties that once united the eastern and Roman churches.

The Crusader Presence

1096-
1290
CE

In Palestine, the Crusaders build Mediterranean harbors at Joppa (now Jaffa) and Acre (now Acco). From these protected ports, English, German, and French knights land their troops and weapons. For the next two centuries, Europeans are able to take and hold all or part of the Holy Land. They erect a string of forts, establish their families in feudal castles protected by the forts, and put yet one more cultural and genetic stamp on Palestine.

I visit two of these impressive forts, one at the site of the Crusader's Acre and one far south at Karak in Jordan on the ancient Kings' Highway trade route between Damascus and Arabia. The Crusader forts are true strongholds, Norman Gothic in style. Massively built, they exhibit great sophistication in architecture and engineering.

However, the Crusader forts cannot hold back the Turks, recent converts to Islam who by 1144 have all but eliminated the Byzantines from Anatolia and have wrested the caliphate from the Fatimids. The Turks themselves become masters at fort building. Led by the brilliant Saladdin, the Turks deliver strong blows to the Crusaders toward the end of the twelfth century. The Crusaders regroup, take Jerusalem once more, and are not finally defeated until the last of the knights departs Acre in 1290.

Legacy of the Crusaders

In all this time, the Muslims in Palestine do not use the term *Crusaders*. They think that they are fighting the *Franks*, and this is what their histories record. The events in Palestine during the Crusades have little more than local significance in most parts of the Islamic Empire. Baghdad, Fez, and Cordoba pay little attention.

Only in the last two hundred years do the words "Crusade" and "Crusaders" come into Muslim vocabularies, learned in studies of Western

Photo 15. The Crusader castle at Karak in western Jordan.

history. These terms are now "red flags" among Muslims, a symbol of the time when Christians dared to impose their rule on the Holy Land. After the events of September 11, 2001, United States President George W. Bush realizes this to his consternation when he uses the word "crusade" in the modern sense to announce a war against terrorism. Muslims everywhere are offended.

While in Palestine, the Crusaders learn to blend the ways of the West with those of the East. They pick up knowledge of Arab medicine and Arab geographical lore, and they become aware of the heritage of Greece and Rome. What the Crusaders lose in territory, they more than gain in knowledge. Returning to Europe, they give vent to ideas that will lead to the Renaissance, the Age of Discovery, and the Reformation.

The Jews fare badly under the Crusaders. The knights of the First Crusade find only a few thousand Jews living in the Holy Land, and many of these they slay. For Christians of the Middle Ages, the Jews are the villains in the crucifixion story, and the Crusaders deem both Jews and Arabs as unworthy occupants of the Holy Land.

Meanwhile, a remnant of Crusader authority remains in the Holy Land to this day: the responsibility accorded by the

Crusader popes to the Franciscan Order for maintaining the Holy Places. Franciscans are present at all of the pilgrimage sites that have come under Roman Catholic protection, and there has never been a time when their presence was not allowed.

The Turks

*The Ottoman Empire advanced rapidly until it spread all
the way from the Euphrates to the Danube. The
Byzantine Empire shrivelled away until it was reduced to
a few territories and a small enclave around
Constantinople. Unlike the Arabs, who thought the use of
firearms dishonorable, the Ottomans became masters of
artillery.*

Hyperhistory Online

Shortly after the Crusaders leave, the Turks surrender   1350 CE
power in the southern part of the Holy Land to the
Mameluks, slave warriors from Egypt. Little happens
under the Mameluks, and as they weaken, a brilliant new
Turkish regime takes over.

The Fall of Constantinople   1453 CE

The Turkish ruler Mehmet II, a masterful strategist, finally
brings about the fall of the almost-impregnable Constantinople in
1453. This ends the last trace of Christian rule in the East, and
the last and much-altered vestige of Rome's once mighty Empire.
In the century following the fall of Constantinople, Europe is awed
and terrified by the military might of Mehmet II, Suleiman the
Magnificent, and their successors. The Turkish Empire, called the

Ottoman Empire by European chroniclers, extends from northern Africa, into the Middle East, and into eastern and southeastern Europe. As late as the mid-seventeenth century, it threatens Vienna.

1550 CE   The land link between the three parts of the Ottoman Empire is Palestine. However, the Ottomans rule an area that slowly turns into a backwater, Palestine with it. Overland caravan trade along the route of the Fertile Crescent, the source of Turkish wealth, gives way to maritime trade on the world's oceans. The ports at the eastern end of the Mediterranean Sea fall into disuse.

The Holy Land under the Ottomans

Suleiman the Magnificent takes great interest in Jerusalem and rebuilds the wall of this ancient city, giving a new definition to its boundaries. He directs that the Dome of the Rock be refurbished. But after Suleiman, the fortunes of the Turks decline, and the Holy Land experiences centuries of partial neglect under Ottoman rule. Cities shrink into towns, and towns disappear. Arab flocks graze the hillsides, and trees are cut for firewood. Malarial swamps border the Jordan River. Roads are neglected, and brigands make travel dangerous.

Palestinian townsmen ply ancient crafts, carry on trade, and perform clerical services for the Ottoman rulers. But the Ottomans do not allow them self-rule. Monks and nuns from both Roman and Orthodox traditions oversee and maintain the places of pilgrimage, and European travelers make sketches that illustrate the extent to which the lands of the Bible have been neglected.

A small number of Jews continue to live in the Holy Land, mostly in the towns. Since their expulsion by the Romans in the first and early second centuries, the remnant left in Palestine has constituted a gradually eroding and politically powerless minority.

In cities of the Ottoman Empire, the Jews are tolerated and generally not ill-treated; their experience especially in banking and finance is valued. Originally by decree but later by convention or preference, the Jews in Ottoman cities live in a separate Jewish Quarter. There they carry on their customs and worship and pass on their traditions to their children. This is the origin of the Jewish

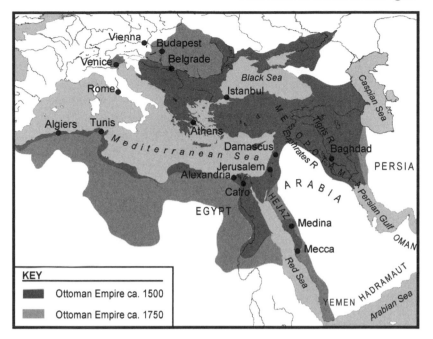

KEY
■ Ottoman Empire ca. 1500
▨ Ottoman Empire ca. 1750

Map 29. The Ottoman Empire.

Quarter in the Old City of Jerusalem. Today about one-third of the city within Suleiman's Wall is occupied by the Arab Quarter. The remainder is divided among the Jewish Quarter, Christian Quarter, and Armenian Quarter. The character of each is distinctive, no less today than during the period of Ottoman rule.

Beginnings of Modernity

Within the limits of their vision, the Ottomans manage to keep order in Palestine and even make early attempts at building a modern infrastructure. They govern Palestine as a part of a much larger territory that extends from Arabia to the southern border of what is now Turkey. They build a rail link between the Hejaz in western Arabia and Damascus in Syria.

I retain an image of Ottoman military barracks erected at the site of the ruins at Gadara. Jordanian authorities have decided that these

Ottoman period pieces should come down so that the focus can be on the Roman character of the site. I feel they should stay so that visitors can get a feel for the more recent history of the site. The truth is there is almost no evidence of nearly five centuries of Ottoman rule, either in Israel or Jordan.

1880

Toward the end of the nineteenth century, Protestant and Catholic organizations from Europe and the United States come to the Holy Land to establish hospitals and schools. Among the Palestinian Arabs, there is now the beginnings of a Western-educated professional class. At the turn of the twentieth century, Ottoman Palestine is overwhelmingly Arab (both Muslim and Christian) and largely rural. Jerusalem is the cultural center of Palestine, but the center of Turkish rule is Damascus.

1914-
1918

During World War I, the Arabs in Palestine side with the British against the moribund Ottoman Empire, which casts its lot with Germany. T. E. Lawrence parleys with the Arab sheiks at Wadi Rum and leads them into battle in 1915, successfully cutting the rail lines between Mecca and Damascus.

1923

At the end of World War I, the Ottoman Empire is no more. Its only remnant is the modern country of Turkey, where a revolution led by Kemal Ataturk installs a new and viable state, secular and on the road to modernity. The rest of the Ottoman Empire must be reordered. Officially, the task falls to the League of Nations. But in reality, it is the British and French who are on the scene.

24

The Mandate Years and After: Roots of Arab Anger

His Majesty's Government views with favour the establishment in Palestine of a national home for the Jewish people and will use their best endeavours to facilitate the achievement of this object, it being clearly understood that nothing shall be done which may prejudice the civil and religious rights of existing non-Jewish communities in Palestine...

Arthur James Balfour,
[British] Foreign Office, November 2, 1917

Out of the eastern remnants of the former Ottoman Empire, the League of Nations creates the modern states of Egypt, Jordan, Lebanon, Syria, and Iraq. Palestine is also intended for statehood, but circumstances there will frustrate the creation of a single national state.

Before World War I, Arab nationalist underground movements are forming throughout the region, opposing Ottoman rule. When the Sharif of Mecca and the Bedouins of the Hejaz (the western mountainous fringe of the Arabian Peninsula) cast their lot with the British against the Turks, they receive widespread support from Arab underground members. The hope among the Syrians, especially, is that out of the defeat of the Ottomans a strong Arab state will emerge.

But the British and French have other ideas. In an 1919-agreement kept secret from the Arabs, they partition the Arab 1923 states into British and French spheres of influence, and by 1923, these are confirmed by the League of Nations. Greater Syria (which once included Palestine) is divided into British- and French-ruled areas and eventually becomes four separate entities: Palestine, Trans-Jordan, Syria, and Lebanon. The League awards a mandate over Palestine and Trans-Jordan to the British and a mandate over Syria and Lebanon to the French. Egypt is already a British Protectorate. At the end of the war, the British also control Mesopotamia, and from this position, they secure a League of Nations mandate over Iraq. The mandates are intended to prepare the new countries for self-government; they are not to be turned into colonies. But their effect is to solidify the British and French presence and to keep the region politically fractured.

There is little or no Arab input into League decision-making, and League planners seem unaware of the impact that the foreign mandates will have on Arab nationalism. In a real sense, Britain and France, working through the League of Nations, lay the groundwork for the resentment toward the West and the political turbulence that has since plagued the region.

The British Sphere: Egypt, Trans-Jordan, Palestine, and Iraq

1882-
1956   **Egypt.** The British presence in Egypt goes back to the mid-nineteenth century. Britain's interest lies in protecting the Suez Canal. An Egyptian royal family from an Albanian line, installed by the Ottomans, is corrupt and unpopular. Britain rules Egypt as a Protectorate from 1882 until 1922, when it officially recognizes Egypt's independence. But Britain continues to maintain control over Egypt's administration and over the Canal. When a popular revolt occurs in 1952, bringing to power General Gamal Abdel Nasser, Britain is ousted. In 1956, Egypt takes control of the Suez Canal. The British try, unsuccessfully, to take it back, and in this context, Israel invades Egypt and acquires Gaza and

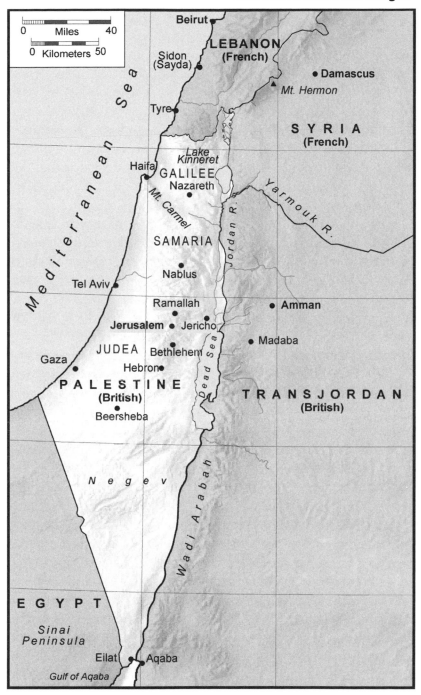

Map 30. The League of Nations Mandates, 1920-1945.

(temporarily) the Sinai Peninsula. Anti-British and anti-Israeli sentiment runs high, and because the United States is allied with both, Egyptian anger also turns toward the U.S. Cairo is the intellectual capital of the Arab world and up to a point exerts leadership. Egypt works out an accommodation with 1978 Israel in 1978 and regains the Sinai Peninsula. But a militant Islamic underground in Egypt bitterly opposes Israel and works to topple the Egyptian government, wanting to install a Muslim state with *Sharia* (Quranic) law in its place. At present, Egypt has broken diplomatic relations with Israel, in sympathy with the Palestinians.

Trans-Jordan. After World War I, Britain receives a League 1919- of Nations mandate to rule over Palestine and the largely desert 1994 land to the east of the Jordan River, called Trans-Jordan. Britain places as king of Trans-Jordan the head of the Bedouin tribe that is loyal to Britain during the war, the Hashemites. In 1943, Trans-Jordan gains its independence as the Hashemite Kingdom of Jordan. The present ruler, King Abdullah, is the great-grandson of the sheik whom the British placed on the throne. Jordan goes to war against Israel in 1948, and although it takes over the West Bank and the Old City of Jerusalem, it pays dearly in the war's aftermath, as Palestinian refugees swell its population and create political problems for the young state. In 1980, Jordan's King Hussein cracks down brutally on Palestinian militants, ousts Arafat's PLO headquarters, and subsequently stabilizes the government. Since 1994, Jordan has had diplomatic relations with Israel.

Palestine. From the beginning of the mandate, Palestine 1919- presents Britain with a situation quite different from Jordan. It is 1948 more urban and its population more diverse, with a growing number of Jewish immigrants. Britain is committed to Jewish immigration into Palestine, but it is also committed to protecting the rights of Palestine's Arabs. In this volatile situation, Britain rules Palestine directly, hoping to set up a parliamentary form of government eventually but with no workable vision for forming a Palestinian state. In Palestine, Arab underground leaders fume. With Jewish Holocaust refugees flooding into the Mandate after World War II and with no ability to stop the violence between Arabs and

Jews, Britain has a tiger by the tail. It dare not let go of its untenable Palestine Mandate. Britain pulls out the same day Israel declares itself independent.

Iraq. Iraq becomes part of Britain's sphere when the British defeat the Ottomans in Mesopotamia in World War I. Afterward, the League of Nations awards Iraq to Britain as a mandate. Aware of oil in the region, the British want to continue to govern. But popular uprisings in Iraq force the British to set up the state of Iraq, and a king is elected in 1921 by plebiscite. The king is cousin to the ruler of Trans-Jordan. In 1932, the British Mandate is officially terminated and Iraq enters the League of Nations as a monarchy. In effect, however, the British continue to exert influence over the Iraqi king. A series of coups, spawned by nationalist military leaders, topple the monarchy in 1958 and by 1979 bring to power a strong man named Saddam Hussein. Hussein is a leader in the Ba-ath Arab Socialist Party, and he uses oil revenue to flex his power. He wars with Iran over territorial disputes for eight years in the 1980s, invades Kuwait in 1990, loses the subsequent Gulf War, but continues to maintain an arsenal of nuclear and chemical weapons. Hussein makes common cause with Syria, opposes Israel, supports the PLO with weapons, and bears deep grievances toward the West. He sees Baghdad as a rival to Cairo as the intellectual capital of the Arab world. But Saddam Hussein has made too many enemies for this to occur in the foreseeable future.

1921-1990

The French Sphere: Syria and Lebanon

Syria. At the end of World War I, France, like Britain, is faced with Arab resistance to its mandates. The Syrians feel betrayed by the British/French agreement to partition Arab lands. Syrian Arab underground independence movements attempt to thwart French rule, and the French have a tough time keeping order in Syria. Syria finally achieves independence at the end of World War II. A series of military coups leave the country unstable for twenty years. Meanwhile, the Ba-ath Arab Socialist Party gains strength in Syria as in Iraq and in 1970 brings General Hafez Assad

1919-1970

1970-2002

183

to power. His son is Syria's president today. Syria opposes Israel, supports Iraq, is involved in Lebanon both militarily and politically, and has deep grievances with the West. For a brief time in the 1970s, Egypt and Syria attempt a political union. Although the union is only short-lived, its existence signified Syria's dream of bringing about Arab unity.

1919-
1943
    Lebanon. Until the French Mandate, and as early as the break-up of Alexander's Empire, Lebanon is part of Greater Syria. Under French rule, the borders of Lebanon are defined to include both the Muslim coastal areas and the Christian hill country. When Lebanon becomes independent in 1943, it is prospering and has a strong framework for democracy. It is the banking and cultural capital of the Arab Middle East. Most of the leaders of the republic that emerges are Christians, and a large number are professionals. The Muslim population, with a higher birthrate, begins to exceed that of the Christians, and Muslims want to lead the government. A shared-rule policy is developed but fails to create stability.

1943-
1982
    Two factors complicate peace in Lebanon: the large number of Palestinians who come as refugees in 1948 (and now live in refugee camps within the country), and the continuing power struggle between Christians and Muslims. All-out civil war between Muslims and Christians tears the country apart from the 1950s to the late 1980s. Syrian military forces intervene in 1976, temporarily imposing peace. The Syrian presence still exists, and most Lebanese want the Syrians there. Meanwhile, the Hezbullah party, based in southern Lebanon among Shi-ite Muslims, makes common cause with the Palestine Liberation Army, headquartered for a time in Beirut. Hezbullah launches terrorist raids across the border into Israel. In 1982, Israel invades Lebanon, bombs and occupies the Muslim areas of Beirut, and ceases military action only after a multinational force of United States and Western European troops arrives to protect Muslim and Palestinian civilians and move the PLO headquarters out of Lebanon. The multinational force withdraws after a bombing kills 300 U.S. and French troops in

1982-
2000
1983. Following a Muslim terrorists' assassination of a Lebanese Christian president that same year, Israeli-backed Christian militia massacre scores of Palestinian civilians in two refugee camps. The

horror of this massacre turns world opinion against the Israelis, who then withdraw to southern Lebanon, where they stay until 2000. Since the early 1990s, Lebanon has known an uneasy peace. With the rebuilding of its capital of Beirut, it may yet again resemble the Jewel of the Eastern Mediterranean it formerly was.

1902-
2002

The Arabian Peninsula

Saudi Arabia. The Bedouin of central Arabia take no part in World War I, nor are they in league with the Hejaz Bedouins of neighboring Jordan. In 1902, Abdul al-Aziz ibn Saud captures Riyadh and sets out on a 30-year campaign to unify the Arabian Peninsula. His grandson rules in Saudi Arabia today, and his progeny and their children command the vast wealth that begins to come to the Peninsula with the discovery of oil in the 1930s. Despite the vast fortunes put away by Saudi princes, oil wealth is also used to build an impressive infrastructure in what was once a land of Bedouin nomads. The Saudis adhere to an extremist Islamic sect named after its eighteenth century leader, the Wahabbis. Saudi Arabia is an Islamic state, governed by *Sharia* law. It accepts responsibility for maintaining the pilgrimage sites of Mecca and Medina, and with its oil money, it supports fundamentalist Islamic causes worldwide, especially madrasas, where its extremist brand of militant Islam is taught. Saudi-funded madrasas in Pakistan and Afghanistan, for example, often serve as the only schooling young boys receive. In Indonesia, traditionally religiously tolerant, Saudi-financed schools and mosques have now spawned a militant Islamism that is precipitating religious wars. To protect his oil resources during the Gulf War with Iraq in 1990, the Saudi king allows the U.S. to deploy its military forces within the kingdom. By doing this, he intensely angers a rich young Saudi named Osama bin Laden, who believes that because the Arabian Peninsula was the home of the Prophet Mohammed, all Saudi soil is holy. Thus, to bin Laden, the presence of U.S. troops defiles holy Saudi soil. He leaves for Afghanistan to fight the Russians, then stays on in Afghanistan to establish and train terrorists for his Al Qaeda network, aimed as much at destabilizing moderate or "reactionary"

185

(read Saudi) Arab regimes as against the West and Israel. Arabia is still a base for U.S. troops, who provide military protection against possible Iraqi aggression and secure Saudi Arabia's oil production. Thus, despite the extreme fundamentalism that it finances in the Islamic world, the Saudi government is also tied to the West. Officially, it opposes the Al Qaeda movement. At the same time, it unites with other Arab countries in opposition to Israel.

The Gulf States. On the fringes of the Arabian Peninsula in the Persian Gulf, other Bedouin rulers have likewise come into great wealth from the oil underneath their desert domains. Like the Saudis, they rule Bahrain, Qatar, the United Arab Emirates, and Oman with absolute authority, and like Saudi Arabia, their infrastructure has undergone spectacular modernization. With oil wealth, they need no taxes and need be responsible to no electorate. Most, like the Saudis, oppose Israel and give assistance to the Palestinians.

Yemen. The southwestern portion of the Arabian Peninsula is occupied by Yemen. This mostly desert kingdom is centered in the better-watered highlands at the south end of the Hejaz, rising to 8,000 feet. It has no oil or other resources on which to build a modern state, though it was the original home of coffee, and from its desert coastlands came the frankincense and myrrh that once dominated caravan trade. The bin Laden family originated in Yemen, and the country today has a reputation for harboring terrorists (though officially it opposes the Al Qaeda movement). In Yemen's port of Aden, a U. S. naval vessel was severely damaged by terrorist action in 2000. Yemen once harbored a sizeable Jewish Diaspora, but Yemeni Jews have now been absorbed into Israel. They form a conservative bloc in the Israeli parliament, and they infuse an exotic element into Israel's ever-evolving popular culture.

The Roots of
Modern Israel

J'Accuse!

Emile Zola,
Public Letter to French Authorities in defense of
Captain Alfred Dreyfus, 1894. The Dreyfus Affair led
directly to the formation of the Zionist Movement.

If you will it, then it [Zionism] is no dream.

Theodor Herzl

Now is the time to make plans to come home to Israel.
Today you can pick up the telephone and make
arrangements to move to Israel. Today you can sell your
home for a fair price. Today you can leave with all your
money, your belongings and your family. Tomorrow may be
too late.

Ahavat Israel Web site, January 2001

What of the people of the Diaspora? By the middle of the fourth century, only five per-cent of all the world's Jews remain in Palestine. This percentage continues to decline in succeeding centuries. As we have seen, there have been many Diasporas, beginning with the

Assyrians when the ten northern Jewish tribes lose their identity. But ever after, in the scatterings brought about by the Babylonians and Romans, or in voluntary emigration through the centuries, Jews everywhere retain their sense of themselves as a separate people, a chosen people, a people whom God once led out of captivity into the Promised Land. Though without a temple in Jerusalem or a central place of worship, the Jews of the Diaspora nevertheless ritually say, "Next year in Jerusalem." Jerusalem is a state of mind, and together with the Talmud, it forges an enduring Jewish identity.

The Diaspora in the Middle East and North Africa

Much of the time following the Roman Diaspora (initiated in 70 CE), the Jews in northern Africa, Yemen, and Mesopotamia live in peace with their neighbors. Until the Roman's adopt Christianity, they recognize Judaism as a legitimate religion even while they persecute the Christians. After Christianity becomes the official religion of the Empire, the Jews have a more difficult time. During the earliest period of Islam, the example set by Mohammed does not bode well for Jewish communities. Very soon, however, Muslim edicts respect both Jews and Christians as People of the Book. With the Crusades, Christians lose this sinecure, but Jewish scholars, physicians, and merchants play a valuable role within Muslim lands, contributing to the growing body of learning coming from the Islamic world, as well as to its wealth. Intolerant rulers, such as the Almohads in Spain, from where the great twelfth-century Jewish philosopher and physician Maimonides is forced to flee, are an exception.

The Diaspora in Europe

Through the centuries, Christians in Europe are rarely so charitable, however. The behavior of the Crusaders toward Jews in Palestine mirrors their massacre of Jews in Europe in the early stages of their march. The Inquisition is aimed as much at Jews as at apostate Christians. Thus, Pope John Paul II's admission and deep apology for past sins of persecution and intolerance by the Catholic Church toward Jews, made earlier in the millennial year and reiterated by the courageous Pope during his visit to Jerusalem, is of the utmost historical significance.

Some in Israel feel that the Pope did not go far enough and that he should have specifically admitted Rome's responsibility in the Holocaust through its failure to act, and worse by documented evidence of complicity. But it would have been impossible to embark on an almost endless litany of evidence of past barbarism, of which the Holocaust is now the most keenly felt.

In Western Europe, the nineteenth century brings a welcome tolerance toward Jews, who become integrated into the fabric of society. But in Eastern Europe, persecution becomes institutionalized, as rulers unleash their armies on Jewish villages in sanctioned *pogroms*. The Diaspora widens as more than four million Jews leave Europe in the nineteenth and early twentieth centuries, joining other Europeans seeking opportunities in the United States, Canada, Middle and South America, South Africa, and Australia.

Zionism and Early Zionist Settlers   1850

The idea of Zionism, that Palestine should be a homeland for Jews, gets its start as a Christian movement in England in the middle of the nineteenth century. The Christians who support it do so not only out of a feeling of sympathy for Jews, but also out of the belief that a return of Jews to the Holy Land and a cataclysmic struggle there must precede the Second Coming of Christ. The Second Coming is predicted in the obscure and symbolic Book of Revelations, the last book of the New Testament, which most fundamentalist Christians use as a guidepost even today.

In the 1890s, Zionism becomes an organized Jewish movement. It is started by Theodor Herzl, an Austrian Jewish journalist and playwright who sees Zionism as a possible answer to the still-existent anti-Semitism that he witnesses in France while covering the Dreyfus affair. In 1894, Captain Alfred Dreyfus, a   1894
French army officer and a Jew, is unjustly accused of treason and sentenced to the French penal colony on Devil's Island, amidst ugly anti-Semitic signs displayed at that time on the

streets of Paris. The Dreyfus Affair splits France. The
government, the army, the Church, and the conservative press
are allied against Dreyfus, despite the fact that the real traitor,
a non-Jew, is identified. The writer Emile Zola champions
Dreyfus's cause and later helps to secure his release. Appalled
by the blatant anti-Semitism he has witnessed, Herzl perceives
that Zionism can offer Jews a political alternative to enduring
persecution, and in 1895 he writes *The Jewish State: A Modern
Solution to the Jewish Question.* The following year he founds
the World Zionist Organization, a movement that divides the
world Jewish community. Some support it and devote their
lives to its cause; others reject the political implications of Jewish
settlement in the Holy Land. The world Christian community is
likewise ambivalent. Some (for theological as well as moral reasons)
give outright financial support to the cause of Zionism, but most
reject the idea as politically unworkable and, in the "enlightened
world" at the beginning of the twentieth century, indeed
unnecessary. Meanwhile, in Eastern Europe and Russia, pogroms
continue in Jewish villages and Jewish urban ghettos.

1895

**1900–
1920**

By the turn of the century, the Zionist movement is supporting
a trickle of Jews from Eastern Europe and Russia who come to
live in Palestine. The Zionist movement aids their immigration
and funds their land purchases. The kernel of the kibbutz way of
life stems from the earliest pioneer settlements in Palestine, born
of the socialist ideas that are beginning to work their way into
Russia in the latter part of the nineteenth century. Settlers on the
pioneer kibbutzim begin to plant trees on slopes that are long
denuded by grazing, a practice that continues in Israel to this day
and has transformed the appearance of the land.

> *There is an overwhelming difference, a great infusion of green, on
> slopes in Israel since I first saw the country more than forty years ago.*

Among other crops, the early settlers plant orange trees, and
very early the large sweet Jaffa oranges are introduced to the
European market.

Through the early decades of the century, Jewish
settlement in the Holy Land grows gradually from a trickle to
a flow, particularly after the British Mandate takes over from

190

the Ottomans. Not all of the early Jewish immigrants become farmers. Some employ skills learned in Europe as merchants or craftsmen in the relatively cosmopolitan and growing port city of Haifa, located at the foot of the ridge known as Mount Carmel, midway between the ruins of ancient Caesarea and the Crusader's Acre. Skilled diamond cutters from Amsterdam and Antwerp set up in Haifa, the beginnings of a new world center for the diamond industry. Another group of pioneer immigrants in Haifa is a German community, whose solidly built houses and shops dating from the early twentieth century indicate they prospered. No other sign of that community remains today.

Haifa today is a thriving industrial city and Israel's chief port. It is not particularly attractive, but it has one of the country's leading universities, and it has a beautiful formal garden leading to the tomb and shrine of the founder of the Baha'i faith. One enters the shrine in total silence, out of respect for a teacher exiled from his homeland in Iran. Followers of the worldwide faith nobly try to synthesize the teachings of all the world's great religions.

Britain's Palestine Dilemma

1920-
1945

Midway into World War I, Britain's Foreign Office attempts to deal with the problem of the growing number of Jewish settlements in Palestine, for the British fully expect that they will be governing post-war Palestine. The British are torn. On the one hand, they are sympathetic to the cause of Zionism, which originated in Britain. On the other hand, they are now the champions and allies of the Arabs. By 1917 when the Balfour Declaration is issued (advocating Palestine as a Jewish homeland), Britain has stated two policies that will prove impossible to execute: At one and the same time, Palestine shall be a homeland for Jews, and Arab rights shall not be infringed.

By the 1920s, Palestinian Arabs begin to react to the presence of Israeli settlers in their midst. Arab tenant farmers and farm workers are losing their homes and jobs as absentee landowners sell their properties to Jewish settlers. Arabs are beginning to fear that what is still a trickle of pioneer Jewish settlement may soon pose a threat to their homeland. Scores of Jewish settlers are killed in an Arab underground action in the mid-1920s, and thereafter Jewish underground groups organize to counter the threat. Both sides use brutal tactics. But at this stage, the British are still able to keep peace, for the most part, in the Palestinian Mandate. Both Arab and Jewish underground members risk imprisonment.

In the years between the end of World War I and World War II, the British try hard to rule their Palestine and Trans-Jordan Mandates with fairness. They improve on the Ottoman infrastructure, and they begin water projects to divert Jordan River water for irrigation. But as more and more Jews come to live in Palestine, Arabs become increasingly resentful. In the 1930s, Jewish immigration steps up as Hitler begins to reveal his plans for exterminating Europe's Jews. As the Jewish refugees from Nazi Germany begin arriving, Arab resentment escalates. Settlers are attacked, and the Jewish underground retaliates. Meanwhile, the British try to keep both the Arab and Jewish undergrounds at bay.

Many young Jews volunteer for World War II service in Britain's Jewish Brigade. Few Palestinians do; they view the British as their enemy and the Mandate as a hindrance to statehood for Palestine. They deeply resent the fact that other Arab Mandates are headed for independence.

1945-
1948 As World War II ends, the full extent of the Holocaust is revealed. Jewish leaders in Britain and the United States struggle over their response. Not all are inclined toward Zionism, but all are in deep mourning over the tragedy. The American Jewish Congress is formed to offer an alternative to Zionism: that resettlement must occur in many places in the world, including Palestine, but that in Palestine Arabs and Jews together should form a democratic society. Arabs should not have to leave their homeland. This more moderate voice, which originally appeals to Reformed Judaism in the United States, is eventually hushed as frantic and organized Zionist appeals open purses of Jews who survive the war in safety.

In Palestine, events rush faster than the British can contain them. Settlers pour into Palestinian lands. The Jewish army assists the settlers, ousting the Palestinians by threats and deception. There is no payment for land taken. Palestinians flee to neighboring Arab states, and the Arab states prepare for war. On May 14, 1948, Israel declares independence. The British pull out. The Arab armies declare war.

Like the warriors of Joshua long ago, the new Israelites claim the Promised Land, wresting it from its present owners. Now they must fight to hold on to it. And they must step up their appeal to Jews in the United States, who will bear much of the financial burden.

"Never Again"

Despite continuing territorial conflicts, the Israelis have succeeded in creating a homeland for Holocaust survivors and for Jews the world over who want to live in what tradition tells them is their Promised Land. In the Yad Vashem Holocaust Museum, the story of the Holocaust lives, and Israelis do not want the world to forget. A group of unevenly truncated square stone columns represents teh children who were victims at Auschwitz, Buchenwald, or Dachau. At the entrance to the museum, a walkway is lined with gnarled trees, each holding stones lovingly placed at the nook where the tree branches. Each tree is dedicated to someone whose courage saved lives. One of these is in honor of Raoul Wallenberg, the Swedish diplomat who helped thousands of Eastern European Jews to escape the Nazis, only to lose his own life in Russian captivity.

One leaves the museum sick at heart, aware that gross inhumanity is not an isolated occurrence, that it has happened, could happen again, and requires the constant vigilance of democratic societies.

Israel continues to assuage the horrors of the Holocaust in a furious and successful effort to build a viable political entity. At the same time, it has assimilated more than 3.5 million immigrants from many different languages and cultures who with great difficulty must learn Hebrew as the ancient/modern common language.

Israel vows "never again." Never again shall there be a Holocaust. Never again shall Jews be forced to leave their homes.

193

Photo 16. Holocaust memorial tree dedicated to Raoul Wallenberg at the Yad Vashem Holocaust Museum

To keep this vow, Israel has what may be the world's best-trained, most-effective military force. Every Israeli male must give three years to the military; every female must give nineteen months. The army is a force for assimilation, and as such has helped Jews from many different cultures and cultural backgrounds to work together.

Wherever I go—on buses, in restaurants, in a northern spa, in the Old City—I see young Israeli military personnel, always with rifles slung over their shoulders. Some wear the small skullcaps that mark an observant Jewish male, but not all do. They are of every hue and of many different racial strains.

194

By having its soldiers ride public buses, Israel reduces the need for military transport. In the event of war, the buses can be commandeered. Many Israeli families point to pictures on their walls of their sons or daughters who have died defending their country. Army service can be hazardous, for the frustration and anger of the Palestinians—who continue to lose larger numbers of sons than the Israelis in the protests of the Intifadeh—remain high.

26
Sharon and Arafat: Antagonists at Seventy

For our part, we will honor our commitments...Our participation in the great peace process means that we are betting everything on the future.

Yasser Arafat,
on the signing of the Oslo II Accord in September 1995 to implement Palestinian rule over a portion of the Occupied Territories

I don't know anyone who has as much civilian Jewish blood on his hands as Arafat since the Nazis' time.

Ariel Sharon, then Israeli Defense Minister, October 1995

I n the late 1920s, two babies are born some 200 miles apart into families with deep attachment to the Holy Land. Seven decades and more later, the two will take center stage as bitter antagonists in the Israeli/Palestinian conflict. Neither will keep his birth name.

    In 1928 on an agricultural settlement north of Tel Aviv in the British Palestine Mandate, Shmuel and Dvora Scheinerman, who have immigrated from Russia six years prior, name their new son Ariel. The family drops "Scheinerman" and takes the name of

1928

the region where they have settled, the "Sharon" Valley.

In Cairo the following year, a successful Palestinian merchant and his wife name their son Mohammed Abdel-Rahman Abdel-Raouf Arafat al-Qudwa, but his family call him "Yasser."

1930's

Lessons in Hatred

Growing up, Ariel Sharon and Yasser Arafat have contrasting experiences that will forever color their viewpoints.

On the agricultural cooperative (the Moshav) where his family has settled, Sharon's father and mother are ostracized by the community for refusing to participate in Bolshevist-style public revilement rallies. Ariel learns to live with rejection. His parents are rich in books but otherwise poor. They save so that Ariel can attend high school, a goal rare among Moshav families of the time. When he is fourteen, he joins a paramilitary group whose duty is to protect the settlement from Arab raiders. His father gives him a knife. "The knife was symbolic," Sharon later writes, "to protect ourselves from our enemies. It was a lesson I have never forgotten." By age seventeen, Ariel has been inducted into the Haganah, the Jewish underground.

Arafat's mother dies when he is five, and he is sent to live with his uncle's family in Jerusalem. His uncle is among many Palestinians who want the British out of their land. He has been active in the underground. Yasser remembers British soldiers breaking into his uncle's house after midnight, beating members of the family and smashing furniture. By 1938, Yasser is back in Cairo, and eight years later, at age seventeen, he is smuggling arms to Palestine to be used against the British and the Jews.

1940's-
1950's **The Cause**

In the Haganah in 1945, Sharon works on missions to harry the British and bring Holocaust refugees into Palestine. He becomes an instructor of police, a regimental intelligence officer, and in the Jewish War for Independence in 1948, a platoon commander in the army. He studies history at Hebrew University

198

and later receives a law degree. But he is never far from military service. He participates in each of Israel's wars, and in between he becomes an expert in gathering intelligence. He organizes and leads "Unit 101," an elite unit that makes bloody retaliatory strikes against Palestinian guerrillas infiltrating Israel. He becomes a general in the army, a strong-willed leader who never makes chief-of-staff.

Arafat is nineteen when Israel declares independence, and he desponds over the results of the first Israeli/Arab war, shocked that the Palestinians now do not even have the state the United Nations has promised them. Arafat (the name he takes after finishing engineering studies in Cairo) is consumed with one idea only: that Palestinians must have their own independent country and the state of Israel must go. Working in Kuwait, Arafat forms the Fatah party, dedicated to this end. Fatah later merges with the Palestinian Liberation Organization (PLO), and Arafat is chosen as leader, representing all Palestinians.

1960's-
1980's

Terrorists

Arafat's union of Fatah with the PLO is a natural alliance, for both groups seek the overthrow of Israel. Leading both organizations, Arafat sets up PLO headquarters in Jordan. Determining to destabilize Israel, he orders night raids across the border into Israeli settlements. But Jordan's King Hussein, feeling that Arafat and his PLO are becoming too powerful, ousts them from Jordan. Arafat turns to Lebanon, where he re-establishes PLO headquarters in Beirut and enlists young Palestinians from refugee camps into the PLO. Under Arafat's direction and working now with the Lebanese Hezbullah, PLO raiders make repeated forays into Israel. They strike abroad also, hijacking airplanes and executing Israeli athletes at the Munich Olympic Games. The more hopeless the lot of the Palestinians becomes, the more Arafat reverts to terror to keep their cause before the world's eye.

Sharon sees Arafat's PLO as Israel's chief enemy. Serving as Defense Minister in the Israeli government in 1982, Sharon leads an invasion of Lebanon and bombs PLO headquarters in Beirut.

199

Arafat survives and moves with the PLO to Tunisia. Sharon makes common cause with the Maronite Christian militia in Lebanon, who in retaliation for the assassination of the Maronite president of Lebanon, carry out a brutal raid on two Palestinian refugee camps outside Beirut, raping women and killing hundreds of refugees. Sharon watches this action within his jurisdiction but does nothing; he probably has a hand in its planning. Israelis are shocked. Sharon orders the army to pull back to Southern Lebanon, then resigns his post. (The shock reverberates internationally, and in 2002, Sharon is being sued by survivors in court action in Brussels on the charge of a crime against humanity.) Sharon is popular with right-leaning Israelis, however, and during the eighties and nineties is given government posts responsible for building Israeli settlements within the West Bank.

From Tunisia, Arafat continues to direct terrorist moves against Israel. But he also gains the attention of the United Nations. A Labor government in Israel is willing to negotiate. The Peace Process starts, but Sharon will have none of it. "No one will touch Judea and Samaria [the occupied West Bank]. They belong to us. They have been ours for thousands of years, eternally." In Israel, Sharon is a hero to the right, an obstacle to peace to the center and 1990's left. He craves leadership, but it is repeatedly denied him. He is too controversial.

The Statesmen

In 1988, Arafat addresses the United Nations, representing the PLO, and in this address, he changes course. He declares that the PLO renounces terrorism and supports the right of both Israel and a Palestinian state to exist. Sharon publicly doubts his sincerity. But at this point Arafat becomes a world statesman. He signs the Oslo Accord in 1993, receives the Nobel Peace Prize (together with Israeli Prime Minister Yitzhak Rabin), and begins negotiations that create the Palestinian Authority. He assumes the Authority's Presidency.

Sharon believes that the Israeli government has sold out. He publicly decries the Oslo Accord. When a conservative government returns, he joins it and resolves to do all he can to delay Palestinian Authority progress. Arafat finds that further negotiations with Israel are going nowhere. The Sharon faction in Israel does not trust him, and Arafat now doubts Israel's sincerity. Within the Authority, he must deal with the growing power and popularity of Hamas and the Islamic Jihad.

2000-
2002

By September of 2000, Arafat is despairing. He has been unable to wrest Jerusalem from the Israelis, his fragmented Palestinian Authority is almost ungovernable, the Israeli military under Sharon's direction is constraining his people, and his own people are questioning his leadership.

In that same month, Sharon, whose house in the Arab Quarter of Jerusalem— heavily guarded and flying the Israeli flag—is a daily provocation to Arabs, undertakes another provocation. He leads a group of right-wing Israeli followers onto the Haram al-Sharif. He knows what he is doing; to the religious Jewish right, the Temple Mount is and must always be Jewish. Here, someday, the Jews will rebuild their Temple. His act is deliberately symbolic.

Hamas and the Islamic Jihad react as Sharon expects, sending boys to throw stones and young men to turn themselves into suicide bombs. Sharon doubts that Arafat will be able to stop the Intifadeh, and in a sense he sets him up for failure. As the Israeli army retaliates, Arafat loses support and Sharon gains strength. Israelis finally vote in Sharon as Prime Minister. At seventy-three, his uncompromising stand has won him the top leadership post. But now, instead of waiting for the Palestinian Authority to collapse from disunity, he must negotiate with Arafat. World opinion demands it.

Does Arafat any longer speak for his people? If not, with whom does Sharon negotiate? Do Sharon and Arafat, lifetime adversaries, stand a chance at the peace table? The dilemma is thrust onto the world stage as Osama bin Laden, responsible for the bombing of the World Trade Center on September 11, 2001, co-opts the Palestinian issue.

Part III
Today:
In the Vortex

I didn't realize, when I was in the Holy Land in the spring of 2000, how fortunate I was. The interminable conflict was simmering, but it was not flaring. Life seemed normal. I was able to move safely and at will. Israeli soldiers were everywhere, giving me a sense of security. But they are everywhere today as well, and security is uncertain.

A Shattering of Dreams

One martyr in the Holy Land is worth seventy martyrs anywhere else.

Yasser Arafat, in a message to Palestinians, December 20, 2001 (cited in New York Times)

A compromise over Jerusalem would lead to uncontrollable violence in the Middle East...No Arab or Muslim can relinquish rights to East Jerusalem or its holy sites.

Hosni Mubarak, President of Egypt, 2001

The Al-Aqsa Intifadeh, which begins in September of 2000, escalates quickly from stones and rocks to mortars and bombs. The delivery medium has shifted, too, as grown men martyr themselves on Israeli streets and buses. The Israelis use weapons of war in retaliation that is not always targeted; they enter Palestinian cities to hunt for terrorists, and they restrict Palestinian movement. Each side charges the other with aggression. Casualties mount, but the toll among Palestinians is higher by far.

2000

Both Israelis and Palestinians are as frustrated now as at any time in the past. The hope of the Oslo Accords has faded, probably collapsed. Neither Israelis nor Palestinians can go about their lives in safety. Arafat's Islands are barricaded. Attaining a viable

Palestinian state, with Jerusalem as its capital, is still a Palestinian dream but only that. In Israel, support for the liberal parties, traditionally more inclined to negotiation, has yielded to the uncompromising parties of the far right, who have never agreed with the premise of Land-for-Peace.

In the Palestinian Authority, Arafat has trouble now controlling the pent-up fury he himself fostered and unleashed as he earlier led the Palestine Liberation Army in militant protest. Hamas and the Islamic Jihad, committed to terrorism and to Israel's total defeat, are winning increasing popular support, and Arafat has little to show for his willingness to negotiate. The Israeli leadership doubts his commitment, and most of his own people doubt he can deliver. Lines are hardening on both sides, and the door to negotiation is almost shut.

#

The Wider Conflict

It's not Islam versus the West
as much as it is Islam versus Islam.

Akibar Ahmed,
former Pakistani ambassador to the United Kingdom,
cited in U. S. News and World Report,
October 1, 2001

Bin Laden changed the game. We need a different
engagement with cultures of the world...We must
acknowledge that religion is a component of most political
conflicts in the world today.

Douglas Johnson, President,
International Center for
Religion and Democracy, 2001

The Israeli/Palestinian conflict is no longer a regional problem only, if indeed it ever was. From plush and distant bunkers, renegade Osama bin Laden and Iraq's Saddam Hussein call on all Muslims to fight a *jihad*, a Holy War against Israel, as did Libya's Muammar Khadafi a decade ago.

The existence of Israel is no threat to the international terrorists personally, nor have they shown that they really care about the Palestinians. Hussein and Khadafi are not even religiously observant, except for public consumption. But all three crave power. Each sees himself as the potential leader of the Arab world. Arab governments are rarely able to achieve unity. They are stressed internally. As they work toward modernization, their poor and poorly educated, embracing extremist versions of Islam learned in madrasas, are left behind, aggrieved and embittered. Terrorist organizations enlist the aggrieved in their cause, using them as they try to destabilize existing regimes.

The Holy Land is one issue on which most Arabs can unite. Almost all Arabs resent the presence of Israel in their midst. They resent the fact that many Palestinians are homeless and are living in surrounding Arab lands. In truth, most Arab countries view the Palestinians as something of a nuisance, taking up space and continually agitating. For this, they blame Israel. The spectrum of Arab attitudes toward Israel runs from measured accommodation (i.e., Jordan and Egypt, and Morocco in North Africa) to refusal to recognize Israel's right to exist (i.e., Lebanon, Syria, Iraq, and Saudi Arabia). In their effort to gain support within the Arab world, bin Laden, Hussein, and Khadafi have taken the Palestinians' cause as their own. Following the attack on the World Trade Center, Arafat publicly rejects bin Laden's support. But Hamas and the Islamic Jihad are in league with the al-Qaeda network, and Sharon charges that Arafat also is continuing to get support from this quarter.

Arab Bitterness

Al-Qaeda's commitment to a Holy War is not only against Israel but also against its Western supporters, especially the United States. Long-held Arab bitterness toward the West stems from European ascendancy beginning in the sixteenth century, the humiliation of colonial or mandate occupation, and present economic disparities. Oil-wealthy Arab rulers, eager to deflect populist grievances away from themselves and toward Israel, support the Palestinian uprising. Bin Laden's role is complex; he wants the West out of the entire Middle East, and he blames Arab rulers for consorting with the West. Particularly, he blames the Saudi rulers for allowing American troops on Saudi soil, which he views as holy soil. The Palestinian cause serves his purpose, but it puts him in bed with the very regimes he wants to oust. More than anything, bin Laden sees himself as a modern-day Saladin, repaying the West for the wrongs of the Crusades. Most leaders in the Arab world are aware of his power game; they recognize it as being as much a threat to their own regimes as to Israel, and they reject his use of terror. But many of their people are powerfully attracted to a charismatic Muslim leader who promises to redress wrong.

Monotheistic Links

We have been able to trace direct ties among the world's three great monotheistic religions, as well as the emotional ties of their adherents to the Holy Land. The God of Jews, Christians, and Muslims is the same God, revealed through Abraham and the Prophets, which all three acknowledge. Jews consider that God has made them his chosen people, and they are divided on whether Jesus was a Prophet. Most certainly, he was not their promised Messiah, whom they still await. Christians believe that Jesus was indeed the Messiah that the prophets foretold, sent by God as his Son to redeem the world; for Christians, the message of Jesus Christ, that God is Love, is meant for everyone, Jews and non-Jews alike. Muslims acknowledge Jesus as a prophet but believe that God's final revelation came through the Prophet Mohammed to his chosen people, the Arabs, whose duty it was (and is) to spread Islam (submission to the One God). The Hebrew Scriptures (the Christians' Old Testament), the New Testament of the Christians, and the Quran of the Muslims are sacred books with many links. All three religions provide a common core of rules by which humans should live together. All ask that believers treat one another as they wish to be treated.

Differences

But it is the differences, not the similarities, that fire zealots. For some forty years after Christ's ascension, Messianic Jews and traditional Jews continued to worship side by side in synagogues. But after the Romans destroyed Jerusalem and the Temple in 70 CE, Jews lost the geographic focus of their entire religion. They needed to reassess their identity, and in doing so, they made a critical decision. The Messianists would have to go. The followers of Jesus would not be welcome in the synagogues. The Gospel of John was written twenty or more years later, when traditional and Messianic Jews were no longer communicating, except as adversaries. The account of the trial and crucifixion in the Gospel of John says that it was the Jews—not "the crowd" or "the people" of the earlier Gospel accounts—who crucified Christ. Although most Christians today believe that it is all sinners who bear responsibility for the crucifixion, this portion of John's Gospel has been used to justify unspeakable past actions and underlies anti-Semitism even today.

Literalist Muslims point out that the Hebrew Scriptures assail the Jews of ancient times for worshipping idols. Can the Quran do less? Christians commit the ultimate blasphemy when they say that the Prophet Jesus is the Son of God. From Morocco to Indonesia, Muslims interpret the Quran literally, and the Quran has some provocative things to say about Jews and Christians. According to the Quran, the Jews try to introduce corruption (Sura 5:64), have always been disobedient (Sura 5:78), and are enemies of al-Lah, the Prophet, and the angels (Sura 2: 97,98). The Christians say, 'The Messiah is the Son of God.'...God assail them! (Sura 9:30) Referring to Jews and Christians, the Quran asks believers to "fight and slay the infidels wherever you find them" (Sura 9:5).

A Matter of Interpretation

Should followers of Islam take literally such Quranic directions? Most Muslims believe that because everything written in the Quran was revealed directly to Mohammed by God, and the Arabic text has not undergone compilation or change, everything in the Quran is true and relevant as written. A literal reading of the Quran, however, sometimes poses a problem for moderate, educated Muslims, who see their faith as one that promotes caring, self-discipline, peace, compassion, love, mercy, tolerance, modesty, and justice. *Islam* means submission to the will of God. *Jihad* is a personal struggle for betterment. Jihad does not mean, say moderate Muslims, a Holy War against others, either People of the Book (Jews and Christians) or unbelievers.

Young Muslims learn piety from their parents, but they learn the Quran in religious schools, verse by memorized verse, in Arabic. In poor societies, they may receive no other education. To Muslim fundamentalists, a Holy War declared against Israel and its Christian allies is sanctioned, even urged, by the Quran.

Most readers of the Hebrew Scriptures view the accounts of bloody battles and harsh treatment of enemies in the distant past as archaic, certainly not a template for action today. But fundamentalist Jews interpret their Scriptures literally when it comes to such matters as imposing Sabbath regulations on the modern Jewish state or determining who can be considered a Jew (for Israeli citizenship). For fundamentalist Jews (and fundamentalist Christians as well), the very existence of the state of Israel is supported by a literal interpretation of God's promise to Abraham and Moses: God has set aside the Promised Land for his chosen people, the Jews.

Hebrew and Christian Scriptures can be read in the original Hebrew or Aramaic or Greek, or in translations in hundreds of languages. Meanings change subtly in translation, and through the centuries interpretations change. Jewish and Christian scholars have continued to examine their texts and to make changes when justified by scholarship. Further, customs change–customs that are not critical to the core of faith–and, therefore, most Jews and Christians can interpret their Scriptures as relevant in today's world without taking literally the portions that are relevant to another time and place.

In history, Judaism underwent two severe and formative trials, both leading to the re-formation of faith and tradition that has enabled it to endure: the Babylonian Captivity and return in the fifth century BCE, and the destruction of the Temple in 70 CE. For Christians, the great cataclysmic upheavals and regenerations were the Reformation and the Counter Reformation, through which human reason took on a "new birth of freedom," with democracy and the scientific revolution as its outgrowth.

Islam has had no such regeneration. To apply critical scholarship to the Quran would be to question God himself. Despite largely politically motivated movements that have split Islam into two major factions (Sunni and Shi'a) and scores of offshoots, the Quran is interpreted much the same today as it was in the seventh century. This is both its strength and its weakness.

Al-Haram al-Sharif/The Temple Mount

Religious fundamentalists of all three faiths approach the Israeli/Palestinian conflict from their own eschatological view. Inevitably, that view centers on the Temple Mount, the Haram al-Sharif. Fundamentalist Jews (who are only a minority in Israel but hold the controlling vote in the government) believe that the rebuilding of the Temple must happen because it is foretold in prophecy. When the Temple is rebuilt (but not until then), the Messiah will finally be revealed, and Jews will enter a long-awaited period of righteousness and fulfillment. With the rebuilding of the Temple will come a restoration of the power of the priestly caste, clerical rule, and animal sacrifice, following literally the Iron-Age practices that prevailed when the Hebrews first occupied the Holy Land.

The rebuilding of the Temple cannot happen until the Dome of the Rock and the Al-Aqsa Mosque are destroyed. Some fundamentalist Jews believe that they should hasten the destruction by militant action, and several times in the past two decades they have attempted to bomb the Dome of

Photo 17. The Dome of the Rock on the Haram al-Sahrif.

the Rock. Although most believe they should wait until God in his good time arranges the destruction, their views strongly underlie Israel's refusal to negotiate on Jerusalem. When Ariel Sharon, whose motivations are always political but rarely religious, walked on the Haram al-Sharif in September of 2000, he knew the symbolism of his action. Sharon's strongest support in Israel has always come from the religious right.

Sharon also gets strong support from those Christian fundamentalists, particularly in the United States, who also believe that the Temple must be rebuilt, but for a different set of reasons. Fundamentalist Christians base their end-time scenario on the opaque and highly symbolic prophesies of the Book of Daniel and the Book of Revelations. Most fundamentalist Christians hold pre-Millennialist views, believing that the Bible foretells the events that must occur in the Holy Land before Jesus returns to earth. Of these events, two have already happened: The nation of Israel has been restored (1948), and the Old City of Jerusalem has become a Jewish city (1967). Only one event remains before end-time events are triggered: The Jews must rebuild the Temple. A pact made with a charismatic world leader, termed the Anti-

215

Christ, and the subsequent rebuilding of the Temple will set in motion a seven-year period known as the *Tribulation*. At first the Jews will revere the Anti-Christ as their long-awaited Messiah, but midway in this seven-year period the Anti-Christ will desecrate the Temple and turn against the Jews. He will then lead a series of attacks on the Jews, aided by world military forces from many parts of the earth. The world will be in turmoil, but most Christians will not know the agony because they will be *raptured*, or taken up to heaven, at the time the Tribulation begins. In the final climactic battle, to be fought north of Jerusalem at Armageddon (on the archaeological site known as Meggido), almost all of the combatants will be killed. After this battle, Christ will return to reign on earth—from Jerusalem—for a thousand years. He will bring with him the raptured saints, who will live in an earthly paradise. With them will be the 144,000 Jews who became Believers and survived the Battle. The end of the world will come after this thousand-year reign, when the dead will rise again, and Christ will be their judge.

Like fundamentalist Jews, fundamentalist Christians differ in how the initiating event, the destruction of the Dome of the Rock and the rebuilding of the Temple, shall come about. Almost all fundamentalist Christians are in sympathy with Zionism and thus with Israel. They see the immigration of Jews to Israel, and the events of 1948 and 1967 as divinely ordained steps toward the prophesied End. In Israel, an organized contingent of Christian Zionists, called the International Christian Embassy in Jerusalem, has strong ties to fundamentalist Christian groups in the United States and elsewhere. Many fundamentalist Christian groups lend financial support to Israeli causes, and some help to finance the immigration of Jewish settlers from Russia and other countries to Israel.

Although fundamentalist Jews and fundamentalist Christians differ greatly in their theology, the Israeli right cultivates and encourages the support of Christian fundamentalists and openly admits the value of their support. In the United States, where according to one poll forty-six percent of all Americans believe that the establishment of Israel is the fulfillment of prophecy, the Israeli/Palestinian conflict has inevitable political overtones. United States support for Israel is probably motivated far less by the so-called "Jewish lobby" than by the eschatology of fundamentalist Christians in the electorate.

Christians who do not hold pre-Millennialist views generally eliminate eschatology from whatever stand they take in the Israeli/Palestinian conflict. Although they are sympathetic to all efforts to redress the horrors of the Holocaust, they tend to be more critical of Israel and more sympathetic to the cause of the Palestinians than their co-religionists on the right. They realize and understand that tourism in Israel is geared to the interests of those who come as pilgrims, to walk where Jesus walked. But they realize, too, that visitors to Israel get little or no opportunity for contact with the struggling Arab Christian community in the Holy Land.

The Israeli military gathers the intelligence that so far has enabled them to foil all attempts on the part of either Jewish or Christian zealots to damage the Dome of the Rock. To the disappointment of fundamentalist Christians and Jews, when Israel took over all of Jerusalem in 1967, it restored control of the Temple Mount to the Muslims on the condition that people of all faiths would be able to have access to the Mount. With difficulty, both the Israeli army and the Muslim clerics who oversee the Haram al-Sharif have kept to this agreement through all the subsequent periods of unrest.

The Islamic view of the Haram al-Sharif is grounded partly in eschatology and partly in Arab nationalism. Whether Mohammed literally ascended to heaven from the site of the Dome of the Rock, as fundamentalist Muslims believe, or merely experienced the Heavenly visit in a vision, the Haram al-Sharif has strong religious connotations for all Muslims. Many believe that on the Last Day the Kaabah will be transported to Jerusalem and that, like Mohammed, Muslims will ascend directly to heaven from the Dome of the Rock. The Dome appears as a logo on most publications that come from the Palestinian Authority. For Palestinians, continued and permanent Palestinian Arab occupancy of the Haram al-Sharif is non-negotiable. This stand underlies Arafat's insistence that Jerusalem, and no other site, must be the capital of the Palestinian state.

Radical Islam had a ready explanation for the wrenching defeat suffered by the Arabs in the Six-Day War in 1967. It was the result of the moral decay of modern secular Arab society. After 1967, religious extremism in the Muslim world began to focus on the Haram al-Sharif, and organizations such as the Islamic Jihad began to swell with adherents. In no small sense, the attraction of bin Laden's al-Qaeda network was an outgrowth of this defeat.

Viewpoints on a Spectrum

To the horror of moderates everywhere, extremists of all three faiths see the struggle for the Holy Land as a struggle between Islam and the Judeo-Christian West.

Secular Israelis, who increasingly are voting with the right, are not interested in such cosmic terms, but they are pragmatic; they accept the support of the Christian right, regardless of its motivation. Palestinians on the right get their support from Muslim extremists (Hamas, the Islamic Jihad, and Hezbullah), as well as extremist groups from surrounding countries who are dedicated to Israel's overthrow.

Moderate voices from the Palestinian community rarely surface, except from the dwindling Arab Christian community. Christians in the Palestinian Authority, in Bethlehem or Ramallah or elsewhere, are having an increasingly difficult time maintaining their programs, and Muslim extremists often unjustly accuse them of collaborating with Israel. Arab Christians within Israel generally do not ally themselves with the Christian right. As Israeli citizens who are both Arab and Christian, they are able to provide a needed bridge of understanding in an increasingly polarized society. Moderate Israelis and Palestinians, who are willing to negotiate Land-for-Peace, seek support and understanding from Christian,

Muslim, and secular moderates everywhere. These are the people who, working behind the scenes, are searching for openings and encouraging dialog.

The Only Way Out

Terrorism has no military solution.

**Israeli security officer, cited in the
New York Times, December 21, 2001**

*The ultimate weakness of violence is that it is a descending
spiral. Instead of diminishing evil, it multiplies it. Hate
cannot drive out hate: Only love can do that.*

Martin Luther King, Jr.

B in Laden's al-Qaeda network has been severely
crippled; it may no longer be a coherent movement.
But the Islamic fundamentalism and the internal
political struggles that gave birth to al-Qaeda remain. So long
as the Israeli/Palestinian conflict is unresolved, the Holy Land
will remain in the vortex of a destabilized world.

In the present International War on Terrorism, the Israeli/
Palestinian conflict is shoved repeatedly to the forefront. The
United States must be able to count on its Arab allies—allies
who are quite ready to tie their cooperation to a just peace in
the Holy Land.

The definition of *just*, of course, depends on who
answers the question posed in the title of this book. No
agreement is ever totally just. Agreement can come about
only through negotiation, through the willingness of both

2001-
2002

parties to give. As I write, statesmen from Europe and the United States, as well as the United Nations, continue to prod the adversaries to the table, to tap the residue of willingness that remains on both sides.

In late 1999 Arafat and [then] Israeli Prime Minister Ehud Barak, prodded by U.S. President Clinton, work out an agreement called by the name of the Egyptian Sinai resort where they are negotiating, Sharm el-Sheik. In this agreement Israel gives Palestinians total control over about eighteen percent of the Occupied West Bank, instead of the three percent that resulted from the Oslo Accord. Further negotiations in 2000—at Camp David, outside Washington D.C.— in which Barak offers to give the Palestinians control over more than 90 percent of the West Bank, break down when Arafat refuses to sign. He refuses because the Israelis, under terms of the failed proposal, would have total control over all roads, and Arafat sees that as unworkable. Shortly after Arafat's refusal the new round of violence begins. With the escalating Intifadeh, Sharon's hardline position, and President Bush's initial reluctance to become involved in the Israeli/Palestinian controversy, negotiations halt. But President Bush has now made the Middle East a priority and has assigned a high-level diplomat to work with both sides. Negotiations must and will resume.

Leading spokesmen both in Israel and Palestine have begun to recognize publicly that the Al-Aqsa Intifadeh and the harsh Israeli retaliatory measures have brought no gains whatsoever, to either side. Even as attitudes harden and negotiation becomes ever more difficult, a growing number of both Palestinians and Israelis now realize that only through talking, and not through guns, can come the peace that both sides crave.

Israelis are in the Holy Land to stay. And so are the Palestinians. Both are deeply attached to the same land. Through negotiations somehow they will find a way to share that land. There will be pain on both sides, for neither will be satisfied with the compromises that they must eventually make. But the alternative is what Martin Luther King has called the "descending spiral of violence."

Yitzhak Frankenthal, an orthodox Israeli and a religious Zionist, is the founder of the Bereaved Families Forum. He has met with political leaders on both sides, and with leaders of Hamas and the Islamic Jihad. "The current situation is dreadful for Israelis and Palestinians alike," says Frankenthal. "That's why there is no alternative to peace."

In 1994 Frankenthal is traveling in the Gaza Strip with his nineteen-year old son Arik, on leave from the army. The son tells his father that if he were a Palestinian in Gaza, what he would most want to do is kill an Israeli soldier. A week later, back in service in the West Bank, Arik is dead, kidnapped and slain by four young members of Hamas. Frankenthal, in his agony, drives back to Gaza. He searches for a family whose son has been killed by Israeli soldiers, and he finds that family. He embraces them, and they weep together. Then Frankenthal decides to form a league of the bereaved.

The Bereaved Families Forum is now 400 strong, its membership roughly half Palestinian, half Israeli. They have made a memorial display of 900 mock caskets, side by side, and they have centered their activities in a Tent of Peace in Tel Aviv's Rabin Square. They sponsor billboards, erected on both sides of the Green Line, proclaiming in Hebrew and Arabic: "Better the Pains of Peace than the Agonies of War."

In the words of the Prophet Mohammed: "If they incline toward peace, incline thou also to it,"

And in the words of Jesus: "Blessed are the peacemakers."

Shalom   Peace   Salaam

Epilogue:
From Suleiman's Wall

It was the last day of my stay in the Holy Land. The late spring sun was already hot. As I sat in a shady niche on the Wall that surrounds the Old City, I was thinking of the three monotheistic faiths that claim Jerusalem as holy, their common ancestor Abraham, the prophets whom all three acknowledge, and Jesus of Nazareth—Messiah to Christians and prophet to Jews and Muslims. Yes, I reassured myself, the teachings of Jesus about the common humanity of all people under One God have the power, even now, to form a basis for peace.

I used the time on the Wall to try to bring together and make sense of what I had experienced. I had benefited from a comprehensive itinerary that let me trace the events of the Old Testament, the interlude between Nehemiah and Matthew, the account in the Gospels of Jesus' life, the Jewish Revolt and the Diaspora, the coming and waning of Christianity, Islam in the Holy Land, the Crusaders' quixotic mission, Ottoman Rule, the impossible task of the British Mandate, the modern state of Israel and the impact it has made on the land, and finally, the tragic conflict between Jew and Arab, between Israeli and Palestinian.

Today, as I recall my time on the Wall, it seems as if it were long ago: before the breakdown of peace efforts between Israelis and Palestinians, before the renewal of the Intifadeh and the daily wailing over caskets carried in disorderly procession through streets of angry mourners, before the concrete barricades and the terror and fear, and before the International War on Terrorism with its ever-present sidebar

225

in the Holy Land. As so often in the past, peace in the Holy Land is once more elusive.

I began writing this account while on the Wall and continued on the long flight home. But only now, nearly two years later, do I muster the courage to bring it to a conclusion. In another sense, it can never be concluded. The Holy Land is living history—past, present, and future—forever linked.

Dorothy Weitz Drummond

GLOSSARY

ABBASSID CALIPHATE. The period [750-1258 CE] when the Arab Empire was ruled from Baghdad. In 909, the Abbassid Caliphate was succeeded in the Holy Land by the Seljuk Turks.

ACTS, BOOK OF. The fifth book of the New Testament, which records the activities of Paul and other apostles from the third to the sixth decades of the first century. It was probably written by the author of the Gospel of Luke.

AELIA CAPITOLINA. The name given by the Romans to Jerusalem in ca 135 CE.

AGE OF DISCOVERY. The period beginning in the fifteenth century when Portuguese, Spanish, English, and Dutch maritime explorers began to map the world as they sought a water route from Europe to the Orient.

AL-AQSA INTIFADEH. The resistance movement started in September 2000 by stone-throwing Palestinians protesting the presence of Israeli Defense Minister Ariel Sharon on the Haram al-Sharif in front of the Al-Aqsa Mosque. It has since been co-opted by militant Islamic groups **HAMAS** (qv) and the **ISLAMIC JIHAD** (qv), with the acquiescence (Israeli charge) of the Palestinian Authority.

AL-AQSA MOSQUE. The mosque located on the **HARAM AL-SHARIF** (qv) in Jerusalem that dates to the seventh century CE.

AL-LAH. For Muslims, the name of the One God. Before Mohammed, the name of the god worshipped in the vicinity of Mecca.

AL-QAEDA. The international movement founded by Osama bin Laden that promotes terrorism in order to destabilize existing governments that it opposes.

AMERICAN JEWISH CONGRESS. The Jewish organization in the United States, particularly active after World War II, that advocated an alternative to Zionism for resettlement of Jewish refugees.

ANNUNCIATION, THE. The event where the virgin Mary learns she is to become the mother of the Messiah.

ANTONIA FORTRESS. The Roman-fortified tower and administrative center overlooking the Temple Mount where Pontius Pilate resided while in Jerusalem. It was destroyed in 70 CE.

APOCRYPHA. A body of text written between the fifth and first centuries BCE, some in Aramaic, some in Greek, that was incorporated within the **SEPTUAGINT** (qv). It is accepted as canonical by Roman Catholics and Anglicans but rejected by other Protestants as not being a portion of the Hebrew Scriptures.

ARAFAT'S ISLANDS. A nickname (somewhat derisive) for the fragmented territories of the Palestinian Authority resulting from the **OSLO ACCORD** (qv).

ARK OF THE COVENANT. A vessel, resembling a chest, in which the ancient Hebrews kept the words of God given to Moses on Mount Sinai. The Ark was enshrined in the holiest portion of the Temple built by Solomon.

ARMAGEDDON. According to the **PRE-MILLENNIALISM** (qv) belief, the climactic battle that will precede the Second Coming of Christ. It will be fought on an archaeological site north of Jerusalem, termed Megiddo.

ASCENSION, THE. The term given to the last appearance of Jesus on earth, when he rose upward and out of view of the disciples. Luke says this event took place on the Mount of Olives.

ASHKENAZI. Jews who lived for centuries in Western and Eastern Europe.

BA-ATH PARTY. The Arab Socialist party that put in power the present-day rulers of Syria and Iraq.

BABYLONIAN CAPTIVITY. The period from ca 591-533 BCE when leaders of Jewish society were held captive in the Chaldean city of Babylonia in Mesopotamia.

BAHA'I. A religion that holds that its founder, Baha'u'llah, is the most recent messenger of those (Moses, Krishna, Buddah, Zoroaster, Jesus, and Mohammed) whom God has chosen to reveal his will to humanity. Baha'u'llah spent the latter part of the nineteenth century in Palestine, exiled from his homeland in Iran.

BALFOUR DECLARATION. The statement issued by Lord Balfour of the British Foreign Office in 1917 supporting Palestine as a homeland for Jews but stating that Arab rights shall not be infringed.

BAPTISM. An ancient Hebrew rite in which water is symbolic of spiritual cleansing. At the beginning of his ministry, Jesus was baptized by John (probably an **ESSENE** (qv)) in the Jordan River. Baptism is now a rite practiced within all branches of Christendom.

BAR KOKBA REVOLT. The final and unsuccessful revolt of Jews in Palestine in 132 CE, protesting the Roman desecration of the Temple Mount where a statue of the Emperor as God was erected.

BCE, CE. Faith-neutral designations of historical time: Before the Common Era and Common Era. These are often used by historians to replace BC (Before Christ) and AD (taken from the Latin Anno Domini, or the Year of Our Lord). The point at which BCE becomes CE is the mistaken date formerly given for the year of Jesus' birth.

BIBLE. The book that for Christians is the revealed Word of God. It includes the Old Testament, which is the same as the Hebrew Scriptures (with some reordering of books), and the New Testament, which begins with the **GOSPELS** (qv) and continues through the Acts of the Apostles and the letters of Paul and other apostles to early Christian communities.

BRITISH PALESTINE MANDATE. *See* Palestine Mandate.

BRONZE AGE. The period of pre-history marked by the use of bronze (a mixture of copper and tin) in weapons and items of decoration. Bronze is softer than iron, at whose discovery the Bronze Age was superseded by the Iron Age.

BYZANTINE. Pertaining to the Graeco/Roman/Christian civilization that characterized the eastern Roman Empire after the removal in 315 CE of the imperial capital from Rome to Byzantium. Byzantium, the Greek name for the city, was changed to Constantinople after the Emperor Constantine took up residence there. During Constantine's reign, the Roman Empire embraced Christianity.

BYZANTINE EMPIRE. The eastern part of the Roman Empire, and after the fifth century, its successor. The Empire was ruled from Constantinople from the early fourth century CE until the final defeat of Constantinople by the Ottomans in 1453.

CAMP DAVID ACCORD (1979). The agreement between Egypt and Israel in which Egypt recognized the existence of Israel, and Israel agreed to return the Sinai Peninsula to Egypt. It was negotiated by former U.S. President Jimmy Carter at Camp David.

CAMP DAVID PROPOSAL (2000). An offer made by Israeli Prime Minister Ehud Barak to give up ninety percent of the West Bank to Palestinian control. It was rejected by Arafat because Israel would have retained control of all West Bank roads.

CANAAN. The land promised to Abraham and his descendents. Its boundaries are indefinite, but the region includes essentially the land from the Mediterranean Sea to the Jordan River (and sometimes beyond), and from the slopes of Mount Hermon to the northern Negev.

CARDO. The main street or way in a Roman-planned city.

CHRISTIAN ZIONISTS. Organized groups of Christians who support the idea of **ZIONISM** (qv) as a precondition for the events that will trigger the **END TIMES** (qv).

CHRISTIANITY. The name given to the community of followers of Jesus Christ. Christianity is the world's largest and most widespread religion. It is divided into three major branches—Roman Catholic, Protestant, and Eastern Orthodox.

CHURCH OF THE HOLY SEPULCHRE. A church in Jerusalem established on the site where its founders, emissaries of the Emperor Constantine, had reason to believe the crucifixion and the burial of Christ took place.

CIRCUMCISION. The removal of the foreskin of the penis. This covenanted rite was announced by God to Abraham and observed by both Jews and Muslims.

CITADEL, THE. A fortified complex inside Jaffa Gate in Jerusalem's Old City, first constructed by Hasmoneans, then repeatedly rebuilt and enlarged by all successive rulers. It is now a museum of the history of Jerusalem.

CODEX SINAITICUS. The oldest existing copy of the Bible, dating to the mid-fourth century. It was written in Greek on parchment and preserved in the Monastery of St. Catherine until its discovery and removal to museums in Leipzig and St. Petersburg in the mid-nineteenth century.

COPTIC. A branch of Christianity followed in Egypt, dating to the first century, and by tradition introduced by Mark the Evangelist.

CRUCIFIXION. A brutal method of execution practiced by the Romans in which the victim was nailed by the hands and feet to a cross beam probably placed on a stationary pole. Jesus Christ was executed in this fashion.

CRUSADES. A series of military expeditions undertaken by European knights in the twelfth and thirteenth centuries to wrest the Holy Land from Muslim control. The Crusaders controlled parts of the Holy Land for almost two centuries, from 1099 to 1291.

CYRUS THE GREAT. The ruler of the Persian Empire from 559 to 530 BCE. He issued a decree in 538 allowing the Jews to return from Babylon to rebuild Jerusalem.

DANIEL, BOOK OF. Probably written during the time of the Maccabeean struggles against the Seleucids, this book tells of the events of the Babylonian Captivity 300 years previously. It is often read as the story of the clash of the kingdom of God with the kingdoms of the earth and the ultimate powerlessness of the latter.

DEAD SEA SCROLLS. Writings on parchment found beginning in 1949 in jars hidden in caves to the west of the Dead Sea, near Qumran. Preserved in the arid climate, the writings date from the third century BCE to the first century CE. Fragments written in Hebrew, Aramaic, and Greek include portions of all the books of the Hebrew Scriptures, as well as the records of a puritanical sect of Judaism known as the Essenes, who compiled the writings.

DECAPOLIS. A region recognized in Greek and Roman Palestine (second century BCE to second century CE) consisting of the territories governed by ten (or more) semi-autonomous trading cities, all but two located east of the Jordan River. The Decapolis is mentioned several times in the Gospels. Its culture was Graeco-Roman, in contrast to the culture of the Jewish communities of nearby Galilee.

DECUMANUS. The grid of streets intersecting the *cardo* in Roman-planned cities.

DEUTERONOMY, BOOK OF. The fifth book of the Torah (the Pentateuch), Deuteronomy means "a retelling." It is purported to be the writings of Moses, forty years after the Exodus, in which he retells the story of the flight from Egypt and the giving of the Ten Commandments, and records the law that the Hebrews are to obey as they take possession of the Promised Land. Modern scholars ascribe to sixth-century compilers the version that exists in the Torah.

DIASPORA. A term that means "scattering," Diaspora can refer to the dispersion of any group of people (e.g., the Palestinian Diaspora) but is usually used to mean the communities of Jewish people living outside the Holy Land. The term can refer both to the events that precipitated the scattering (as in the Roman Diaspora), and to the lands where Jews settled.

DOME OF THE ROCK. Completed in 691, the Dome of the Rock is built on the Haram al-Sharif over the rock where Muslims believe Abraham trussed Ishmael for sacrifice, and from where Mohammed in *The Night Visit* ascended to heaven. One of the earliest and most beautiful examples of Islamic architecture. Under the Abbasids the Dome of the Rock was completely retiled, with its walls and dome completely repaired, along with those of the adjacent Haram al-Sharif compound, by builders, craftsmen, and mosaic artists from all parts of the expanding Arab caliphate. The dome was most recently retiled in the mid-sixteenth century during the reign of Suleiman the Magnificent.

DREYFUS AFFAIR. Circumstances surrounding the unjust sentencing in France of Army Captain Alfred Dreyfus, a Jew, to the penal colony on Devil's Island on false charges of treason. His cause was taken up by the novelist Emile Zola, who succeeded in winning his release. The anti-Semitism revealed during the Dreyfus Affair led Austrian reporter Theodor Herzl to found the International Zionist movement in 1895.

END TIMES. The events that, according to prophecy, will be associated with the end of the world.

ERETZ ISRAEL. A term used by Zionists to indicate all the territory commonly included in the **PROMISED LAND** (qv).

ESCHATOLOGY. That branch of theology or belief systems that deals with the End Times, or "last things."

ESSENES. A reformist and pietistic sect of Jews in the third century BCE and later who lived in separate communities isolated from others in order to practice their understanding of the Law. Knowledge of the Essenes has come from the **DEAD SEA SCROLLS** (qv).

ESTHER, BOOK OF. Written in the third or second century, the Book of Esther tells the story of a Jewish woman during the Babylonian Captivity who becomes the queen of the king of Persia and subsequently saves Jews of the kingdom from the designs of the wicked Haman. The story is celebrated by Jews in the Feast of Purim.

EXODUS, BOOK OF. The second book of the **TORAH** (qv), which relates the story of the deliverance of the Hebrews from slavery in Egypt, the giving of the Ten Commandments to Moses on Mount Sinai, and the subsequent 40-year period of wandering in the desert. Most scholars give a late sixth century date for the final compilation of Exodus in its present form, from written sources dating to the ninth century.

EXODUS, THE. The escape of the Hebrew tribes from Egypt, where they had been held as slaves, an event (probably occurring in the thirteenth century BCE) for which there is strong evidence in tradition but none in archaeology or historical record.

EZRA, BOOK OF. A book of the Old Testament where Ezra narrates the history of the Jews from the return from Babylonian Captivity in 538 BCE to about 458 BCE. It names the families that returned, tells of the rebuilding of the Temple, and of the efforts of Ezra, an emissary of the Persian ruler, to restore the observance of the Law to Israel.

FATAH.The leading Palestinian political party and the most important faction of the **PLO** (qv). Led by Yasser Arafat, Fatah carried out numerous acts of international terrorism in the 1970s and 1980s. Then in 1993, Arafat renounced terrorism and violence. Arafat maintains that Fatah has since carried on no authorized terrorist operation. However, Tanzim, the armed wing of Fatah, acts as an unofficial army of the Palestinian Authority and serves as a counterbalance to the activities of the Islamist parties Hamas and the **ISLAMIC JIHAD** (qv). Tanzim has played an active role in the Al-Aqsa Intifadeh.

FRANCISCAN ORDER. A monastic order within the Roman Catholic Church founded by St. Francis of Assisi. In the fourteenth century, a papal decree gave the

Franciscans the responsibility for maintaining all Christian holy places in the Holy Land. Those under Roman Catholic care are maintained by Franciscans to this day.

FRANKINCENSE. A gum resin that seeps from a low, small-leaved thorny tree that is found in better-watered parts of the Hadramaut, now in southern Oman. Frankincense was prized in ancient times for its scent when burned and for its medicinal and cosmetic qualities.

FUNDAMENTALISM. A global religious impulse that seeks to recover and publicly institutionalize aspects of the past that modern life has obscured. Fundamentalism in any religion insists on the literal truth of its sacred books. Fundamentalism tends to proclaim itself as the guardian of truth, usually to the exclusion of others' interpretations. In the United States, fundamentalism has been the most successful of the religious movements of the past hundred years. In other countries and among other religions fundamentalism is likewise a growing movement.

GENESIS, BOOK OF. The first book of the Hebrew Scriptures and the Old Testament containing accounts of the Creation, the Flood, and the Patriarchs Abraham, Isaac, and Jacob.

GOSPELS. The first four books of the New Testament, which tell of the life, ministry, death, and resurrection of Jesus Christ. The Gospels are named Matthew, Mark, Luke, and John.

GRAECO-ROMAN WORLD. A term referring to the culture of the lands of the eastern Mediterranean following the conquests of Alexander in the fourth century BCE. Although two hundred years of Greek rule was followed in 63 BCE by Roman conquest, and later by **BYZANTINE RULE** (qv), in the eastern lands the Greek language continued to prevail and Greek culture blended with that of Rome. The Graeco-Roman world faded after the Muslim conquests of the seventh century CE but continued in Asia Minor until the coming of the Turks in the twelfth century.

GREAT COMMISSION, THE. The missionary command of Jesus, given just before his ascension, telling his followers to go into all the world to preach the gospel.

GREEN LINE. A term that refers to the pre-1967 border between the Occupied Territories and Israel.

HADITH. The sayings of Mohammed and the traditions concerning his life, collected in books called the Hadith books.

HAGANAH. The underground military organization of the Jewish community in Palestine from 1920 to 1948.

HAJJ. The pilgrimage to Mecca required of all Muslims who are able. A person who makes such a pilgrimage is thereafter accorded the title Hajji.

HAMAS. An underground organization in Palestine formed in 1987. Hamas uses both political and violent means, including terrorism, to pursue its goal of establishing an Islamic Palestinian state in place of Israel. Hamas has an unknown number of hardcore members but tens of thousands of supporters and sympathizers.

HARAM AL-SHARIF. An Arabic name meaning "Noble Sanctuary," given about 638 CE to the area of Jerusalem that the Jews call the Temple Mount and until 70 CE was the site of the Jewish Temple. The Haram al-Sharif contains both the **DOME OF THE ROCK** (qv) and the **AL-AQSA MOSQUE** (qv).

HASHEMITE. A tribe of Bedouins from the Hejaz of Arabia who aided the British in World War I and in turn were rewarded with leadership of the state of Jordan that emerged from the British Palestinian Mandate.

HASMONEAN KINGDOM. The period in Jewish history following the **MACCABEEAN REVOLT** (qv) during which a priestly family known as the Hasmoneans ruled in Palestine. They ruled an autonomous part of Syria (142-129 BCE) and an independent kingdom (129-63) until they fell to the Romans.

HASSIDIM. A spiritual movement within Judaism that began in Eastern Europe and Russia in the eighteenth century, revived Judaism in those areas, and afterward spread throughout the world. Hassidic followers in Israel are among the most conservative of religious Jews.

HEBREW SCRIPTURES. The books that collectively form the sacred writings of Judaism. The first five books of the Hebrew Scriptures are known as the **TORAH** (qv). The canon of the Hebrew Scriptures was fixed in its present form about 150 BCE, but much of the work of assembly was accomplished following the return of the Jewish priests and scribes from captivity in Babylon, in the latter part of the sixth century. The Old Testament of the Christian Bible is essentially the Hebrew Scriptures, with slightly altered format.

HEGIRA. The flight of Mohammed and his followers from Mecca to Medina in the year 622 CE. Muslims date their calendar from this year.

HELLENIC. A term used to describe Greek civilization as spread by Alexander the Great and his successors.

HEROD'S TEMPLE. An inaccurate term for the second Temple, built by the Jews after they returned from Babylon in the sixth century. Herod the Great modified and enlarged the Temple in the last decades of the first century, and it was this modified version of the Temple that existed at the time of Christ.

HEZBULLAH. A militant, armed terrorist organization based in southern Lebanon, drawing its strength from the Shi'ite community and much of its financial support from Iran. The Hezbullah (Party of God) carries on an extensive program of social services in addition to its military concerns.

HIGH ALTAR. The inner part of the Temple, which in Solomon's time enshrined the Ark of the Covenant.

HOLOCAUST, THE. The systematic slaughter by the Nazis of six million Jews in Europe during World War II.

HOLY LAND. The land with associations sacred to three world faiths: Judaism, Christianity, and Islam. Geographically, it includes all of present-day Israel and also western Jordan, southern Syria and Lebanon, and the Sinai Peninsula.

HOLY WEEK. The week that begins with Palm Sunday, commemorating the entrance of Jesus into Jerusalem, includes the commemoration of the crucifixion on Good Friday, and ends with the commemoration of the resurrection on Easter Sunday.

HOSANNA! The message shouted by people along the way as Jesus entered Jerusalem on Palm Sunday. An ancient Hebrew acclamation, accompanied by the waving of palm branches, its meaning can vary. A literal translation is "Lord, Save!"

IN-GATHERING. A term referring to the immigration of Jews from lands of the Diaspora into modern Israel.

INQUISITION. Inaugurated in the twelfth century by the Roman Catholic Church, the Inquisition was an attempt to rid Christendom of heresy. Many Christians and Jews suffered in the brutality of the Inquisition, particularly in sixteenth-century Spain.

INTIFADEH. An uprising of Palestinians against Israeli rule. Beginning with the throwing of rocks and stones, it has escalated into suicide bombings. The first Intifadeh lasted from 1988 until 1993. The second, called the Al-Aqsa Intifadeh, began in September of 2000 and at publication is ongoing.

IRGUN. A militant armed Jewish underground organization, founded in 1931, by dissident **HAGANAH** (qv) commanders in the Palestine Mandate. Trying to end the British Mandate and bring about Israel's independence, it performed such terrorist acts as blowing up the King David Hotel in Jerusalem.

IRON AGE. The stage in the development of civilization marked by the use of iron in weapons and tools. The Iron Age reached Egypt by about 1500 BCE.

ISLAM. The monotheistic religion founded by Mohammed in the seventh century CE. Islam means "submission" to the will of God. Its Scripture, the

QURAN (qv), reveres the patriarchs and prophets of the Hebrew Scriptures, as well as Jesus Christ, as Prophets who were leading humans toward an understanding of God but teaches that the Prophet Mohammed has been given the final revelation. Islam is the world's second most widespread religion and currently the fastest growing.

ISLAMIC JIHAD. A militant Palestinian organization founded in the Gaza Strip during the 1970s. It is committed to the creation of an Islamic Palestinian state and the destruction of Israel through a Holy War (*See* Jihad). It also opposes moderate Arab governments that it believes have been tainted by Western secularism.

ISLAMISM. An ideology that demands complete adherence to the Quran and rejects, as much as possible, outside influence, with some exceptions (such as access to military and medical technology). It is imbued with a deep antagonism towards non-Muslims and has a particular hostility toward the West.

JEREMIAH, BOOK OF. The book of the Old Testament named after the prophet who lived in Jerusalem prior to and during the fall of Judah to the Babylonians (ca 620–587 BCE). He was frequently in danger from the political and religious leaders who were angry because of his prophetic messages of the coming catastrophe. Jeremiah was not taken to Babylon, and it is thought that he died in Egypt.

JEWISH LOBBY, The. Formal and informal attempts by American Jewish citizens to influence public policy in favor of Israel. The most powerful lobbying group is the American Israel Public Affairs Committee.

JIHAD. An Arabic word meaning "struggle," it can refer both to the continuing internal struggle of humans for personal betterment and to the struggle of Muslims against unbelievers. In the latter context, a Jihad is considered to be a Holy War, invoked by fundamentalist Muslims against the leaders of modernizing Arab states, or against Israel.

JOHN, GOSPEL OF. The fourth book of the New Testament, one of the four Gospels that deals with the life and teachings of Jesus. It differs in many respects from the other three Gospels and is probably based on sources different from those used by the authors of Matthew, Mark, and Luke.

JUDAISM. The oldest of the three monotheistic faiths, Judaism derives its name from the tribe of Judah, whose descendents were taken to Babylon and later returned to rebuild the Temple. As a result of this formative experience, the spiritual leaders of the returnees oversaw the final compilation of the **HEBREW SCRIPTURES** (qv) and put their stamp on Jewish worship practices. Judaism survived the **DIASPORA** (qv). Today, as always, Judaism as understood and practiced has liberal, moderate, and conservative factions.

KAABAH. The large square structure, covered with a black cloth, in the center of Mecca, Arabia. A black meteorite is set in the eastern face of the Kaabah. The

Kaabah, and in particular the meteorite, is the geographic center of Islamic worship. Muslims all over the world face the Kaabah when they pray. One of the rites of the **HAJJ** (qv) involves circumambulating the Kaabah seven times and kissing the black meteorite. Muslims believe that the Kaabah was built by Abraham (Ibrahim) when he went to visit his son Ishmael (Ismail). It is certain that its existence long predated the coming of Islam.

KAFFIYEH. A traditional Bedouin head covering worn by many Arab men, including Yasser Arafat.

KIBBUTZ, KIBBUTZIM. A type of collective farm introduced into Israel by Zionist settlers from Russia during the early part of the twentieth century. On a kibbutz, members share land ownership, most possessions, work responsibilities, and profit. Less than one percent of Israelis now live on kibbutzim.

KNESSET. The Israeli Parliament, housed in Jerusalem.

LAND-FOR-PEACE. The basis for the **OSLO ACCORD** (qv) by which Israel would surrender to a Palestinian state all land taken in the 1967 Six-Day War, including the West Bank and Gaza. Israelis who agree with the Land-for-Peace concept do not agree that it includes East Jerusalem. Palestinians insist that Jerusalem is an essential part of Land-for-Peace.

LEAGUE OF NATIONS. An international organization established after World War I. Although its demise came with World War II, many of the concepts that underlie its structure were incorporated within its successor organization, the United Nations. The headquarters of the League of Nations was in Geneva, Switzerland.

LEVITICUS, BOOK OF. The third book of the **TORAH** (qv) and the **PENTATEUCH** (qv).

LINGUA FRANCA. A common language by which people of different linguistic groups can communicate. A lingua franca often originates as a trade or administrative language. In the Holy Land during the time of Christ, both Aramaic and Greek were used as common languages.

LUKE, GOSPEL OF. The third book of the New Testament, it includes many of the instances in Jesus' life related by Matthew and Mark but also relates additional material. For this reason, it is thought that the writer of the Gospel of Luke had access to a source unknown to Matthew and Mark. Luke's Gospel, written in the seventh or eighth decade of the first century, is considered to be the first part of a narrative continued in the **BOOK OF ACTS** (qv).

MACCABBEAN REVOLT. An uprising of Jewish militants against the Seleucid ruler King Antiochus IV Epiphanes, led by the sons of a priestly family known as the Hasmoneans, beginning in 167 BCE. The term Maccabees comes from a Hebrew word meaning "hammers."

MADABA MAP. A mosaic map, covering all the territory from Mesopotamia to the Nile, set into the floor of a Byzantine church in Madaba (Jordan) during the sixth century. Much of the map survived subsequent earthquakes and attempts at reconstruction. Its jewel for historians is a representation of Jerusalem at the time, showing the street plan imposed by the Romans in the second century.

MADRASES. Religious schools, usually associated with a mosque, in which boys learn to recite the Quran.

MANDATE. A temporary rule over a territory lost by Axis powers (Germany and Turkey) during World War I and assigned by the League of Nations to Britain or France for the purpose of leading the mandate to self-government.

MARK, GOSPEL OF. The second book of the New Testament and oldest of the four Gospels. It was probably written shortly after 70 CE. With similarities to the Gospels of Matthew and Luke, it is called one of the three **SYNOPTIC GOSPELS** (qv).

MARTYR. A person who dies or is killed because of his/her faith.

MASADA. Rising above the shores of the Dead Sea, Masada is the most visited of all archaeological sites in Israel. It can be reached by cable car or on foot, from the east via the original and steep "snake path" or from the west on a path built from the old Roman ramp. Herod the Great fortified Masada and turned it into a luxurious mountain resort. In 66 CE, during the Jewish Revolt against the Romans, Masada was captured by a small group of Jews known as the Zealots. They and other refugee families held out until 72 CE when the Romans finally breached the fortress. All of the Masada defenders committed suicide rather than submit to the Romans.

MASORITIC TEXT. The traditional Hebrew Old Testament text of both Judaism and Protestantism. (The Catholic Church, historically, used the Latin translation of Jerome based on the Greek Septuagint.) Masoritic comes from the word *Masora*, which usually refers to the notes printed beside the Hebrew text by Jewish scribes and scholars. Until recently, the oldest existing manuscripts of the Hebrew Old Testament dated from the ninth century CE and onward. However, the **DEAD SEA SCROLLS** (qv) provide manuscripts that predate the previous manuscripts by about 1,000 years. A large number of the Dead Sea Scroll manuscripts agree with the Masoritic Text.

MATTHEW, GOSPEL OF. The first book of the New Testament, it is one of the four Gospels that records the life and ministry of Jesus. Scholars think that when he wrote, Matthew had access to the **GOSPEL OF MARK** (qv), as well as an additional source now lost. (*See* Synoptic Gospels.) The Gospel of Matthew was probably composed in the seventh or eighth decade of the first century. It was addressed primarily to the community of Jewish Christians in the Diaspora.

MESSIAH. A Hebrew word meaning "anointed one" and referring to a person who will deliver his people from oppression. Old Testament prophets foretold that a messiah would come into the world to save the Jewish people.

MIDDLE AGES. A loosely used term that covers the period in Europe from about 1000 CE to 1350 CE (the beginning of the Renaissance in Italy).

MILLENNIALISM. Christian fundamentalist teachings based on interpretations of prophecies in the Biblical Book of Revelation about the coming of a new millennium, when evil will be vanquished and true believers will enter a 1,000-year period of peace and harmony marking the return of Christ to earth.

MISHNA. A codified collection of oral legal interpretations of portions of the **TORAH** (qv) made in Palestine about 200 CE by Rabbi Yehudah haNasi (usually referred to simply as "Rabbi"). Together with the commentary on the Mishna, it comprises the Talmud. Next to the Scriptures, the Mishna is the basic textbook of Jewish life and thought, and is traditionally considered to be an integral part of the Torah.

MODUS VIVENDI. A way of living together.

MONOTHEISM. The concept that there is only One God, almighty and all-powerful. Judaism came earliest to this understanding. Christianity developed the concept of the Trinity (Father, Son, and Holy Sprit) in one Unity. In rejecting the Christian understanding, Islam developed a concept of One God that is closer to that of Judaism.

MOSAIC LAW. The laws given to Moses on Mount Sinai and incorporated within the **TORAH** (qv).

MOSHAV. A type of cooperative farm unit in Israel that allows some private holding of property. A moshav arrangement is halfway between the collectively owned **KIBBUTZ** (qv) and a privately owned farm.

MOSQUE. A building in which Muslims worship. Traditionally, a mosque includes an outer courtyard or area for prescribed ablution. The direction of Mecca (the qibla) is always indicated in a mosque by a niche called a mihrab. A mosque always contains a large open area where worshippers pray, facing the mihrab.

MYRRH. A gummy substance that flows from the bark of a low, thorny tree found in Arabia and Somalia. It has been used since ancient times as an ingredient in incense and perfume. Liquefied, it was the holy oil used in Hebrew ceremonies.

NEHEMIAH, BOOK OF. The book of the Old Testament that tells of the rebuilding of the walls of Jerusalem and the reform of Judaism in the middle of the fifth century, as led by the Jewish governor **NEHEMIAH** (qv) who was appointed by the Persian king.

NEW TESTAMENT. The portion of the Bible that tells of the birth, ministry, death, resurrection, and ascension of Jesus Christ (the Gospels of Matthew, Mark, Luke, and John); chronicles the spread of the early church in the first century (the Acts of the Apostles); preserves the letters of Paul and other missionaries to early Christian congregations (including Ephesians, Corinthians, Romans); and concludes with the vision of John, a mystic exiled to the island of Patmos (Revelation).

NIGHT VISIT, THE. The tradition that Mohammed ascended to heaven from Mount Moriah (the Mount where Isaac or Ishmael was trussed for sacrifice), there met Abraham, Moses, and Jesus, then returned to earth. His wife later said that he never left his bed at the time of the Night Visit, so many Muslims believe the Visit was a vision. Others believe that it actually happened, miraculously. The site of the Night Visit is memorialized in the **DOME OF THE ROCK** (qv).

NOBEL PEACE PRIZE. A prize awarded each year under the terms of the will of Swedish philanthropist Alfred Nobel to the person or persons who have made the greatest contributions to World Peace. Yitzhak Rabin and Yasser Arafat shared the Nobel Peace Prize in 1995.

NORTHERN KINGDOM. The kingdom that was formed in 930 BCE by the Hebrew tribes that lived in Galilee and Samaria following the split that occurred after the death of Solomon. The northern kingdom was often referred to as Israel, in contrast with the southern kingdom, termed Judah. In 721, the Assyrians defeated the northern kingdom and deported almost all of its population, after which they disappeared from history.

NUMBERS, BOOK OF. One of the books of the **TORAH** (qv) and the **PENTATEUCH** (qv).

OCCUPIED TERRITORIES. Territories won by Israel in the Six-Day War of 1967 and since termed "Occupied Territories" by the United Nations. Israel claims the right to build settlements in the Occupied Territories and has done so. Palestinians want Israel to surrender the Gaza Strip and the West Bank to a new Palestinian state, and Syria wants Israel to return the Golan Heights. East Jerusalem (the Old City) is also a part of the Occupied Territories.

OLD CITY OF JERUSALEM. The eastern portion of the modern city of Jerusalem, contained within the walls built by the Ottoman ruler Suleiman the Magnificent in the sixteenth century CE. The street plan of the Old City was laid out by the Romans in 135 CE (*See* Madaba Map).

OLD TESTAMENT. The first part of the Christian Bible, based on the books of the **HEBREW SCRIPTURES** (qv), slightly rearranged. For Catholics, the canon of the Old Testament (including the Apocrypha) is based partly on the **SEPTUAGINT** (qv); for Protestants, the Old Testament canon is identical to that of the Hebrew Scriptures, using the **MASORITIC TEXT** (qv).

OMAYYAD CALIPHATE. The period (661-750 CE) when the Arab Empire was ruled from Damascus.

ORIENTAL JEWS. Jews of the Diaspora who settled in North Africa and the Middle East. In present-day Israel, the culture of Oriental Jews is distinctive from that of the **ASHKENAZI** or **SEPHARDIC JEWS** (qv).

ORTHODOX. Religious or political convictions that are hued to original or standard interpretations. Orthodox Christian churches, sometimes called Eastern Orthodox churches, have their roots in the rituals and conventions that evolved when the Christian church was headquartered in Constantinople. In 1054, Orthodox churches split from the Roman Catholic Church. Among Orthodox churches today that trace their origin to Constantinople are those with ecclesial headquarters in Athens (Greek Orthodox), Erevan (Armenian Orthodox), Antioch (Syrian Orthodox), Bucharest (Romanian Orthodox), and Moscow (Russian Orthodox).

OSLO ACCORD. An understanding between Israel, represented by former Prime Minister Yitzhak Rabin, and the Palestine Liberation Organization, represented by Yasser Arafat, reached in Oslo in 1993, signed in Washington the following year, and first implemented in Palestine in 1995. The Accord created the **PALESTINIAN AUTHORITY** (qv).

OTTOMAN EMPIRE. The Empire ruled by the Turks from about 1450 to 1918. After Sultan Mehmet II captured Constantinople in 1453, the Ottoman Sultans ruled from the former Byzantine capital, which they renamed Istanbul. The most famous Ottoman sultan was Suleiman the Magnificent, who ruled in the sixteenth century. At its height in the eighteenth and nineteenth centuries, the territory of the Ottoman Empire included North Africa, southeastern Europe, western Arabia, the Holy Land, Syria, and Mesopotamia.

PALESTINE. First named "Palestine" by the Romans about 135 CE (after the long-disappeared Philistines), the region that includes the land from the Mediterranean Sea to the Jordan River, and from the slopes of Mount Hermon south to the northern reaches of the Negev Desert.

PALESTINE LIBERATION ORGANIZATION (PLO). Founded in 1964, the PLO was originally an umbrella organization of refugee and military groups, joined later by professional, labor, and student associations. Its stated purpose is to help Palestinians "to recover their usurped homes" and to replace Israel with a secular Palestinian state. To that end, it has been responsible for terrorist acts both in Israel and in other countries. Yasser Arafat has headed the PLO since 1968, when his **FATAH PARTY** (qv) merged with the PLO. Becoming a threat to national stability, the PLO was ousted first from Jordan (1970), then from Lebanon (1982). From then until the creation of the **PALESTINIAN AUTHORITY** (qv), it was headquartered in Tunisia. PLO headquarters are now in Ramallah.

PALESTINE MANDATE. The temporary rule of the former Ottoman province of Palestine awarded to Britain by the League of Nations. British rule was *de facto* as of the end of World War I but was ratified by the League in 1923. The Mandate extended east of the Jordan, where it was termed the **TRANS-JORDAN MANDATE** (qv). The League intended that Britain prepare the Mandate for self-government.

PALESTINIAN AUTHORITY. Established under terms of the **OSLO ACCORD** (qv), it exercises self-government in urban areas of Gaza and the **WEST BANK** (qv). The territory under its rule is not currently independent but is under the sovereign control of the state of Israel until its final status is settled.

PASSOVER. An ancient Hebrew celebration commemorating the exodus of the Israelites from Egypt. The term "Passover" signifies that the Angel of Death, who was to kill all first-born males, passed over the homes of the Israelites, whose doorframes were smeared with the blood of a newly slaughtered lamb or goat.

PATRIARCHS. The founding fathers of any significant movement. *See* Patriarchs, The in "People in the Holy Land Story."

PAX ROMANA. The stable conditions that accompanied Roman rule, allowing commerce to flow freely on well-maintained roads.

PENTECOST. An ancient Hebrew first-fruits festival, celebrating the harvest of winter wheat, it was usually held fifty days after **PASSOVER** (qv). It also became a celebration of the giving of the Law on Mount Sinai, traditionally fifty days after the escape from Egypt. Fifty days after the first Easter, Jews from all parts of the **DIASPORA** (qv) were assembled in Jerusalem to celebrate the festival that by this time had acquired the Greek name of Pentecost. At this festival, the Apostles, gifted by the Holy Sprit, were able to tell the story of the resurrected Jesus to the assembled crowd, each hearing it in his/her own language. Pentecost has since become a leading Christian festival.

PEOPLE OF THE BOOK. A term that includes Jews, Christians, and Muslims, whose Scriptures share the same patriarchs and prophets. During the Arab conquests, most conquerors acknowledged that the Quran grants special dispensation to People of the Book that is not to be extended to "unbelievers."

PERSIAN EMPIRE. From the mid-sixth century until the time of Alexander the Great (ca 560 to 330 BCE), the most extensive Empire the world had yet known, extending far east of Mesopotamia, almost to India, and far west of the Nile River in North Africa. In one of history's turning points, the Persian advance was stopped by the Greeks at the battles of Marathon and Salamis, thereby placing Western Europe in the debt of Greek rather than Persian culture. The Old Testament records that the Persian ruler Cyrus the Great freed the Jews from captivity in Babylon and ordered them to return home and rebuild their Temple.

PFLP Acronym for the Popular Front for the Liberation of Palestine, one of the constituent groups of the Palestine Liberation Organization (PLO). It is second in size and influence to Arafat's **Fatah party** (qv).

PILGRIMAGE. A journey to a site holy or meaningful to one's faith.

PILLARS OF ISLAM. The five duties required of every Muslim: To acknowledge that there is only One God and that Mohammed is his Prophet, to pray five times daily in the direction of the **KAABAH** (qv), to perform acts of charity, to observe a total fast from sunup to sundown during the month of Ramadan, and (if physically and financially able) to make a pilgrimage to Mecca.

POGROM. A systematic and politically sanctioned persecution of Jews, carried out particularly in cities and towns of Eastern Europe and Russia in the nineteenth and early twentieth centuries. In these pogroms, many Jews were killed and their villages were razed. Survivors fled to cities, where they were forced to live in restricted areas or ghettos.

POLYTHEISM. The worship of or belief in the existence of many gods.

PRE-MILLENNIALISM. The variant of **MILLENNIALISM** (qv) that posits a series of events that must precede the Second Coming of Christ: the return of Jews to the Holy Land, Jewish rule in the Holy Land, the rebuilding of the Temple, the deception of the Anti-Christ, the mustering of forces of evil from all parts of the world, the period of Tribulation, the **RAPTURE** (qv) of believing Christians, the climactic battle of **ARMAGEDDON** (qv) in which almost all people on earth will be killed, and the conversion of 144,000 Jews.

PROMISED LAND. The Land of Canaan, promised to Abraham and his descendents, as recorded in the Book of Genesis. It is roughly equivalent in area to the land known as **PALESTINE** (qv).

PROPHET. A man or woman with unusual abilities to predict the future. In the Old Testament, prophets were chosen by God to bring his messages to the rulers. All of the Old Testament prophets, as well as Jesus, are accepted as prophets by Muslims, who believe that the last of the prophets to whom God revealed truth directly was Mohammed.

PROTESTANTISM. The Christian community that is an offshoot of the **REFORMATION** (qv). As religious leaders broke from the churches of the Reformers, Protestant churches proliferated. Protestantism today prevails in northern Europe and in those parts of the world settled primarily by emigrants from northern European countries.

PSALMS. Poems and songs recorded in the Old Testament Book of Psalms distilling the relationship of humans to God. It is thought that some of the Psalms were composed by David as early as 1000 CE. For others, the date of composition varies. Many were written during the **BABYLONIAN CAPTIVITY** (qv) or later.

PTOLEMYS. The descendents of Alexander's generals who ruled from Alexandria in Egypt. The Ptolemys ruled much of Palestine and Trans-Jordan for several decades after Alexander's death in 330 BCE, but by 200 they had lost control of most of Palestine to the Seleucids, based in Syria.

PURIM, FEAST OF. A Jewish festival celebrating the victory of Queen Esther, wife of a Persian king, over the villainous court minister Haman, who had given orders for the mass slaying of Jews in the Empire. The event, dating to the latter years of the **BABYLONIAN CAPTIVITY** (qv) is narrated in the Old Testament **BOOK OF ESTHER** (qv).

QURAN. The Holy Book of **ISLAM** (qv). The Quran was revealed by the Angel Gabriel to Mohammed over a 22-year period from 610 to 632 CE, first in Mecca and after 622 in Medina. Because Mohammed was illiterate, he dictated the revelations to scribes, who recorded them in Arabic. Although the Quran has been translated into many languages, believers prefer to recite it in Arabic. The Quran is divided into 114 Suras, or Chapters, of varying length.

RAIN SHADOW. An area that is cut off from rain-bearing winds.

RAMADAN. A month-long period of spiritual renewal required of all Muslims (*See* Pillars of Islam). Set according to the lunar calendar, its date varies. During Ramadan, Muslims must abstain from food and drink from sunup to sundown, which can be an especially trying discipline when Ramadan falls during the heat of the summer.

RAPTURE, THE. A **PRE-MILLENNIALIST** (qv) belief that just before the period of Tribulation, which will precede the Second Coming of Christ, Christians will be raptured, or taken directly to heaven, thus being spared the horrors of the **TRIBULATION** and **ARMAGEDDON** (qv). After Armageddon, the raptured Christians will return to earth with the Second Coming and will experience his millennial reign.

RECONQUISTA. The 600-year period during which Christian rulers and armies slowly wrested the Iberian Peninsula (Spain and Portugal) from Islamic control. The Reconquista (reconquest) ended in 1492 with the defeat of the last Muslim ruler in southern Spain.

REFORMATION. A period in European history, during the sixteenth century, when the absolute authority of the Roman Catholic Church was questioned by reformers, such as Martin Luther and John Calvin, using as their authority *sola scriptura* (Scripture only), and accepting tradition or papal decrees only when they did not disagree with Scripture. Translations of Scripture into the vernacular by Tyndale (into English) and Luther (into German) were made widely available through the medium of the newly invented printing press. Out of varying interpretations of Scripture, various **PROTESTANT** (qv) groups formed. The Counter-Reformation, which followed within the Roman Catholic Church in the late sixteenth and seventeenth centuries, instituted to stem the effects of the Reformation, nevertheless led Catholic theologians to similarly examine their own traditions and sources of authority. The Reformation and Counter-Reformation led to the elevation of reason in the Age of Enlightenment.

REGISTERED REFUGEE. A refugee who seeks United Nations assistance.

RENAISSANCE. A period of cultural awakening and renewal in Europe, beginning in the fourteenth century in Italy and spreading rapidly to all parts of the continent. The Crusades led directly to the Renaissance. As the writings of the ancient Greeks came to be known through Arab translation, and Arab advances in mathematics and the sciences also reached Europe, European writers and artists began to tap sources of knowledge and cultural inspiration that had been "lost" during the long period following the fall of the Roman Empire. Art and literature flourished during the Renaissance.

RESURRECTION. The act of coming back to life after death. Christians believe that on the third day after his burial, Jesus Christ rose from the dead. An account of the Resurrection of Jesus is given in each of the four **GOSPELS** (qv).

REVELATION, BOOK OF. The last book of the New Testament, written by a seer named John (not the writer of the Gospel of John) who in the last decade of the first century was living in exile on the island of Patmos in the Ionian Sea. He writes to seven named churches in Asia Minor, setting down the visions he has received. The visions are apocalyptic (dealing with the end of the world) and highly symbolic. The attempt of some early Christians to place a literal interpretation on his images delayed the acceptance of the Book of Revelation into the New Testament Christian canon until the end of the fourth century, when it was championed by Augustine. In doing so, Augustine provided what would become the normative interpretation of the book by reading the symbolism in the Book of Revelation as just that, symbolism and not literal history. His view is the one that would eventually prevail throughout most of later Christian tradition, but it would also be rejected by the large number of Christians who look to Revelation for a literal prediction of end-time events (*See also* Pre-Millenialism).

RIFT VALLEY. A geological term indicating the down thrust that occurs between two block-fault mountains. In the case of Palestine, the hills to the east and west of the Jordan River, rising to 3,000 feet, are separated by the rift valley occupied by the river. The rift valley continues southward, where in its lowest portion it is occupied by the Dead Sea. This structural rift in the earth's crust continues through the Wadi Arabah, the Gulf of Aqaba, and the Red Sea, into Ethiopia, and into East Africa, where it is marked by a series of longitudinal lakes that occupy the rift.

ROMAN CATHOLIC. The worldwide branch of Christendom headquartered from the mid-first century in Rome and governed by an ecclesiastical hierarchy headed by a Pope. The Roman Catholic Church split from the Eastern church, headquartered in Constantinople in 1054. In the sixteenth century, the development of Protestantism further fractured Christian unity under Rome. Roman Catholicism spread to Latin America and elsewhere as Spain and Portugal developed colonies. Among branches of Christendom, Roman Catholicism has the largest number of adherents today.

SALAAM. An Arabic greeting meaning "Peace!"

SAMARITAN HERESY. The belief held by Jewish leaders, following their return from Captivity in Babylon in the late sixth century BCE, that the religious leaders of Samaria had strayed from the truth and the Samaritans were to be shunned. The Samaritans were a blend of the various peoples whom the Assyrians had settled in the central hill country two centuries previously, together with the small Jewish population who had escaped the Assyrian deportation. The Samaritans built a Temple on Mount Gerazim, and their forms of worship varied from those of ancient Judaism.

SECOND COMING OF CHRIST. A Christian belief with many variations, ranging from the view that the Second Coming is an ongoing spiritual occurrence in human lives to the literal interpretation of portions of Scripture that associate the Second Coming with predictable cataclysmic events (*See* Pre-Millennialism).

SEDER. The commemorative meal by which Jews everywhere celebrate the **PASSOVER** (qv).

SELEUCIDS. The generals who inherited the northern portion of Alexander's Empire and their descendents. The Seleucids, who ruled from what is now Syria, extended their domain into Palestine by the beginning of the second century.

SEMITIC. A subdivision of the Caucasian grouping of early peoples, with links that are primarily linguistic. Semitic languages can be grouped into a northern branch—including Akkadian (also called Assyro-Babylonian), Aramaic (including Syriac), Moabite, Hebrew, and Phoenician (now a dead language)— and a southern branch, which includes Arabic, Sabaean, and Ethiopic (Amharic). All Semitic languages are written from right to left except Amharic and Assyrian, which are written from left to right.

SEPTUAGINT. A translation of the Hebrew Scriptures into Greek, authorized by Ptolemaic rulers in Alexandria about 200 BCE but supplemented by additional material during the hundred and fifty years. It contains books not in the Hebrew Scriptures. Together, these books are called the **APOCRYPHA** (qv).

SHALOM. A Hebrew word meaning "Peace!"

SHARIA. The body of rules laid down in the **QURAN** (qv) that are the basis for a civil code in certain Muslim countries. The Sharia contains the rules by which a Muslim society is organized and governed, and it provides the means to resolve conflicts among individuals and between the individual and the state. Countries presently ruled by Quranic law are Saudi Arabia, Sudan, Iran, and the northern provinces of Nigeria.

SHARIF. A regional or tribal ruler in Arab society.

SHARM EL-SHEIKH Agreement. An understanding reached in Israeli/Palestinian negotiations in 1999 at Sharm el-Sheikh resort at the southern tip of the Sinai Peninsula. Implemented in early 2000, the agreement increased the percentage of land in the West Bank over which the Palestinian Authority has sovereignty.

SHI'A. A branch of Islam whose adherents are primarily in Iran but also in scattered communities throughout the Middle East. Shi'a broke early with the dominant **SUNNI** (qv) faction over the issue of succession. The Shi'a faction believed that Mohammed should have been succeeded by his brother-in-law, Ali. The Sunni faction backed a ruler elected by local tribal leaders. For the most part, Shi'a and Sunni understandings of Islam differ little.

SIX-DAY WAR. The war that Israel fought against Arab invaders in 1967. At the end of this war, Israel held the Golan Heights, the West Bank, and the Gaza Strip, areas now called the "Occupied Territories" by countries other than Israel.

SOLOMON'S TEMPLE. The first Temple to be built on the Temple Mount in Jerusalem about 925 BCE.

SOUTHERN KINGDOM. The remnant of the kingdom of Solomon after the northern tribes seceded to form the **NORTHERN KINGDOM** (qv) in 930 BCE. The southern kingdom was called Judah, the name of the largest of its two tribes. The other tribe that made up the southern kingdom was Benjamin. The southern kingdom lasted until 587 BCE, when it was destroyed by the Chaldeans.

STATIONS OF THE CROSS. A form of devotion that commemorates the Passion and death of Jesus. Each of the stations stands for an event that occurred, either as recorded in Scripture or by tradition. As early as 400 CE, pilgrims in Jerusalem were walking the **VIA DOLOROSA** (qv) and halting to pray at each marked Station.

SULEIMAN'S WALL. The wall surrounding Jerusalem that was rebuilt many times since the time of Christ. The Romans rebuilt the city in 135 and extended the walls at that time. Subsequent rulers repaired the walls and added gates such that the present wall little resembles the wall of 2,000 years ago. The most recent reconstruction was carried out by Suleiman the Magnificent in the mid-sixteenth century.

SUNNI. The largest and most numerous of the two major divisions of Islam (*See also* Shi'a), who early split over the issue of succession. Sunnis were those who endorsed the elected leader, Abu Bakr.

SURA. A chapter, or section, of the Quran. There are 114 separate Suras in the Quran, each divided by numbered verses.

SYNAGOGUE. A place of worship for Jews.

SYNOPTIC GOSPELS. The first three Gospels, Matthew, Mark, and Luke, whose accounts of the life of Jesus have strong concurrences and may have been taken from similar early sources, now lost.

TALMUD. A collection of rabbinical studies of the **TORAH** (qv), which date from the second century CE.

TANZIM. The militant armed wing of Arafat's **FATAH PARTY** (qv).

TELL. An archaeological term indicating a mound or low hill formed by the debris of an ancient settlement.

TEMPLE, THE. The historic center of Jewish worship. It was constructed by Solomon in Jerusalem in the eleventh century BCE, destroyed by the Babylonians in 587, rebuilt by the Jews in the latter part of the sixth century, and renovated and enlarged by Herod the Great toward the end of the first century. The Temple was destroyed by the Romans in 70 CE.

TEMPLE MOUNT. The natural rise within the city of Jerusalem where Abraham once offered Isaac (for Muslims, Ishmael) for sacrifice. Originally known as **MOUNT MORIAH** (qv), the rise was used by Solomon as a platform on which to build his Temple. The Temple Mount was the center of Jewish worship from the tenth century BCE to 70 CE, when the Romans razed the Temple. It was later (135 CE) the site of a Roman temple, but during the Byzantine period it was ignored. With the coming of Islam, the site became the Haram al-Sharif, its present designation. Over the former site of the Temple, the Muslim conquerors built the **Dome of the Rock** (qv) and facing it the Al-Aqsa Mosque.

Ten Commandments. The ten laws given to Moses on Mount Sinai, as recorded in the Book of Exodus.

Torah. The first five books of the Hebrew Scriptures as well as the Christian Old Testament (where they are designated as the Pentateuch). Included are the Books of Genesis, Exodus, Leviticus, Numbers, and Deuteronomy.

Trans-Jordan Mandate. The part of the **British Mandate of Palestine** (qv) that was east of the Jordan River. In 1946, the Trans-Jordan Mandate became the independent Hashemite Kingdom of Jordan.

Tribulation, The. According to the eschatology of **Pre-Millennialism** (qv), the period of warfare and natural disasters that will come to a climax in the Battle of Armageddon.

UNDOF (United Nations Disengagement Observer Force). A force stationed along the eastern border of the Golan Heights to keep peace between Israel and Syria. Since 1974, it has successfully carried out its mission.

United Nations. An international organization founded in 1945 as a successor to the **League of Nations** (qv). The UN is headquartered in New York City, but many of its agencies are based in Geneva, Switzerland.

UNRWA (United Nations Relief and Works Agency). The agency responsible for the welfare of refugees. A separate branch, titled **UNRWA** for Palestine Refugees in the Near East, is devoted exclusively to the maintenance of camps and welfare programs for Palestinian refugees.

Via Dolorosa. The route followed by Jesus from the Antonia Fortress to Golgotha, the place of execution. It is a pilgrimage route from early Christian times. *See also* Stations of the Cross.

Wadi. A valley in a desert area. Usually dry, it can hold a torrent of water after a sudden rain.

Wahabbi. An ultra conservative religious faction of Sunni Islam that emerged in Arabia in the eighteenth century. Wahabbi was embraced by Abdulaziz ibn Saud as he fought for control of the Arabian Peninsula in the early part of the twentieth century and established the kingdom of Saudi Arabia. Wahabbi clerics are much involved in the government of Saudi Arabia through the Ulama, or council of religious elders. Most Saudis are religiously conservative, and Saudi Arabia is governed by **Sharia law** (qv).

WEST BANK. Part of the Occupied Territories that Israel gained from Jordan in the Six-Day War in 1967. The West Bank lies west of the Jordan River. Ninety-two percent of the population of the West Bank are Palestinian, eight percent Israeli. The Palestinian Authority has responsibility for government and security in cities in the West Bank, but Israel maintains control over intervening territory.

WESTERN WALL. The only portion of the original Temple Mount that the Romans left standing when they destroyed the Temple in 70 CE. In most periods since, the Western Wall has been a destination for Jewish pilgrims. After 1967, when Israel again had control of East Jerusalem, the Western Wall once more became available to Jews who wish to pray there.

YAD VASHEM HOLOCAUST MUSEUM. Located on the Mount of Remembrance in Jerusalem, the museum exists so that the world will never forget the horrors and cruelty of the Holocaust. Its principal missions are commemorating and documenting the events of the Holocaust; collecting, examining, and publishing testimonies to the Holocaust; and collecting and memorializing the names of Holocaust victims.

ZIONISM. The idea that Palestine should be a homeland for Jews (*See* Zion, Mount). The Zionist Movement began in Britain in the nineteenth century. It gained impetus in 1895 when, following the **DREYFUS AFFAIR** (qv), Theodor Herzl organized the World Zionist Organization. In 1917, the **BALFOUR DECLARATION** (qv) put the British government officially in favor of Zionism. Supported by the movement, settlers especially from Eastern Europe began arriving in Palestine around the turn of the century and continued gradually until 1945 and 1946, when the flood of Holocaust survivors began arriving. Since Israel became independent, its national policy has been guided by Zionism.

PEOPLE IN
THE HOLY LAND

ABBASSIDS. Rulers of the Arab Empire based in Baghdad, 750-1258. They ruled in Palestine until 909.

ABDULLAH, Crown Prince of Saudi Arabia. Brother of ailing King Fadh and frequently his spokesman.

ABDULLAH, King of Jordan. First ruler of the Hashemite Kingdom of Jordan (1946-1952). Grandfather of King Hussein (1952-1999) and great grandfather of present King Abdullah II.

ABRAHAM. The first of the patriarchs, considered by both Jews and Muslims to be the founding father of their nations. (*See also Isaac and Ishmael*)

ABU BAKR. According to **SUNNIS** (qv), the first successor to Mohammed.

ALEXANDER THE GREAT. Macedonian conqueror who spread Greek culture over the known world, 333-323 BCE. In 332, he marched through Palestine, defeating the Persian contingents stationed there.

ALI (Ali ibn Abi Talib). Son-in-law of Mohammed. Believed by Shi'ites to be the legitimate successor of Mohammed.

AMMONITES. Semitic people who occupied the Trans-Jordan Plateau of Moab and frequently clashed with the Israelites.

AMOS. A prophet in the northern kingdom, beginning about 750 BCE.

ANNAS. Father of **CAIPHAS** (qv).

ARABS. A Semitic people who from ancient times occupied the Arabian Peninsula. Arabs spread northward into Palestine and Mesopotamia and westward into North Africa in the seventh century CE, following the founding of Islam.

ARAFAT, YASSER. Founder of the Fatah Party, head of the PLO, and leader of the Palestinian Authority.

ASHKENAZIM. Descendents of Jews whose migrations in the Diaspora led to settlement in Western and Eastern Europe.

ASSAD, HAFEZ. Head of the Arab Ba-ath Socialist Party and President of Syria from 1974 until his death in 2000. Succeeded by his son, Bashir Assad.

ASSYRIANS. A Semitic people whose imperial ascendancy lasted from about 1000 to 600 BCE, when they were defeated by the Chaldeans. In 723, the Assyrians overran Israel's northern kingdom and scattered its inhabitants. A few pockets of modern-day Assyrians exist today in Iraq, but the largest contingent has immigrated to the United States. They are found mostly in and around Detroit.

BABYLONIANS. A Semitic people whose empire was centered in Babylon in Mesopotamia. After defeating the Assyrians, the Babylonians ruled in the Fertile Crescent from about 600 to 650 BCE. During this period, they defeated the southern kingdom of Judah and took many of its inhabitants into exile. Babylonia was a Chaldean city-state.

BALFOUR, JAMES. Head of the British Foreign Office in 1917. He issued a declaration favoring Palestine as a homeland for Jews, providing that Arab rights would not be infringed.

BARAK, EHUD. Prime Minister of Israel from 1999-2001; succeeded by Ariel Sharon.

BATHSHEBA. Wife of King David and mother of Solomon. Enamored with Bathsheba, David arranged to have her husband, Uriah, sent to certain death in an assault on the walls of Rabboth Ammon.

BEDOUINS. Arabs who are nomadic and tribally organized. They live in arid lands of the Middle East, but they form no more than five percent of the total population.

BENJAMIN. Youngest son of Jacob, as well as the name of the tribe formed by his descendents. The tribe of Benjamin settled an area north of Judah and joined with Judah in forming the southern kingdom.

BIN LADEN, OSAMA. Saudi engineer and radical Muslim who joined Afghans in ousting the Soviets. Then with the approval of the Taliban rulers of Afghanistan stayed to organize Al-Qaeda, an international training program for terrorism. Took part in planning the World Trade Center bombing. A target of the International War on Terrorism beginning September 11, 2001, he may no longer be alive.

CEASAR AUGUSTUS. Born in 63 BCE Octavian was named Caesar Augustus, the first emperor of Rome, in the year 27 and ruled until his death in 14 CE. He was the ruler of Rome at the time of the birth of Christ.

CAIAPHAS. The High Priest in Jerusalem before whom Jesus was brought for a hearing. Caiaphas remanded him to Pontius Pilate.

CALEB. One of two named spies sent by Moses to assess circumstances in Canaan during the period of wandering in the desert.

CANAANITES. A Semitic people with iron-age technology who were living in the plateau country between the Mediterranean Sea and the Jordan River at the time when the Israelites arrived (about 1260 BCE).

CHALDEANS. A Semitic people of lower Mesopotamia who formed an empire that defeated the Assyrians about 600 BCE. Babylon was a city-state within the Chaldean Empire, and the name Babylonian is thus often given to the Chaldean Empire.

CHRISTIAN ZIONISTS. Groups of Christians organized to support Israel, believing that Palestine should be a homeland for Jews because the land of Canaan was promised by God to the Children of Israel.

CONSTANTINE. Roman emperor who in 313 CE made Christianity the official state religion. In 325, he moved the capital of his empire to Byzantium, renaming the city Constantinople.

CRUSADERS. European knights who attempted to reclaim the Holy Land for Christendom. They remained in the Holy Land from 1096 to 1290, but were ultimately defeated by the Seljuk Turks under Saladdin.

CYRUS THE GREAT. Founder and first ruler of the Persian Empire (580-529 BC), formed by uniting the two original Iranian tribes, the Medes and the Persians. Remembered for his unprecedented tolerance and magnanimous attitude towards those he defeated. Under his rule, the Jews in Babylon were freed and allowed to return to Jerusalem.

DAVID. Ruler of the united kingdom of Israel from ca 1010–970 BCE. Writer of many Psalms.

DREYFUS, ALFRED. Jewish French army captain unjustly accused of treason in 1894 and sent to Devil's Island. The Dreyfus Affair, in which his freedom was ultimately won by the author Emile Zola, triggered the organized beginning of the Zionist Movement. (*See also Herzl, Theodor*)

EDOMITES. A tribal people on the plateau east of the Dead Sea with whom the Israelites contended as they worked their way north during their wanderings. By tradition, the Edomites are descendents of **ESAU** (qv).

Esau. Oldest son of Isaac and twin brother of **Jacob** (qv). Esau, a hunter, was cheated out of his inheritance by Jacob and his mother. After, he goes to live in Edom and becomes the father of the Edomites.

Esther. As told in the Old Testament Book of Esther, a Jewish Queen in the court of a Persian ruler, who saves her people from the persecutions planned by a wicked court minister named Haman. Her story is commemorated in the **Feast of Purim** (qv).

Ethiopian Jews. A community of some 30,000 Jews in Israel, representing an ancient community of Jews in highland Ethiopia whose origins are obscure. It is thought that they may be descendants of Jews who fled Israel for Egypt after the destruction of the first Temple in 586 BCE and eventually settled in Ethiopia.

Ezra. A Jewish priest and scholar living in Babylon who led a large company of Jewish exiles back to Jerusalem in ca 458 BCE, receiving substantial Persian assistance in the undertaking. In Israel, he undertook reforms that changed the course of Judaism. Jewish tradition, unsubstantiated by modern scholarship, credits him with establishing the canon of the Hebrew Scriptures and with the authorship of the books of Ezra, Nehemiah, and Chronicles.

Fatimids. Islamic rulers in Egypt from the tenth to the twelfth centuries. Expanding into Palestine, Fatimid Sultan Hakim reversed the previous Omayyad and Abbassid tolerance towards Christians. His destruction of the Church of the Holy Sepulchre in 1009 led to the First Crusade.

Four Evangelists. The writers of the four Gospels, the first books of the New Testament, by tradition Matthew, Mark, Luke, and John.

Franciscans. Members of the clerical order established by St. Francis of Assisi.

FRANKS. Name used in the Middle Ages to designate the people who would later be called French. Among Arabs in twelfth-century Palestine, it was used as a general name to designate the Crusaders.

FUNDAMENTALISTS. Persons whose religious beliefs are based on strict and literal interpretation of the writings in their Holy Book.

GADARENES. People living within the territory under the jurisdiction of the Decapolis city of Gadara.

HAGAR. Servant of Abraham and mother of his first-born son **ISHMAEL** (qv). Later exiled by Abraham, she goes to live in Arabia, where Arabs believe her son becomes the father of the Arab nation.

HAMAN. Persian court minister whose edict against the Jews is foiled by **QUEEN ESTHER** (qv).

HASSIDIM. Members of a fundamentalist Jewish community in Israel who have a strong influence on right-wing political parties in the **KNESSET** (qv). The Hassidim were among immigrants to Israel from Russia, where Hassidism originated.

HASMONEANS. A priestly family who rebelled against the **SELEUCIDS** (qv) and established an independent kingdom in the Holy Land (167-63 BCE). (*See also Maccabees*)

HELENA. The mother of Emperor Constantine. Her journey to the Holy Land in 324 established the site of places connected with the life of Jesus.

HEROD ANTIPAS. Son of Herod the Great. Roman tetrarch in the province of Galilee and the Trans-Jordan province of Perea. Herod Antipas imprisoned John the Baptist and had him beheaded. During the week of Passover, Herod Antipas was in Jerusalem, and Pontius Pilate sent Jesus to Herod for questioning.

HEROD THE GREAT. Appointed King of Judea by the Roman Emperor Augustus. Reigned for more than thirty years until his death, either in 6 or 4 BCE. Enlarged and refurbished the Temple, built amphitheaters and baths, and established the port of Caesarea. At the time of the birth of Christ, he ordered the death of all males in the kingdom less than two years of age.

HERZL, THEODOR. Austrian Jewish playwright and reporter who was present in Paris during the **DREYFUS AFFAIR** (qv). His subsequent call for Zionism was articulated in The Jewish State: A Modern Solution to the Jewish Question. Herzl is considered the founder of Zionism.

HITTITES. People of the Hittite Empire, based in central Anatolia, who vied with Egypt for control of the Fertile Crescent during the latter part of the second millennium BCE. As individuals, Hittites are mentioned frequently in the Old Testament.

HOSEA. Prophet in the northern kingdom in the eighth century BCE. Successor to the prophet Amos.

HUSSEIN, KING OF JORDAN. Ruler of Jordan from 1952 to his death in 1999. (*See also Abdullah*)

HUSSEIN, SADDAM. Military ruler of Iraq since 1979. A member of the Ba-ath Arab Socialist Party.

IBN SAUD, Abdul Al-Aziz. Founder in 1902 of the country that bears his name, Saudi Arabia.

ISAAC. One of the patriarchs, son of Abraham and Sarah in their old age and half-brother of **ISHMAEL** (qv). As a child, Isaac was offered by Abraham for sacrifice on **MOUNT MORIAH** (qv), but at the last moment an angel stayed Abraham's hand. Nine hundred years later, the traditional place of sacrifice became the site of Solomon's Temple.

ISAIAH. Prophet in Judah, the southern kingdom, beginning about 740 BCE. Christians read Isaiah's prophesies as foretelling the birth and mission of Jesus.

Ishmael. Son of Abraham by his servant-woman Hagar and half-brother of Isaac. Sent away from Abraham's family at the insistence of **Sarah** (qv), Ishmael and his mother flee southward into Arabia. There, by tradition, he becomes the father of the Arab nation.

Israelis. Citizens of the country of Israel. Five-sixths of the population are Jews, one-sixth Arabs.

Israelites. Name given to the descendents of the twelve sons of **Jacob** (qv). Spent four hundred years in Egypt, part of the time in slavery, then escaped to wander in the wilderness for forty years before entering Canaan, the land promised to their ancestors by God.

Jacob. Third of the patriarchs, son of Isaac, grandson of Abraham. He went from the Holy Land to Haran to find a wife, stayed there twenty years, fathered twelve sons (eleven of them born in Haran). Wrestling with an angel in a dream, he realizes that the angel was really God, who tells him that henceforth he shall also be called "Israel," a name meaning "to strive with God."

Jeremiah. Prophet in Judah before and during the Babylonian conquest and deportation. He foretold the destruction of Jerusalem and the coming years of exile.

Jesus Christ. The name Jesus is a Greek version of the Hebrew name Joshua, which means "one who saves his people." The name Christ is Greek for the Hebrew word "Messiah." Jesus lived in Palestine for about thirty-three years until his death by crucifixion, his resurrection, and his ascension, about the year 29 CE. Christians believe that Jesus was the son of God, sent to redeem all people from the burden of sin. Jews acknowledge that Jesus probably lived, and may have been a prophet, but was not the Messiah promised in the Hebrew Scriptures. Muslims consider Jesus the most important of the prophets next to Mohammed but reject his divinity.

JEWS. Name given to the exiles from Judah living in Babylon. When the exiles return, and thereafter, the descendents of the remnant of the Children of Israel (the tribe of Judah, the tribe of Benjamin, and the Levites) are called Jews. Jews form the majority of the population of present-day Israel.

JOHN PAUL II. Pope of the Roman Catholic Church since 1978, he is the most traveled Pope in the history of the Church. He was born Karol Joseph Wojtyla in Poland in 1920. In the year 2000, he spent ten days on a personal pilgrimage to the Holy Land.

JOHN THE EVANGELIST. Writer of the fourth Gospel.

JORDANIANS. Citizens of the Hashemite Kingdom of Jordan. More than half are Palestinians.

JOSEPH. Eleventh son of Jacob, first son of his mother, Rachel, his father's favorite son. Sold by his brothers into Egyptian slavery, he rises to be a chief minister of Pharaoh and brings his father and brothers to live in Egypt.

JOSEPH OF ARIMATHAEA. Man who gave his family's tomb as a burial place for Christ after the crucifixion.

JOSEPH, FATHER OF JESUS. Carpenter in Nazareth (Galilee), a Judean from Bethlehem by birth, and husband of Mary, the mother of Jesus.

JOSEPHUS, FLAVIUS. Jewish historian writing after 70 CE for a Roman audience. He mentions Jesus Christ in his *Antiquities of the Jews*.

JOSHUA. One of the two named spies sent by Moses to assess the fertility of the Promised Land. Appointed by Moses to assume leadership of the Israelites, he leads them into battle against the Canaanites, about 1260 BCE. His exploits and the conquest of Canaan are narrated in the Book of Joshua, probably written at least five hundred years later.

JUDAH. One of the sons of Jacob and subsequently the largest of the Twelve Tribes of the Israelites. The territory allotted to

Judah dominated the southern part of the Promised Land and included Jerusalem. King David was of the tribe of Judah. Together with the tribe of Benjamin, Judah formed the Kingdom of Judah, the remnant of the once united kingdom of David after the northern tribes seceded. Judah was conquered by the Babylonians in 587 BCE.

KENYON, KATHLEEN. Oxford archaeologist whose discoveries concerning the age of Jericho and the location of the probable site of the crucifixion and burial of Jesus are documented in her book *Archaeology in the Holy Land,* 1970.

KHADAFFI, MUAMMAR. Ruler of Libya since 1969, Khadaffi has used oil revenues for his country's economic betterment. But in the 1980s, he became a terrorist, attempting to strike at Western targets, including an airplane shot down over Lockerbie, Scotland.

KHADIZA. Wife of Mohammed, a strong supporter, and the first to believe in his revelations.

LAWRENCE, T.E. British officer who in World War I united the tribes of the Hejaz in Arabia in revolt against the Ottomans.

LAZARUS. Friend of Jesus in the town of Bethany, brother of Mary and Martha. In one of his miracles, Jesus raised Lazarus back to life after he had been four days dead.

LEAH. The less-attractive sister of the woman whom Jacob preferred as his wife. His uncle Laban gave Leah to Jacob, then required him to work an additional seven years for Rachel.

LEBANESE. The people of Lebanon, Arabic-speaking, about one-third of whom are Christian, two-thirds Muslim.

LOST TRIBES. The descendents of the Hebrew tribes that once occupied the regions known as Samaria and Galilee. From north to south, they included Dan, Naphtali, Asher, Zebulun, Issachar, Manasseh, Ephraim, and (in Trans-Jordan) Gad and Reuben. Allied in the **NORTHERN KINGDOM** (qv), they were conquered by the Assyrians in 723 BCE and dispersed throughout the Assyrian Empire, subsequently losing their identity. A tenth tribe that has also disappeared, but was not among those captured by the Assyrians, was Simeon, whose original territory was in the northern reaches of the Negev Desert.

LOT. The nephew of Abraham, who accompanied him on his wanderings and who settled in the vicinity of the two eventually doomed cities of Sodom and Gomorrah.

LUKE THE EVANGELIST. The writer of the third Gospel as well as the Book of Acts.

MACCABEES. The leaders of the Hasmonean priestly family who led the Maccabeean Revolt beginning in 167 BCE. *Maccabee* is from a Hebrew word meaning "hammer."

MACCABEUS, JUDAS. Renowned for his generalship in the Maccabeean Revolt against the Seleucids, as well as his subsequent skill at governing.

MAIMONIDES, MOSES. Famed Jewish physician and philosopher (1135-1204) who was forced to leave Spain during the rule of the Almohads and subsequently moved to Egypt.

MAMELUKS. Rulers of the Holy Land during two centuries following the end of the Crusades. Created as a warrior caste by Saladin, the Mameluks were Caucasians purchased or captured as infants and trained as superior soldiers who owed allegiance only to their ruler. Eventually they took power and, based in Egypt, created a strong state, defeating the Crusaders and keeping the Mongols out of Palestine. They were incorporated into the Ottoman Empire in 1517 but continued to hold positions of power under the Turks.

MARK THE EVANGELIST. Writer of the second of the four Gospels that begin the New Testament.

MARONITES. Members of a Syrian Christian community whose ties are to the Roman Catholic Church in Rome. Several thousand Maronite Christians live in Israel.

MARTHA OF BETHANY. Friend of Jesus living in a town near Jerusalem; sister of Mary and Lazarus.

MARY OF BETHANY. Friend of Jesus living in a town near Jerusalem; sister of Martha and Lazarus.

MARY OF MAGDALA. Woman from the Galilean town of Magdala, whom Jesus healed of a mental illness. She became a loyal follower, was present at the crucifixion, and was among those who found the empty tomb on Easter morning.

MARY, MOTHER OF JESUS. Nazarene, of Davidic stock, who as a virgin learns that she is to become the mother of Jesus. She gives birth in Bethlehem. Mary is mentioned many times in the Gospels, most notably at the wedding of Cana and as a witness of the crucifixion. Jesus assigned her care to John, and by tradition at the end of her life, Mary lived in Ephesus.

MATTHEW THE EVANGELIST. Writer of the first of the four Gospels that begin the New Testament.

MEHMET II. Early Ottoman ruler, skilled warrior and builder, who in 1453 captured Constantinople, changed its name to Istanbul, and made it the capital of the Ottoman Empire.

MELKITES. Syrian Catholics in communion with the Roman Catholic Church who nevertheless follow Byzantine worship traditions. Melkite clergy are free to marry.

MESSIAH, The. The savior whom the Old Testament prophets foretold would come into the world to save the Jewish people. The prophecies were variously understood so that some of the Jews looked for a Messiah who would rescue them from political tyranny, while others waited expectantly for a spiritual reformer. Jesus Christ was considered the Messiah by many Jews during his lifetime but opposed by many as well.

MESSIANISTS. Jews in first-century Palestine, as well as in the **DIASPORA** (qv), who accepted Jesus Christ as the Messiah foretold by Old Testament prophets. Eventually they were to become known as Christians, along with non-Jewish believers.

MESSIANIC JEWS. Jews of present times who have converted to Christianity but who nevertheless are hued to Old Testament Jewish traditions.

MICAH. Prophet in the southern kingdom in the middle of the eighth century BCE.

MOHAMMED. Founder of the monotheistic religion called **ISLAM** (qv). Mohammed is called "The Prophet" by his followers, who are known as Muslims. Born in Mecca in 578 CE, Mohammed was a trader who could neither read nor write. Over a 22-year period, from 610 until his death, he received revelations that were written down by his followers. The revelations have been preserved in the Quran, the Holy Book of Islam. His flight from Mecca to Medina, known as the **HEGIRA** (qv), marks the beginning of the Islamic calendar.

MOSES. Chosen by God to lead the Children of Israel out of Egyptian captivity, Moses later received the **TEN COMMANDMENTS** (qv) on Mount Sinai. He led the Hebrew tribes during the forty years they wandered in the desert but died without entering the Promised Land. He is revered alike by Jews, Christians, and Muslims.

MUSLIMS. The name given to the followers of **ISLAM** (qv).

NABATEANS. A Semitic people who established a wealthy kingdom in the southern desert area of what is now Jordan. For four centuries (200 BCE to ca 200 CE), the Nabateans profited from trade between Arabia, Palestine, and the Fertile Crescent. Their kingdom was conquered by the Romans in the late first century, but they continued to function as traders.

NATHAN. A prophet who lived in the time of David and Solomon.

NEBUCHADNEZZAR. King of Babylon from 605–562. Under his reign, the southern kingdom was conquered and Judeans were taken as captives to Babylon. Nebuchadnezzar built the famous Hanging Gardens of Babylon.

NEHEMIAH. Jewish leader in the service of the Persian king in Susa. Learning of the sorry state of affairs in Jerusalem, Nehemiah asked and received permission to go to Jerusalem in 445 BCE. He supervised the repair of the walls, introduced law and order, and reformed abuses; he returned to Persia in 443 but soon after came back to Jerusalem and continued with his reforms. (*See also Ezra*)

OMAYYADS. The caliphs who ruled the Arab Empire from Damascus from 661 to 750.

ORIENTAL JEWS. Jews from the Diaspora who lived (or live) in North Africa, Ethiopia, and the Middle East.

OTTOMANS. The rulers of the Ottoman Empire, centered in Istanbul, from ca 1453 to 1918. The Ottomans were Turks, and their remnant after World War II became the modern country of Turkey.

PALESTINIAN REFUGEES. Palestinians who were displaced by Israelis as the new state of Israel was being formed (1946–1948) and after the Six-Day War in 1967.

PALESTINIANS. A blend of all the Semitic and other peoples who have lived in the Holy Land from earliest times. After the coming of Islam in the seventh century, the Palestinians adopted Arabic as their spoken and written language.

PATRIARCHS, The. Founding Fathers of both Judaism and Islam, and revered also by Christians because of Old Testament accounts. Included are Abraham; his two sons, Isaac and Ishmael; Isaac's two sons, Jacob and Esau; and Jacobs Twelve Sons, the progenitors of the Twelve Tribes of Israel. According to tradition, Abraham is the founder of both the Jewish and Arab nations, the former through Isaac, the latter through Ishmael.

PAUL. Leading early Christian missionary who founded churches throughout Asia Minor and traveled widely in the Mediterranean world. A Roman citizen from Tarsus, Paul was also a Jew schooled in theology. In an epiphany on the way to Damascus, where he was going to help eradicate the new Christian faith, his encounter with Christ changed his life and subsequently the future of Christianity.

PEOPLE OF THE BOOK. A designation that includes Jews, Christians, and Muslims, all of whose faith is grounded in Holy Books that revere the same prophets.

PHILISTINES. The "Sea Peoples" whom the Egyptians encountered on the coastlands of the eastern Mediterranean about 1450 BCE. Many scholars think they were remnants of the Minoan civilization. Technologically more advanced than the Israelites who settled on the plateau, the Philistines maintained their supremacy until they were annihilated by the Assyrians in 723.

PHOENICIANS. A Semitic people who settled in the northern coastlands of the eastern Mediterranean, they developed a maritime empire that expanded to outposts in North Africa and Spain. By the time the Assyrians defeated the Phoenicians in the eastern Mediterranean, their center had already shifted to Carthage, where they founded the Carthaginian Empire.

PILATE, PONTIUS. The Roman legate under Tiberius Caesar in command of Palestine from 26 to 36 CE. After vainly attempting to set Jesus free, he sentenced him to be crucified. Tiberius later recalled him, and he was banished by Caligula to the Danube provinces, where he died in 43 CE.

PTOLEMYS. The line of kings who ruled in Egypt upon the breakup of Alexander's Empire, beginning after 310 BCE. For the next 200 years, they fought with the **SELEUCIDS** (qv) for control of Palestine.

RACHEL. Wife for whom Jacob worked an extra seven years in Haran, in servitude to his uncle Laban. Mother of Joseph, born in Haran, and Benjamin, born in Hebron. She died giving birth to Benjamin.

RAMSES II. Pharaoh whose building projects in the Nile Delta required the labor of many slaves, including the Israelites. It is thought that Ramses II was Pharaoh at the time of the EXODUS (qv).

SALADDIN. Crusader transliteration for Salah al-Din, the commander of the Seljuk Turks who successfully captured most of the Christian forts in Palestine in the mid-thirteenth century. The Crusaders never recovered from the blows inflicted by Saladdin.

SAMARITANS. The people who emerged in the hill country between Galilee and Judea after the Assyrian defeat and dispersion of the people of northern Israel in 723 BCE and subsequent resettlement of the area with peoples from other parts of the Assyrian Empire. The Samaritans adopted a version of Judaism that the exiles, on their return from Babylon, refused to acknowledge.

SAMUEL. The prophet who in the eleventh century BCE picked Saul to begin to unite the Israelite tribes and subsequently anointed the shepherd boy David as Saul's successor.

SARAH. Wife of **ABRAHAM** (qv) and mother (in her old age) of Isaac, her only child.

SAUDIES. People who live in Saudi Arabia.

SAUL. The first king who tried to unite Israel (1020-1000 BCE). He was killed in a battle with the Philistines on Mount Gilboa near Beit Sha'an.

SCYTHIANS. Horsemen from the plains north of the Black Sea who served the ancient Egyptians as mercenaries. (*See Scythopolis*)

SEA PEOPLES. Name given by the Egyptians to the maritime invaders, the **PHILISTINES** (qv), who reached the eastern Mediterranean coast in the mid-fifteenth century BCE.

SELEUCIDS. Rulers descended from Seleucia, the general who received much of Mesopotamia, Syria, and Asia Minor as their share to rule following the breakup of Alexander's

Empire. In the third and second centuries, the Seleucids struggled with the Ptolemys for control of Palestine.

SEMITES. The term applied to a group of peoples closely related in language whose original habitat is southwest Asia. The expression is derived from the Biblical table of nations (Genesis 10), in which most of these peoples are recorded as descendants of Noah's son Shem.

SEPHARDIM. Descendents of Diaspora Jews who settled in Spain and subsequently fled to settle in North Africa or southeastern Europe.

SHARON, ARIEL. Prime Minister of Israel, 2001, and former Defense Minister and Minister in Charge of West Bank Settlements. Politically far to the right. Sharon was born in 1928.

SHI'ITES. Members of the branch of Islam centered in Iran. (*See Shi'a in Glossary*)

SOLOMON. Son of David and last ruler of the united kingdom (961-922 BCE). Under Solomon, the kingdom expanded in all directions and wealth poured into the capital in Jerusalem. Solomon built the first Temple.

SULEIMAN THE MAGNIFICENT. Sultan of the Ottoman Empire, 1520-1566. His rule was noted for opulence. In Jerusalem, he repaired the Dome of the Rock and built a new wall around the city, the one still standing today.

SUNNIS. Muslims who belong to the Sunni branch of Islam, the largest branch.

SYRIANS. Citizens of Syria.

TURKS. Descendents of Central Asian Turkic peoples who first began to occupy the Anatolian Peninsula in the eleventh century. Under their leader Saladdin, the Seljuk Turks were successful in defeating the Crusaders. The Ottoman Turks came later to power. (*See Ottomans*)

TWELVE TRIBES. The descendents of the twelve sons of Jacob, also called the Children of Israel, who following the escape from Egypt and the subsequent wanderings in the desert, came to occupy parts of the Promised Land (the Land of Canaan) allotted by Moses to each. (*See also Lost Tribes*)

UNIATES. Members of churches that follow rites derived from ancient traditions of Christian churches in the East. They are considered to be Catholic Christians and are allied with the Catholic Church in Rome. (*See Melkites, Maronites*)

URIAH. A Hittite, husband of **BATHSHEBA** (qv). Sent by David to die in the assault on the walls of Rabboth Ammon.

ZIONISTS. Those who are motivated by **ZIONISM** (qv).

ZOLA, EMILE. French author who played a leading role in the **DREYFUS AFFAIR** (qv).

PLACE NAMES

Abila. Northernmost of the Decapolis archaeological sites in Jordan.

Acco. City in Israel, north of Haifa, pop 46,000. Ancient Mediterranean Port called Ptolemais during the period when the Ptolemys occupied Palestine. Called Acre by Crusaders. Archaeological site.

Acre. *See* Acco.

Aden. Arabian seaport in Yemen.

Aelia Capitolina. Roman name for Jerusalem after 135 BCE.

Afghanistan. Country where Al-Qaeda operatives trained under Osama bin Laden.

Al-Aqsa Mosque. Mosque built in seventh century CE on the Haram al-Sharif.

Alexandria. City in western part of Egypt's Nile delta, founded by Alexander the Great Pop 3.3 million.

Al-Haram al-Sharif. Arab name for the former Temple Mount in Jerusalem. In Arabic, "The Noble Sanctuary."

Amman. Capital of Jordan, located in the central west portion of the country, pop 1.3 million. Called Philadelphia in Graeco-Roman times.

AMMON. Ancient kingdom west of the Jordan River within the plateau area known as Moab.

ANATOLIA. Name for the area included within the Anatolian Peninsula.

ANATOLIAN PENINSULA. Westernmost peninsula of Asia, bordered by the Black, Ionian, and Mediterranean Seas. Also known as Asia Minor. Occupied by the modern country of Turkey.

ANTIOCH (Antakya). City in southeastern Turkey on Syrian border. Site of early Christian churches.

AQABA. Jordan port city located on the Gulf of Aqaba.

ARAB MIDDLE EAST. Includes the Arab-speaking countries of the Middle East: Egypt, Jordan, Lebanon, Syria, Iraq, Yemen, Saudi Arabia, Oman, Qatar, Bahrain, and the United Arab Emirates. Excludes Israel, Turkey, and Iran.

ARAB QUARTER. Arab section of the Old City of Jerusalem.

ARAB STATES. Countries where Arabic is the chief spoken language. In addition to the **ARAB MIDDLE EAST** (qv), Arab States include Libya, Algeria, Morocco, Mauritania, and Sudan.

ARABIA. Loosely defined in ancient times to include all desert areas south of the Fertile Crescent and east of the better-watered Trans-Jordan Plateau areas.

ARABIAN DESERT. The area of very low rainfall extending from the Red Sea to the Persian Gulf. The highlands of Yemen are excluded from the "Desert" designation.

ARABIAN PENINSULA. The landmass bordered by the Red Sea, the Arabian Sea, and the Persian Gulf.

ARAFAT'S ISLANDS. Term sometimes used to designate the noncontiguous urban areas over which the Palestinian Authority has complete control.

ARAM. Ancient kingdom within the Fertile Crescent, north and east of Damascus.

ARMENIAN QUARTER. Smallest of the four sections of the Old City of Jerusalem.

ASHDOD. Israeli port city, pop 188,000. Site of ancient Philistine port.

ASHKELON. Israeli port city, pop 104,000. Archaeological site revealing bronze and iron age Egyptian and Philistine occupation.

ASIA. As distinguished from Europe, all the land east of the Dardanelles, the Bosporus, and the Sea of Marmara. The Middle East is sometimes designated as Southwest Asia.

ASIA MINOR. The **ANATOLIAN PENINSULA** (qv).

ASSYRIA. Ancient kingdom centered in northern Mesopotamia with its capital at Nineveh.

BABYLON. Ancient Chaldean city-state on the Euphrates River that expanded into the Babylonian Empire (BCE) and the Neo-Babylonian Empire (BCE).

BAGHDAD. City on the Tigris River, est. pop 5,000,000. Capital of Iraq. Seat of the **ABBASSID CALIPHATE** (qv).

BAHRAIN. Island in the Persian Gulf off the coast of Saudi Arabia; a sovereign country whose territory is Bahrain Island.

BALKAN LANDS. Countries of the mountainous peninsula of southeastern Europe known as the Balkans. Present day countries include Croatia, Serbia, Macedonia, Bosnia, Albania, and Bulgaria. The Balkan appellation does not usually include Greece.

BANIAS. Part of a natural park on the slopes of Mount Hermon in far northern Israel. Springs in Banias are one of the sources of the Jordan River. Called Caesarea Philippi during Roman times.

BEATITUDES, Mount of the. A hillside near Capernaum where Jesus preached his Sermon on the Mount, which included the Beatitudes (Blessed are…) as well as the Lord's Prayer.

BEERSHEBA. A town in the Negev, south of the Dead Sea, occupying an ancient site of the same name.

BEIRUT. The capital of Lebanon, located on the Mediterranean Sea. Est. pop 1,600,00.

BEIT SHA'AN. Town south of Sea of Galilee occupying strategic position in Jezreel Valley between Jordan River and Mediterranean coast. Important archaeological site. Pop 16,000.

BETHANY. Village east of Jerusalem on the way to Jericho.

BETHLEHEM. Town about ten miles south of Jerusalem, pop 25,000. Birthplace of Jesus.

BIBLICAL PROMISED LAND. The territory promised to the descendents of Abraham: from the southern slopes of Mount Hermon in the north to the Negev Desert in the south, and from the Mediterranean Sea in the west to the Jordan River and the Dead Sea in the east.

BITHYNIA. Roman province in the northern part of Anatolia.

BOSPORUS. Strait separating Europe from Asia, and Turkey's European provinces from its Asiatic mainland. Istanbul is on the west side of the strait.

BYZANTIUM. Greek name for the city on the west side of the **BOSPORUS** (qv) that became Constantinople in 315 CE and Istanbul in 1453.

CAESAREA. Mediterranean port city used by the Romans when they ruled Palestine. Now an archaeological site, about twenty miles south of Haifa.

CAESAREA PHILIPPI. Resort in far northern Galilee built by the son of Herod the Great. Now known as Banias and included within an Israeli national park.

CAIRO. Capital of Egypt, located on the lower Nile River. Est. pop 7 million.

Camp David. Presidential retreat in Maryland frequently used as a site of international conferences.

Cana. Village three miles north of **Nazareth** (qv) where Jesus performed his first miracle. Now the Arab town of Kafr Kanna, pop 11,500.

Canaan. *See* Biblical Promised Land.

Capernaum. Village on the northern shore of the Sea of Galilee around which Jesus' ministry was centered. Now an archaeological site.

Cappadocia. Early Christian site in central Anatolia.

Carmel, Mount. A ridge, rather than a mount, that marks the south side of the Jezreel Valley and terminates in Haifa.

Carthage. Phoenician colony on the coast of North Africa in what is now Tunisia.

Central Highlands. Hill country between the Mediterranean Sea and the Jordan Valley.

Chaldea. The area in the southern part of Mesopotamia inhabited by the Chaldeans in the early part of the first millennium BCE. Its chief city was Babylon.

Chaldean Empire. Synonymous with the Neo-Babylonian Empire (*See* Babylon).

Christian Quarter. Section of the Old City of Jerusalem that contains the Church of the Holy Sepulchre.

Constantinople. City that was the capital of the Byzantine Empire. Located on the western side of the **Bosporus** (qv) in what is now Turkey. Called **Istanbul** (qv) after 1453.

Cordoba. City in southern Spain that was once an Arab city of culture and learning.

Corinth. City in ancient Greece and site of an early Christian community.

Cyprus. Large island in the eastern Mediterranean.

DAMASCUS. Ancient and modern city in Syria, pop 3.5 million. Located on Fertile Crescent trade route.

DAN. The northernmost location in ancient Israel, on the lower slopes of Mount Hermon.

DEAD SEA. Lowest surface on earth, 1,290 ft. below sea level, occupying a geological trough that also includes the Sea of Galilee, Jordan River, Wadi Arabah, Gulf of Aqaba, and Red Sea.

DECAPOLIS. A regional name given in Graeco-Roman times to the (mostly) Trans-Jordan location of the league of ten semi-autonomous trade cities collectively called by that name.

DECAPOLIS CITIES. Of the ten cities that once were considered part of the **DECAPOLIS** (qv), Amman (once Philadelphia) is now the capital of Jordan, Damascus is the capital of Syria, and Beit Sha'an (once Scythopolis) is a small city in Israel. The remainder are archaeological sites: Gerasa (Jerash), Pella, Abila, and Gadara in Jordan, Capitolia and Dium in Syria, and Hippos in Israel.

DIASPORA, JEWISH. Countries or regions where Jews displaced from their homes in Palestine settled or to which they or their descendents were subsequently scattered.

DIASPORA, PALESTINIAN. Countries or regions, chiefly in the Middle East, where Palestinians displaced from their homes in Israel are now living.

EAST JERUSALEM. The Old City, retained by Jordan in the Arab-Israeli war of 1948 but taken by Israel in the Six-Day War in 1967.

EDOM. Ancient name for the area of the Jordan Plateau, east of the Dead Sea.

EGYPT. Country in the northeastern corner of Africa, adjacent (in the Sinai Peninsula) to Israel.

EILAT. City at the southern tip of the Negev Desert on the Gulf of Aqaba, pop 43,000.

EPHESUS. Greek and Roman city on the west coast of Asia Minor. An archaeological site today.

ETHIOPIA. Country in the highlands of East Africa, west of the Red Sea.

EUPHRATES RIVER. One of the two rivers that encompasses Mesopotamia (the Land Between the Rivers) and joins to flow into the Persian Gulf. With its headwaters in Turkey, it flows through Syria into Iraq.

FERTILE CRESCENT. The ancient route between the Persian Gulf and the Mediterranean Sea, beginning in the irrigated lowlands of **MESOPOTAMIA** (qv) and following the grasslands between the mountains to the north and the desert to the south to reach the hill country and coastlands of Palestine. The route continues along the Mediterranean coastlands southward and westward into the Nile Valley.

FEZ. City in northern Morocco, pop 413,000. Early Arab center of learning and culture.

GADARA. Archaeological site in northern Jordan, near the Yarmouk River. Once a Decapolis city.

GADARENES, LAND OF THE. Term in the Gospel of Luke (8:26) referring to the area along the south coast of the Sea of Galilee in the territory administered by the Decapolis city of **GADARA** (qv).

GALATIA. Roman province in Asia Minor.

GALILEE. Northern part of Israel.

GAZA. City in the Gaza Strip, serving as the Gaza Strip headquarters of the Palestinian Authority. Pop 367,000.

GAZA STRIP. Occupied Territory in the southwest part of Israel, fronting the Mediterranean Sea. Under partial control of the Palestinian Authority.

GENNESARET, LAKE OF. One of the names given in the Gospels for the Sea of Galilee.

Gerasa. A Decapolis city. Now an archaeological site in west central Jordan. The Arabic name for the site is Jerash.

Gerazim, Mount. Mountain in Samaria on which the **Samaritans** (qv) built a Temple.

Germanic Lands. Lands in Europe north of the Roman Empire.

Gethsemane, Garden of. Located at the base of the Mount of Olives, across the Kidron Valley from Jerusalem.

Gilboa, Mount. Overlooks the Jezreel Valley, near Beit Sha'an.

Golan Heights. Occupied Syrian Territory in the northeast part of Israel.

Golgotha. Stated place of the crucifixion, outside the walls of Jerusalem.

Gomorrah. One of two ancient cities (the other Sodom) said to have been located near the southern end of the Dead Sea.

Goshen. Fertile area in the northeast part of the Nile delta.

Graeco-Roman World. Particularly refers to the eastern part of the Roman Empire.

Greater Syria. In ancient times included Lebanon, northern Palestine, and northern Trans-Jordan.

Gulf of Aqaba. Northward extension of the Red Sea, giving both Israel a southern port and Jordan its only port.

Gulf of Eilat. Name sometimes given by Israelis to the Gulf of Aqaba.

Gulf of Suez. Extension of the Red Sea into Egypt. The Gulf of Aqaba and the Gulf of Suez border the Sinai Peninsula.

Hadramaut. The exceedingly dry southern coast of the Arabian Peninsula, shared by Oman and Yemen.

Haifa. Chief port city of Israel on the Mediterranean Sea. Pop 276,100.

HARAM AL-SHARIF. *See* Al-Haram al-Sharif.

HARAN. Ancient site in the northern part of the Fertile Crescent; now within Turkey but at the time of Abraham within the kingdom of Padan Aram.

HASHEMITE KINGDOM OF JORDAN. Official name of the country to the east of Israel, bound on the west by the Jordan River.

HASMONEAN KINGDOM. The territory, roughly equivalent to the ancient United Kingdom of Israel, ruled by the Hasmonean kings from 167 to 63 BCE.

HEBRON. City in the southern part of the Palestinian Authority, pop 406,000.

HEJAZ. Western mountainous region of the Arabian Peninsula.

HELLESPONT. Ancient name for the Bosporus, connecting Europe and Asia.

HERMON, MOUNT. Mountain in Syria, north of Israel. Mount Hermon's lower slopes are within Israel.

HILL COUNTRY. Designation for the higher rolling country between the Mediterranean Sea and the Jordan Valley. The elevation rises to 3,000 feet.

HIPPOS. A Decapolis city in the hills east of the Sea of Galilee. Now an archaeological site.

HIRA, MOUNT. Mountain near Mecca where Mohammed received his first revelations.

HOLY LAND. The land with associations sacred to three world faiths: Judaism, Christianity, and Islam. Geographically, it includes all of present-day Israel and also western Jordan, southern Syria and Lebanon, and the Sinai Peninsula.

HOREB, MOUNT. Alternate name for Mount Sinai.

HULA LAKES. Small lakes in the lowlands of far northern Israel that collect the waters from Mount Hermon and send them southward to the Sea of Galilee and the Jordan River.

IBERIAN PENINSULA. Peninsula shared today by Spain and Portugal.

IDUMEA. Roman province in the northern Negev.

INDUS RIVER. River that flows southward in Pakistan to reach the Arabian Sea.

IRAN. Ancient Persia. Bordered today by Iraq on the west, Afghanistan and Pakistan on the east.

IRAQ. Country that contains ancient Mesopotamia. Its borders are with Iran, Kuwait, Saudi Arabia, Jordan, Syria, and Turkey.

ISLAMIC LANDS. The part of the world to which Islam has spread. Includes all of North Africa, northern parts of sub-Saharan Africa, all of the Middle East except Israel, Afghanistan, Pakistan, Bangladesh, Malaysia, Indonesia, and the southern Philippines.

ISRAEL. The name given to the northern kingdom in the tenth to eighth centuries BCE. Now the name of the modern country of Israel.

JAFFA. Ancient port city, south of Tel Aviv.

JEBEL MUSA. Means "the Mount of Moses." An alternative name for Mount Sinai.

JENIN. City in the northern part of the West Bank, pop 203,000.

JERASH. Arab name for the archaeological site of **GERASA** (qv).

JERICHO. Ancient city west of the Jordan River near where it empties into the Dead Sea. Now within the Occupied Territories. Pop 32,700.

JERUSALEM. Located in the southern part of the plateau that rises from the Jordan Valley, about 25 miles from Jericho, 50 miles from Tel Aviv. Israel's capital and largest city. Includes the **OLD CITY** (qv) in the eastern part and a modern western part. Pop 675,000.

JERUSALEM, Old City of. *See* Old City of Jerusalem.

JEWISH QUARTER. The Jewish section of the Old City of Jerusalem.

JEWISH SETTLEMENTS. Scattered throughout the West Bank, the Golan Heights, and the Gaza Strip.

JEZREEL VALLEY. Ancient east-west route south of the Sea of Galilee, leading from the Jordan Valley to the Mediterranean Sea.

JOPPA. Ancient Philistine port, now known as Jaffa. Forms the southern part of Tel Aviv.

JORDAN. *See* Hasemite Kingdom of Jordan.

JORDAN PLATEAU. Highlands to the east of the Jordan Valley and the Dead Sea.

JORDAN RIVER. Flows out of the Sea of Galilee into the Dead Sea.

JORDAN VALLEY. Broad valley in which the Jordan River flows, bordered to east and west by highlands.

JUDAH. Name of the southern kingdom that followed the breakup of the united kingdom ruled by Solomon.

JUDEA. Romanized name of Judah; the southern of the three parts of Palestine: Galilee, Samaria, and Judea.

JUDEAN DESERT. The eastern slopes of the Judean hills, fronting the Jordan Valley. The Judean Desert lies in a rain shadow, cut off from moisture that reaches the Plateau.

KARAK. City in Jordan on the King's Highway in the area once known as Edom. Site of a Crusader castle. Pop 22,700.

KHAN YOUNIS. Second most populous city in the Gaza Strip. Located in the south central part of the territory. Pop 204,700.

KIDRON BROOK. Watercourse intervening between the Mount of Olives and the Old City of Jerusalem.

KINGS' HIGHWAY. Ancient route from Damascus southward in Jordan, along the western edge of the Plateau, leading to

Petra and the Gulf of Aqaba. Used as early as the second millennium BCE.

KINNERET, LAKE. Official Israeli name for the Sea of Galilee.

KUWAIT. Small oil-rich country on the Persian Gulf, bordered by Saudi Arabia and Iraq.

LEBANON. Country bordered by the Mediterranean on the west, Israel on the South, and Syria on the north and east.

LEVANT. Term referring to the coastal areas of the eastern Mediterranean.

MADABA. City in Jordan west of Amman. Site of the **MADABA MAP** (qv). Pop 80,300.

MAGDALA. Town near the western shore of the Sea of Galilee in the time of Jesus.

MALTA. Island in the Mediterranean Sea, south of Sicily and east of Tunisia.

MASADA. Archaeological site. Knoll rising west of the Dead Sea, fortified by Herod the Great, captured and defended to the death by zealots in 73 CE.

MECCA. City in Saudi Arabia, about 40 miles inland from the Red Sea. Birthplace of Mohammed. Site of the **KAABAH** (qv).

MEDINA. City in Saudi Arabia about 200 miles north of Mecca. Mohammed fled from Mecca to Medina in 622 CE, the date on which Muslims begin their calendar.

MEDITERRANEAN COASTLANDS. Lowlands bordering the Mediterranean Sea.

MESOPOTAMIA. Name given to the fertile land between the Euphrates and Tigris Rivers. One of the earliest centers of civilization.

MIDDLE EAST. Term that generally includes the Arab-speaking countries from Egypt to Iraq, plus Turkey, Israel, and Iran.

Some scholars also include the countries of Libya, Tunisia, Algeria, and Morocco in North Africa.

MIDIAN. The southernmost and driest part of the Jordan Plateau. An ancient designation, not in current usage.

MOAB. The well-watered part of the Jordan Plateau west of the Dead Sea. An ancient designation, not in current usage.

MOAB PLATEAU. *See* Moab.

MORIAH, MOUNT. The name of the hilly area where Abraham was told to sacrifice Isaac (Ishmael to Muslims). On a high part of the area, Abraham built an altar and prepared to slay his son. The area was subsequently named Mount Moriah, or The Mount of Sacrifice. The city of Jerusalem grew up around Mount Moriah. Solomon chose it as the site of his Temple, on the **TEMPLE MOUNT** (qv). After 638 BCE, Muslims built the **DOME OF THE ROCK** (qv) there. *See also* Zion, Mount.

MUSLIM WORLD. *See* Islamic Lands.

NABATEA. Empire controlled by the Nabateans from their capital at Petra, now an archaeological site, in southern Jordan.

NABLUS. City in the West Bank that was once knows as **SHECHEM** (qv), pop 262,000.

NAZARETH. City south and west of the Sea of Galilee, pop 64,000.

NEBO, MOUNT. Mountain peak in Jordan overlooking the northern edge of the Dead Sea. From this height, Moses got a view of the Promised Land before he died. Elevation 2,700 ft.

NEGEV DESERT. The dry area of southern Israel, extending roughly from Beersheba to Eilat.

NETANYA. City in Israel on the Mediterranean coast, north of Tel Aviv, pop 171,000.

NORTHERN KINGDOM. Territory of the tribes who split from the united kingdom ruled by Solomon. The territory included all of Galilee and Samaria.

OCCUPIED TERRITORIES. Areas won by Israel in the Six-Day War of 1967 and since termed "Occupied Territories" by the United Nations. Israel claims the right to build settlements in the Occupied Territories and has done so. Palestinians want Israel to surrender the Gaza Strip and the West Bank to a new Palestinian state, and Syria wants Israel to return the Golan Heights. East Jerusalem (the Old City) is also a part of the Occupied Territories.

OLD CITY OF JERUSALEM. The eastern portion of the modern city of Jerusalem, contained within the walls built by the Ottoman ruler Suleiman the Magnificent in the sixteenth century CE. The street plan of the Old City was laid out by the Romans in 135 CE (*See* Madaba Map).

OLIVES, MOUNT OF. Hill to the east of the Old City of Jerusalem.

OMAN. Country occupying the southeast portion of the Arabian Peninsula.

OTTOMAN EMPIRE. At its peak in the eighteenth century, held suzerainty over southeastern Europe, Anatolia, Palestine, the Fertile Crescent, Mesopotamia, and North Africa from its base in Istanbul.

PADAN ARAM. Name of the area north and east of Damascus controlled by the Arameans from the early part of the second millennium. Subsequently changed to **ARAM** (qv).

PAKISTAN. Country to the east of Afghanistan and Iran, including within its territory the fertile valley of the Indus River.

PALESTINE. Name given by the Romans in the early second century to their province at the eastern end of the Mediterranean, from the sea to and beyond the Jordan, and from the slopes of Mount Hermon southward to the northern

Negev. Name based on the Philistines, who by that time were extinct as a people.

Palestine Mandate. The mandate given to Britain by the League of Nations after World War I to rule over Palestine. The mandate extended from Lebanon and Syria on the north to the Gulf of Aqaba on the south, and from the Mediterranean Sea on the west to the Arabian Desert in Jordan on the east. The portion of the mandate east of the Jordan River became the Trans-Jordan Mandate.

Palestinian Authority. The areas of the West Bank and Gaza over which the Palestinian Authority has total or partial control.

Paran, Wilderness of. Area in the southern part of the Negev mentioned in the Exodus account of the wanderings of the Israelites.

Pella. Decapolis city during the Graeco-Roman period, now an archaeological site under restoration in Jordan. Located east of the Jordan River and north of Jerash (Gerasa).

Perea. Roman district centered in the Jordan Valley, east of the river and north of the Dead Sea.

Persia. Empire ruled from Susa in what is now Iran, from ca 550 to 330 BCE, extending eastward to the Indus and westward to include the Fertile Crescent, Asia Minor, portions of Greece, Palestine, the Nile Valley, and the North African coastlands.

Persian Gulf. Body of water that separates Arabia from Iran and connects through the Straits of Hormuz with the Arabian Sea.

Petra. Capital of the Nabatean Empire. Archaeological site in southern Jordan.

Philadelphia. Greek name given to **Amman** (qv), ancient city of Ammon and now the capital of Jordan (*See* Amman).

Philippi. City in the northeastern part of Greece during Graeco-Roman times.

Philistia. Territory ruled by the **Philistines** (qv). *See* Land of the Philistines.

Philistines, Land of the. Term referring to that part of the Mediterranean coastlands and adjacent highlands inhabited by the Philistines.

Phoenicia. Territory inhabited in the second and first millennia by the maritime peoples known as the Phoenicians, roughly equivalent to coastal Lebanon and northern Israel.

Poitiers. City in France that marked the furthest northward advance of Arab conquest. The Arabs were turned back at the nearby battle of Tours in 732 CE.

Pontus. Northeast province of Roman Asia Minor, with the Black Sea on the north, Cappadocia on the south, and Galatia on the west.

Portugal. Country in the western part of the Iberian Peninsula. Bordered on the west and south by the Atlantic Ocean, on the east and north by Spain.

Promised Land. *See* Biblical Promised Land.

Qatar. Persian Gulf country occupying a small peninsula projecting into the Persian Gulf from Arabia.

Qumran. Location of the first site where the Dead Sea Scrolls were found. In rough, cave-riddled country west of the northern part of the Dead Sea.

Quneitra. Town now in Syria on eastern border of the Golan Heights, within territory monitored by the United Nations. From 1967 to 1974 within territory occupied by Israel. Destroyed by Israelis in 1974.

Rabbath Ammon. Ancient walled city of the **Ammonites** (qv). Site of present-day **Amman** (qv), capital of Jordan.

Rafah. City near the southern border of the Gaza Strip, pop 123,000.

Ramallah. West Bank city located about ten miles north of Jerusalem, pop 214,000.

Red Sea. Body of water separating the Arabian Peninsula from Africa.

Riyadh. Capital of Saudi Arabia. Located in an oasis in the center of the country. One of the world's fastest-growing cities, est. pop 4.6 million.

Roman Empire. Extended at its height in the second century CE from Britain to Mesopotamia and Palestine, and from all of southern Europe to all of North Africa.

Roman Palestine. Land from the Mediterranean Sea eastward to the western portions of the Jordan Plateau, and from Syria in the north to Nabatea and the Negev in the south.

Rome. The capital of the Roman Empire, now the capital of Italy, and (in the Vatican) the headquarters of the Roman Catholic Church.

Russia. Country of origin of most immigrants to Israel in the past two decades.

Russian Steppes. Grasslands north of the Black Sea. Homeland of mercenary mounted Scythian warriors.

Samaria. Hill country of central Palestine. Included within the West Bank portion of the Occupied Territories. Historically the central of the three regions of the ancient kingdom of Israel. Included within the northern kingdom after the kingdom of Solomon was divided.

Saudi Arabia. The largest country in the Arabian Peninsula.

Sayda. *See* Sidon.

Scythia. The grassland region north of the Black Sea from which Scythian mercenaries were recruited by Hittites, Egyptians, and other ancient empires.

Scythopolis. Greek name for **Beit Sha'an** (qv). One of two **Decapolis** (qv) cities in what is now Israel.

SEA OF GALILEE. Actually, a lake, receiving the waters flowing southward off the slopes of Mount Hermon and sending them south in the Jordan River to the Dead Sea. Other names for the Sea of Galilee are the Lake of Tiberius, the Sea of Gennesaret, and Lake Kinneret.

SEA OF REEDS. Swampy area north of the Red Sea mistranslated in early Old Testament sources as the Red Sea.

SECOND TEMPLE. The Temple built by the Jews who returned from Babylon on the site of Solomon's Temple. Completed in 515 BCE. Enlarged by Herod the Great in the last two decades of the first century. Destroyed by the Romans in 70 CE.

SEPPHORIS. City of hellenized Jews, with evidence of wealth and sophistication, located about four miles north of Nazareth during the time of Christ. Now an archaeological site.

SHARM EL-SHEIKH. Egyptian resort at the southern tip of the Sinai Peninsula. Occasional site of international meetings involving Israel and the Palestinian Authority.

SHARON VALLEY. Broad area of the coastal plain of Israel, between Tel Aviv and Haifa.

SHEBA. Homeland of the Queen who is said to have visited Solomon in the tenth century BCE. Generally assumed to be Saba, the highlands of present-day Yemen. But may possibly have been located in the highlands of Ethiopia.

SHECHEM. Ancient name for the present West Bank city of **NABLUS.**(qv). Located in the central highlands. Abraham stopped in Shechem, and Israel's kings were crowned there.

SICILY. Island portion of Italy separated from the mainland by the Straits of Messina. Its chief city in Graeco-Roman times was Syracuse.

SIDON. Ancient Mediterranean port city in Lebanon, pop 200,000.

SILK ROAD. Caravan route that led from the Mediterranean through Central Asia into China. Lost some of its importance when maritime contacts were established between Europe and the Far East.

SINAI DESERT. A continuation of the Arabian Desert.

SINAI, MOUNT. Mountain peak in the southern part of the Sinai Peninsula. Also called Mount Horeb and Jebel Musa (the Mount of Moses). Here Moses received the Ten Commandments.

SINAI PENINSULA. Peninsula between the Gulf of Suez and the Gulf of Aqaba, fronting the Mediterranean Sea on the north.

SLAVIC LANDS. Countries where Slavic languages are spoken. These include Russia, Poland, the Czech and Slovak Republics, Serbia, Croatia, Bosnia, Macedonia, and Bulgaria. Serbs, Bulgarians, and Russians use the Cyrillic alphabet, based on Greek and introduced from Constantinople. Most of their population is **EASTERN ORTHODOX** (qv). Other Slavic countries use the Latin alphabet, and most of their population is Roman Catholic.

SODOM. One of two ancient cities (the other Gomorrah) said to have been located near the southern end of the Dead Sea.

SOLOMON'S TEMPLE. The first Jewish Temple, built in Jerusalem by Solomon on **MOUNT MORIAH** (qv).

SOUTHERN KINGDOM. The part of the united kingdom that remained when the northern tribes seceded in 931 BCE. Included the territories of the tribes of Judah and Benjamin. Thereafter named Judah, after the larger of the two. Included the hill country in the southern portion of the united kingdom, from the vicinity of Jerusalem into the northern part of the Negev.

SPAIN. Larger of the two countries that occupy the **IBERIAN PENINSULA** (qv).

St. Catherine's Monastery. Located high on a mountainside within view of Mount Sinai, in the southern part of the Sinai Peninsula.

Suez Canal. A big ditch (without locks) connecting the Mediterranean Sea and the Red Sea via the Gulf of Suez.

Suleiman's Wall. The most recent of the many walls built, modified, or reinforced through the centuries to surround Jerusalem. Suleiman's Wall dates to the mid-sixteenth century.

Sumer. Most ancient of Mesopotamian civilizations, comprising a number of city-states whose welfare depended on irrigated agriculture and trade. The Sumerian civilization dates to 3500 BCE. It was still in existence at the time of Abraham, about 1850 BCE, when Abraham left the Sumerian city-state of **Ur** (qv). By that time, however, the Babylonians were in ascendancy in the region.

Susa. Capital of the Persian Empire. Located in western Persia, about 75 miles west of the Tigris River and about 250 miles north of the Persian Gulf.

Syria. In its present configuration, Syria as a country is bordered by Lebanon, Turkey, Israel, and Iraq. In Seleucid and Roman times, it was a region north of Palestine with shifting boundaries.

Tel Aviv. Located in the central part of Israel's coastal plain facing the Mediterranean Sea. Tel Aviv is a modern city founded by Jewish settlers in 1909, pop 348,000.

Temple. Structure on the Temple Mount built by Solomon in the tenth century to house the **Ark of the Covenant** (qv). Destroyed by the Babylonians in 587 BCE. *See also* Second Temple.

Temple Mount. An elevated area in the eastern part of the Old City of Jerusalem that once held the **Temple** (qv). See *also* Moriah, Mount. Since the Muslim conquest in 538 BCE, the site has been known to Muslims as **Al-Haram al-Sharif** (qv). The total area of the Temple Mount is about 45 acres.

TIBERIUS. Roman city on the west shore of the Sea of Galilee, now a city in Israel. Pop 40,000.

TIBERIUS, LAKE OF. Roman name for the **SEA OF GALILEE** (qv).

TIRAN, STRAITS OF. Narrow passageway into the Gulf of Aqaba from the Red Sea, between the Sinai Peninsula and Saudi Arabia.

TOURS. City in southern France. Site of the decisive battle in 732 CE that marked the farthest northward push of the Arabs in Western Europe.

TRANS-JORDAN. A general term for the area east of the Jordan River.

TRANS-JORDAN MANDATE. Eastern Trans-Jordan portion of the British Palestine Mandate, which led to the founding of the **HASHEMITE KINGDOM OF JORDAN** (qv).

TRANS-JORDAN PLATEAU. The plateau that comprises most of the eastern part of Jordan, rising to 3,000 feet. It presents a sheer face east of the Jordan River.

TULKAREM. Palestinian city in the northern part of the West Bank, near its western border, pop 134,000.

TUNISIA. Country in North Africa, bound by Libya on the west and Algeria on the east. Site of ancient Carthage. The PLO was based in Tunisia from 1982 until 1993.

TURKEY. Country that occupies the **ANATOLIAN PENINSULA** (qv), extends across the Bosporus, Sea of Marmara, and the Dardanelles Strait to border Greece and Bulgaria, and extends eastward to border Syria, Iraq, and Iran. Its capital is Ankara.

TYRE. Ancient Phoenician seaport on the Mediterranean coast of Lebanon. Now a modern city, pop 100,000.

UNITED ARAB EMIRATES (UAR). Country occupying a portion of the eastern part of the Arabian Peninsula fronting the southern part of the Persian Gulf. Its desert border is with Saudi Arabia and Oman. The capital of the UAR is Abu Dhabi.

Via Dolorosa. Route followed by Jesus as he walked from the **Antonia Fortress** (qv) to Golgotha, the place of crucifixion. A pilgrim route since early Christian times, it begins in what is now the Muslim quarter of the **Old City** (qv) and ends at the **Church of the Holy Sepulchre** (qv).

Wadi Arabah. Southward continuation to the Gulf of Aqaba of the structural trench occupied by the Sea of Galilee, Jordan River, and Dead Sea. A route used by both Israel and Jordan, it marks a division between the area in southern Israel called the Negev Desert and the Arabian Desert of southern Jordan.

Wadi Rum. Area in the desert of southern Jordan of great beauty, where cliffs of black basalt and white and red sandstone overlook a network of wadis that rarely contain water.

West Bank. Part of the Occupied Territory that Israel gained from Jordan in the Six-Day War in 1967. Lies west of the Jordan River. As the result of Israeli settlement policy, seventeen percent of the West Bank population is now Israeli. The Palestinian Authority has responsibility for government in cities in the West Bank, but Israel maintains control over intervening territory.

West, The. A term that includes Europe and the countries once settled by Europeans and embraces the common aspects of the culture evolved from their political, economic, and religious history.

Yarmouk River. River flowing into the Jordan River from the east, forming a boundary between Jordan and Israel's Golan Heights Occupied Territory. Its deep gorge serves as a barrier to travel. The Byzantines lost the battle with the Arabs fought at the Yarmouk River in 638, and thereafter Palestine came under Muslim domination.

Yemen. Country in the southwest corner of the Arabian Peninsula, bordering Saudi Arabia and the Red Sea. It includes the highest and wettest portion of the Peninsula, with elevations to 8,000 feet.

Zin, Wilderness of. Area in the southern part of the Negev mentioned in the Exodus account of the wanderings of the Israelites.

Zion. Mount. A rise in the topography of the Old City of Jerusalem, culminating outside the southwest corner of the city's walls. In the Psalms and elsewhere in the Hebrew Scriptures (Old Testament), the term Zion was often used to mean Jerusalem, so a return to Zion meant a return to Jerusalem. **Mount Zion** and **Mount Moriah** (qv) were both part of the low hills on which the city was built.

SOURCES

Achtemeier, Paul J., Editor, *Harper's Bible Dictionary* HarperCollins, New York, 1985.

Ajami, Fouad *The Arab Predicament: Arab Political Thought and Practice since 1967.* Cambridge University Press, New York, 1992.

Armstrong, Karen. *A History of God: The 4000-Year Quest of Judaism, Christianity and Islam.* Ballentine Books, New York, 1993.

Armstrong, Karen. *Islam: A Short History.* Modern Library, New York, 2000.

Cahill, Thomas *The Gift of the Jews: How a Tribe of Desert Nomads Changed the Way Everyone Thinks and Feels.* Doubleday, New York, 1998.

Cahill, Thomas. *Desire of the Everlasting Hills: The World Before and After Jesus.* Anchor Books, New York, 1999.

Chacour, Elias. *We Belong to the Land: The Story of a Palestinian Israeli Who Lives for Peace and Reconciliation.* HarperCollins, New York, 1990.

Friedman, Thomas L. *From Beirut to Jerusalem.* Farrar, Straus & Giroux, New York, 1990.

Lewis, Bernard *The Middle East: A Brief History of the Last 2000 Years.* Paperback Reprint Edition, Touchstone Books, New York, 1997.

Lewis, Bernard. *Islam and the West* Oxford University Press, London, 1994.

Lewis, Bernard. *What Went Wrong: Western Impact and Middle Eastern Response.* Oxford University Press, New York, 2001.

Shipler, David K. *Arab and Jew: Wounded Spirits in a Promised Land.* Random House, New York, 1986.

The New Jerusalem Bible. Doubleday, New York, 1985

The New Oxford Annotated Bible. Oxford University Press, New York, 1994.

The Koran Interpreted. Translation by A. J. Arberry. Macmillan, New York, 1955. Touchstone Edition, Simon & Schuster, New York, 1996.

Internet

Lewis, Bernard, *"The Roots of Muslim Rage," Atlantic Monthly* Sept. 1990. Available at:

http://www.theatlantic.com/issues/90sep/rage.htm

NPR Interview with Bernard Lewis: "What Went Wrong with Islam?":

http://www.npr.org/programs/atc/features/2002/jan/ lewis/020103.lewis.html

An Overview of the Geopolitical Situation in the Palestinian Areas. May 2001:

http://www.poica.org/casestudies/ geopolitical%20situation/

MEPP/PERN *Refugees in the Middle East Process:*

http://www.arts.mcgill.ca/MEPP/PRRN/prmepp.html

Palestinian sources:

http://www.palestinecenter.org

http://www.washington-report.org

http://www.nad-plo.org

Israeli sources:

http://www.jewishgates.org

http://www.etzel.org.il/english/

http://www.aish.com/literacy/jewishhistory/

On Yasser Arafat:

http://wee.nobel.se/peace/laureates/1994/arafat-bio.html

http://search.biography.com/print_record.pl?id=3931
http://abcnews.go.com/reference/bios/arafat.html

On Ariel Sharon:

http://www.redress.btinternet.co.uk/sharon4.htm

http://www.cnn.com/2000/WORLD/meast/10/25/sharon.profile/

http://www.mallat.com/articles/blanford%20csm.htm

UN General Assembly Resolution 181 November 29, 1947

http://www.ariga.com/treaties/part181.html

Weber, Timothy P., *"How Evangelicals Became Israel's Best Friend,"* Christianity Today, October 5, 1998. Available at:

http://www.christianitytoday.com/ct/8tb/8tb038.html

Wolf, Aaron T. *Water, War, and Arab-Israeli Peace Negotiations.* Available at:

http://www.pnl.gov/ces/academic/midleas2.htm

Wright, Lawrence, "Forcing the End," *New Yorker*, July 20, 1988. Available at:

http://www.pbs.org/wgbh/pages/frontline/shows/ apocalypse/readings/forcing.html

INDEX

A

F

M

N

S

T

U

V

W

The typefaces used in this book are from the
Garamond family, designed in the sixteenth century
by Parisian Claude Garamond (1480-1561), a type
designer, publisher, and printer. Most types of his
time emulated the gothic, uncial, or black letter
styles, which were derived from hand lettering styles.
However, Garamond's Roman and Italic type designs,
with their sinuous, elegant curves, and optically
balanced forms were so admired they helped the
Roman characters become the letter forms we
commonly use to this day.